CURRICULUM MAKING IN POST-16 EDUCATION

British post-16 education in the mid- to late 1990s has been dominated by a New Right agenda and its search for the teacher- and student-proof curriculum, for political accountability and for uniformity of 'outcome'. This book highlights inadequacies in that thinking. It points to the serious short-comings of 'top-down' prescription and proposes a very different approach to curriculum reform. It celebrates agency, professionalism and diversity in educational practice and acknowledges the essential contributions of teachers and students to the making of knowledge, learning opportunities and curricula. It offers a critical examination of a number of centrally important questions in a manner suited to informing debate among professionals, politicians and academics at all levels.

Martin Bloomer is currently Dean of the Faculty of Education and Director of the Centre for Educational Development and Co-operation at the University of Exeter. He has directed three research projects on students' experiences of post-16 education and is co-author, with James Avis, Geoff Esland, Denis Gleeson and Phil Hodkinson, of *Knowledge and Nationhood: Education, Politics and Work* (1996).

CURRICULUM MAKING IN POST-16 EDUCATION

The social conditions of studentship

Martin Bloomer

London and New York

First published 1997
by Routledge
11 New Fetter Lane, London EC4P 4EE

Simultaneously published in the USA and Canada
by Routledge
29 West 35th Street, New York, NY 10001

© 1997 Martin Bloomer

Typeset in Garamond by Routledge
Printed and bound in Great Britain by
Hartnolls Ltd, Bodmin, Cornwall

British Library Cataloguing in Publication Data
A catalogue record for this book is available from the British Library

Library of Congress Cataloguing in Publication Data
Bloomer, M. (Martin)
Curriculum making in post-16 education: the social conditions of
studentship / Martin Bloomer.
p. cm.
Includes bibliographical references and index.
1. Post-compulsory education–Great Britain–Curricula. 2. Post-
compulsory education–Social aspects–Great Britain.3. Educational
change–Great Britain. 4. Teacher participation in curriculum
planning–Great Britain. 5. Student participation in curriculum
planning–Great Britain. 6. Education and state–Great Britain. I. Title.
LC1039.8.G7B56 1997
373. 19–dc21   97–6438
CIP

ISBN 0–415–12022–5 (hbk)
ISBN 0–415–12023–3 (pbk)

CONTENTS

ILLUSTRATIONS

FIGURE

TABLES

ACKNOWLEDGEMENTS

I am most grateful for the financial support I have received from The Leverhulme Trust for the research project, 'Teaching and Learning in 16–19 Education', and from the Further Education Development Agency (formerly the Further Education Unit) for 'The Experience of the Learner in FE: A Longitudinal Study'. The continued support of bodies such as these for pure and exploratory research is essential if we are to generate new and relevant insights into ever-transforming problems of educational need and opportunity.

Equally, I am grateful to members of the numerous schools and colleges which participated in the researches. Unfortunately, I am not able to name them here since I have undertaken to preserve the anonymity of all. However, I should like to point out that despite the trials of teaching and learning in the 1990s, my colleagues and I were never once refused a request to observe or interview. Instead, the students and teachers we met not only allowed us access to their experiences of post-16 education, but frequently gave more time and energy to our project than we would have considered reasonable to request. I hope that we have repaid their faith in us, at least in some small measure.

The composition of the research team changed over the course of the projects referred to in this book. The major fieldwork was carried out by Ali Harwood, initially, and by Bruce Butt and Debbie Morgan, latterly. I am particularly grateful to them all, not merely for discharging their formal responsibilities to the projects but for the integrity, sensitivity and intelligence with which they exercised judgement when, as was frequently the case, they were called upon to do so. I am also grateful to Rosie Turner-Bissett and Marios Goudas for their conscientious assistance with data collection and analysis, respectively.

My gratitude extends, also, to that network of friends and colleagues who reside for the most part in the subconscious of my 'generalised other' but who, from time to time, step forward to impinge upon my life in some more tangible form. They are too many to mention, except a few whose practical help, moral support or wisdom has had a direct bearing upon this work:

Pam Barnard, Gill Bunting, Mike Golby, Phil Hodkinson, Martin Johnson, Rob Lawy and Nina Wroe.

While my loss of the original first five chapters of this book provided a stern but effective lesson in computer file management, it did little to enhance my humour at that time. For this reason, among *many* others, I am especially indebted to Alison, Ellen and Rachael for their tolerance and understanding.

Finally, but by no means least, my thanks to Helen Fairlie and Routledge for their patience, faith and encouragement.

1

INTRODUCTION

Developments in British post-16 education in the mid- to late 1990s have been dominated by a New Right agenda and its search for the teacher- and student-proof curriculum, for political accountability and for uniformity of 'outcome'. This book, drawing from the findings of recent research, highlights inadequacies in that thinking and proposes a very different approach to curriculum reform. It celebrates agency, professionalism and diversity in educational practice and acknowledges the essential contributions of teachers and students to the making of knowledge, learning opportunities and curricula.

THE PROBLEM AND THE APPROACH

My attention, throughout this book, is tightly focused upon students' and teachers' experiences of learning and teaching. It might seem strange that I should want to draw attention to students and teachers following the widespread reforms of curricula and administrative arrangements for post-16 education in the late 1980s and 1990s. After all, one could reasonably expect that their experiences had already received exhaustive examination and evaluation prior to and during this period of reform. The deplorable fact is that they have not; students' and teachers' experiences have been largely ignored in the processes of policy making.

Of course, I do not deny that some notions of 'student' and 'teacher' have figured in the much publicised reforms of recent years. But I do question what notions these are, how informed they are, and what value they hold for any critical evaluation of post-16 education or for the development of policy. In the chapters that follow, I shall examine the concepts of 'student' and 'teacher' which have informed recent policy making and illustrate the ways in which these have served to promote and sustain an impoverished concept of education. I shall argue that the structurally deterministic theories in which such concepts are firmly located, and which treat students and teachers as objects in some grand technocratic design, are not only blinded to key purposes of education but devalue educative processes themselves.

1

But my aim is not merely to heap criticism upon the faithful slaves of determinism. Rather, it is to try to learn from recent experiences, to come to know learning and teaching more thoroughly and to point to opportunities for their enhancement. I attempt this in the belief that, one day, post-16 education will be revisited by people of greater vision than the reformers of the 1980s and 1990s. To assist my analysis, I shall draw heavily from research evidence collected for the 'Teaching and Learning in 16–19 Education' research project funded by the Leverhulme Trust, referred to below as the 'Leverhulme Study'. This evidence adds considerable weight to the claim that curriculum making does not begin and end with policy makers. It indicates how teachers act critically, in varied ways, upon the curriculum prescriptions presented to them as they create opportunities for their students; and how students act upon those opportunities as they each carve out their own personal learning careers. Students and teachers 'make' rather than 'take' their roles and the making of the curriculum is their essential business. I have, therefore, chosen the term 'studentship' to describe the active and critical engagement of students in these processes but I fear I must draw the line at using 'teachership' in my accounts of what teachers do.

In the following chapters, I shall draw from many particular cases of students and teachers. In the course of illuminating studentship and teaching I shall try to make explicit some of the techniques and strategies that individuals have used in the course of their learning and teaching. While I hope that readers might find something here which prompts reflections on their own practices, it is not my intention that the exemplar cases I use should be treated as models. Neither teaching nor learning are acts of technicianship, acquired through modelling technical skills, through the uncritical adoption of rules or procedures or through the rehearsal of prescribed roles. Both are achieved and continually refined through the critical examination of one's own and others' practices, a claim that I shall return to in due course.

Throughout this book, I shall use the Leverhulme Study to illustrate certain flaws in contemporary policy, planning and theorising. But my use of empirical evidence is by no means confined to illustrating and verifying. Its greater usefulness, as far as I am concerned here, is in the generation of an explanatory theory of studentship and of learning and teaching in post-16 education.

If my work is to assist readers in their own evaluations of practice, whether as teachers or researchers or even as learners, it is important that I make the processes of my own theorising quite explicit. I have, therefore, presented my own interpretive accounts alongside the research data at various stages throughout the book and have attempted to weigh these against evidence and theory from other sources. My theoretical standpoint in this work is that of interpretivism and my principal aim the generation of theory from research data. Much of the data that I have used for this purpose are qualitative: students' and teachers' accounts of their work and observers' accounts of life in post-16 classrooms. But the analytical categories and concepts by which the data have been ordered are not borne simply from my own preconceptions; nor are they unduly governed by pre-existent theories of teaching and learning. They have been elicited from the data by means of comparative analysis, my handling of which I hope to make clear in later chapters. It is my intention, therefore, that the reader will have full access to the interpretive processes that I have employed and, hence, be able to view my work as critically as they might their own.

THE LEVERHULME STUDY

A rationale for the study

The Leverhulme Study was conceived at a time of central government commitment to the expansion of participation in post-16 education. It was also a period of growing interest in more broadly based post-16 curricula and in proposals for addressing the so-called 'academic–vocational divide'. There were also major developments in 14–16 education and the higher education system was in a state of some considerable flux. It was even anticipated that the significance of research in this field would grow as the Single European Market became more firmly established and the prospect of a 'harmonisation' of curriculum planning in the 16–19 sector in Europe became an ever closer reality.

The research was designed to examine relationships between curriculum planning and students' experiences of learning. If, as my previous research had suggested, these relationships were fundamentally weak, there would follow very clear and strong implications for reforms of post-16 education, particularly those concerning relationships between 'academic' and 'vocational' tracks and those concerning the 'broad-based sixth' (see DES *et al.*, 1988a, 1991; Finegold *et al.*, 1990; Richardson *et al.*, 1995). The research was also designed to identify factors having a significant bearing upon students' learning and to explain the processes underlying their relationship with learning. Of course, the explanatory theory to be generated would be only a partial theory given the infinite number of factors likely to have some bearing upon learning. However, it was to be a theory firmly grounded in evidence of students' experiences of learning and, for that reason at least, would provide an essential contribution to debates and decisions affecting post-16 education. Without such a contribution, the course of post-16 education would be as likely to be steered by folk-lore and New Right dogma as by anything else.

Studies of classroom life in post-16 education are vastly under-represented in the research literature and, certainly, have had little impact upon curriculum planning and development. There are many reasons for this: not

3

least among them is the long-standing preoccupation of university depart-
ments of education with teacher education and research in the compulsory
sector and their consequent lack of involvement in the affairs of further
education. Thus, the explosion of interest in ethnographic studies in the
1970s was confined largely to secondary and, to a lesser extent, primary
education. The post-16 sector was not well served in the process, with only a
few works (e.g. Willis, 1977) having any recognised relevance.

Bereft of a significant history of classroom research, planners in the post-
16 sector at both national and local levels rarely draw upon empirical
evidence of students' experiences. Instead, knowledge of the student experience is largely taken for granted, informed more by inferences from the
stated purposes of grand curriculum designs than by systematic study of
practice. What is planned to happen is widely assumed to determine what
happens in practice (Bloomer and Morgan, 1993). Not surprisingly, in the
absence of hard knowledge of students' experiences, much of the literature
which serves the sector is marked by the uncritical use of descriptors such as
'BTEC', 'GNVQ', 'A-level', 'academic', 'vocational', 'theoretical' and 'practical' in accounts of students and learning. Such usage serves to reify 'types'
of course, group, student or activity; it deflects attention from the purposes
and experiences of individual students and, by accentuating the significance
of normative knowledge of student experience, casts the student into the
role of passive recipient rather than active participant.

But there is a recently expanded body of more discerning work in the
field, much of which is referred to elsewhere in this book. These works
include 'structural' demographic studies of trends in participation rates,
examination performances and such like (e.g. Audit Commission, 1991;
Audit Commission and OFSTED, 1993; Smithers and Robinson, 1991,
1993); critical analyses of the principles underpinning current post-16
curricula, often with particular reference to 'vocationalism' (e.g. Holt, 1987;
Spours and Young, 1988; Maclure, 1991a; Hyland, 1993a, 1994a); studies
of curriculum innovation, design and management (such as the work of the
Further Education Development Agency (FEDA, formerly FEU), often based
on some form of 'top-down' or 'centre-periphery' model of evaluation);
studies of specific key curriculum issues such as provision for students with
special educational needs, multi-cultural education, assessment, information
technology in the curriculum (where, again, the work of FEDA figures
significantly); and 'local' evaluations of specific curriculum initiatives,
particularly TVEI. However, important as these works are, few have taken
serious account of students' experiences of learning. Those that have been
grounded in research into students' experiences have, very often, focused on
vocational courses and students' transition into work (e.g. Sims, 1987;
Stoney, 1987; MacDonald and Coffield, 1991; Hodkinson and Sparkes,
1993; the studies reported in Bates and Riseborough, 1993; and Hodkinson
et al., 1996). Few have concentrated attention on 'general' (often referred to

as 'academic') education or attempted to review the experiences of students across a range of courses or subjects.

Given the far reaching reforms to the 14–19 curriculum, recently completed, in hand or in prospect (e.g. National Curriculum, AS levels, Baccalauréats, NVQs, GNVQs, A-level reform, Diplomas, modular courses, reforms of assessment practices and the pervading influence of the 'enterprise culture' and the educational 'market place') it is especially important that serious attempts are made to comprehend students' and teachers' experiences of teaching and learning in order to describe and explain the real effects of educational planning/provision upon learning across a range of 'general' ('academic') and 'vocational' courses. The Leverhulme Study was planned with these considerations in mind.

Previous work

My earlier work in this field (e.g. Bloomer, 1991, 1992) revealed considerable variation in the pedagogic practices of teachers. This is no profound revelation in itself and is frequently acknowledged at the 'common sense' level as natural, inevitable and even justifiable. There is indeed a rhetoric, readily available at this level, which accounts for pedagogic variation in post-16 education in terms such as the 'academic–vocational divide', the 'nature of the subject', the characteristics of particular curriculum designs or the 'qualities of the students concerned'. But such explanations (or rationalisations) are not confined purely to staff room discourse; they are reproduced in similar forms in ministerial pronouncements, publications by government-funded agencies, the media and the professional journals. As such, they have a significant bearing upon curriculum development and evaluation at both national and institutional levels.

From my earlier work, it was apparent to me that variation in pedagogic practices and in students' experiences of learning is by no means solely attributable to curriculum design or even to the 'nature of the subject'. I found far greater variation in classroom organisation, classroom discourse, students' learning tasks, assessment practices and teachers' pedagogic plans to exist within A-level courses and within vocational courses than between them. I found a similar range of practices in both, suggesting that the widespread use of the terms, 'academic' and 'vocational', to denote 'types' of course was to some extent misplaced and that popular claims about the 'academic–vocational divide' warrant careful re-examination, at least in respect of their assumptions about pedagogy and students' experiences of learning. As far as specific subjects were concerned, I found pedagogic practices to vary both between and within them. I found the practices of English teachers to vary to the greatest extent despite the fact that all of the teachers observed and interviewed were 'following' the same syllabus. A similar story can be told of mathematics and, certainly, of 'vocational' course tutors. It was also very apparent to me that such variation as existed between subjects was only weakly related to the crude yet widely held belief (grounded, perhaps, in the literature of the 1970s and 1980s which examined aspects of pedagogic practice in secondary schools in terms of subject paradigms, orientations or cultures – e.g. Bernstein, 1971; Barnes and Shemilt, 1974; Ball, 1981, 1982) that teachers of science, mathematics and foreign languages adopt more 'teacher-centred' practices while their colleagues in the arts, humanities and social sciences work in a more 'student-centred' fashion.

But, just as the practices of teachers were not tied securely to courses, subjects or curricula, it was apparent that variations in students' experiences of learning were not to be explained solely by reference to subject, courses or course groups. In a small study based on nineteen class meetings involving about 250 students, I found that students' experiences of learning varied more noticeably within courses than they did between courses. Not only were students found to differ in the value that they accorded to different learning activities but, although exposed to the same experience as others in the same group, often gave quite different accounts of what they had learned. Some identified 'factual' knowledge as the significant content while others pointed more readily to the underlying principles that contributed to their understanding. This was apparent regardless of teacher or subject and it was quite clear that the teachers were, at most, only partly aware of the 'mis-match' between the learning that they had planned would take place and the quality of learning that had actually taken place among many of their students. The essential point here is that students' perceptions, experiences and evaluations of learning were not simply the products of the curricula that had been designed for them; nor were they, for that matter, the fulfilment of plans of the teachers who had interpreted such designs. Other factors, such as students' personal and career ambitions, their perceptions of knowledge, their evaluations of learning opportunities, their previous schools, social background and such like appeared to have combined to have a far more profound effect upon their learning than did the 'grand curriculum designs' which had generated the labels by which their learning experiences were commonly described.

The aims and outline methodology of the study

The initial aims of the Leverhulme Study were to examine ways in which teachers interpreted and acted upon externally prescribed curricula, to examine how students experienced the demands placed upon them, and to explain relationships between the two. Given my concern with the processes by which students and teachers achieved mutually satisfactory (or unsatisfactory) working relationships, it was necessary to gain access to their perceptions and evaluations of curriculum aims, pedagogic plans and practices and to gain insight into students' personal experiences of learning. It was through such insights that an understanding of processes was to be developed.

The first, brief, phase of the study focused on students' first encounters with their tutors and peers and on their induction into post-16 courses at a tertiary college. Some ten classes, drawn from a range of A-level and BTEC National (some of which were shortly to be designated GNVQ) courses were observed and recorded on audio tape. Each tutor was interviewed before and after the observed session and, in each case, two students were interviewed afterwards. In addition, questionnaires seeking background information, students' reasons for their choices of course, their expectations of course content, teaching, learning, assessment and classroom management, and their evaluations of their GCSE experiences, were completed by 816 new students during their induction week.

Information yielded from observations and interviews was used to inform the development of the observation and interview techniques employed in the second phase of the project. Data obtained from the questionnaires were analysed, reported (Bloomer and Morgan, 1993), utilised in a full comparative analysis, described below, and used as the basis from which a student questionnaire for use in phase two of the study was developed.

The second, major, phase of the study entailed ninety observations of A-level and BTEC/GNVQ class meetings across two tertiary colleges, a selective school sixth form and an independent school sixth form. The observations, by course and subject, are shown in Table 1.1. The subjects were selected on the grounds that they provided a reasonable representation of the range of different courses available at A-level and BTEC National/Advanced GNVQ and that they were likely to yield sufficient numbers of students for the study. The decision to confine the scope of the project, in effect, to young people who had secured four or more grade Cs at GCSE level was based purely on pragmatic considerations. The scope of the study had to be confined to manageable proportions somehow and, given that my previous work had focused almost entirely upon this same range of courses, manageability was readily achieved by confining the project in this way. Moreover, since the study was partly concerned to examine the nature of teaching and learning in 'academic' and 'vocational' courses, there was much to be gained from limiting the focus of the study to students who, on the face of it, had been eligible to make a choice between 'academic' and 'vocational' routes. Most of the vocational course students in the study could have elected to take A-levels by virtue of having achieved at least minimum entry requirements for those courses.

Prior to each observed class meeting a twenty-minute tape-recorded semi-structured interview was conducted with the tutor for the purposes of confirming the conditions of the observation, providing assurances about confidentiality, identifying the tutor's principal aims in the class meeting to

Table 1.1 Numbers of observations by course and subject

Subject	A-level	BTEC National/ Advanced GNVQ
Mathematics	6	–
English	9	–
Physics	6	–
Chemistry	12	–
History	10	–
French	9	–
Sociology	6	–
Art	7	–
Business and finance	–	8
Leisure	–	2
Hotel and catering	–	3
Engineering	–	4
Social care	–	2
Nursery nursing	–	2
Other	4	–
Total	69	21

be observed, her/his accounts of course knowledge and personal view of the learning 'processes' appropriate to the students in question, and other matters concerning the background and previous experiences of tutor and students. The ninety observations were each recorded by the use of a schedule with a mixed structured and semi-structured format and at the end of each session, ten minutes was set aside for the students to complete a short session evaluation schedule. After the observed session, a further interview was conducted in order to enable the tutor to verify the observer's record of the structure and apparent purposes of each stage of the class meeting, to identify the tutor's intentions for the future development of the work covered in the observed session, to obtain the tutor's view of the nature and origins of the significant knowledge of the observed session, to re-examine the tutor's previous comments on learning processes and significant knowledge in the light of the observed session, and to obtain the tutor's responses to questions formulated during the observation. In addition, two students (normally one male, one female) were, subject to their agreement, interviewed separately after the session. The students were asked to offer their accounts of the significant knowledge of the observed session and of their course as a whole, to comment on 'critical incidents' and to compare the observed session with their previous experiences of GCSE courses. They were also invited to elaborate upon answers provided in the student questionnaires (above) and their session-evaluation schedules.

Throughout the second phase, the accumulated qualitative data were continually subjected to analysis. This preliminary analysis was guided initially by the principles of comparative analysis and theoretical saturation

(Glaser and Strauss, 1968). The research methods employed in the study were fine-tuned in the process in order to yield the evidence necessary for the clarification and verification of critical concepts, categories and their properties and for the generation of more clearly focused hypotheses. Through theoretical sampling, the evidence was used to verify emergent hypotheses as the emphasis of the study shifted slightly from 'exploration' towards 'verification'.

The final source of data were student questionnaires completed by 1,680 A-level and BTEC National/Advanced GNVQ students from the four institutions participating in the study. The questionnaires asked students to provide background information about themselves, to state their reasons for embarking upon their present courses and to indicate, depending upon the timing of the questionnaire, their expectations, experiences and evaluations of prior (notably GCSE) and present course learning activities. The questionnaires were adapted for use with students in the light of the course, the institution and the year of study concerned. The distribution of student responses by course and year group is shown in Table 1.2.

Most of the data yielded by the questionnaires were in quantitative form and, in certain cases, such as students' reasons for choosing courses, and their expectations, experiences and evaluations of learning activities, facilitated the construction of scales. Some of these are referred to in later chapters. Additional quantitative data, such as students' ages and their GCSE and post-16 course results broadened the scope of the quantitative analysis while information from course syllabuses, course planning documents and teaching materials extended the range of qualitative data. However, it is important to bear in mind the relationship between quantitative and qualitative data in the study. The research was essentially exploratory, seeking to identify those categories and concepts most adequate for the purposes of describing and explaining teachers' and students' experiences of learning. The qualitative data were central to this task. Comparative analysis of qualitative data allowed those concepts and categories which proved most relevant to, and most powerful in, an explanatory account to be scrutinised and validated. The progressive refinement and validation of key concepts and hypotheses

Table 1.2 Distribution of questionnaire responses by course and year group

Stages of distribution	A-level	BTEC National/ Advanced GNVQ	Total
Induction day, year one only	307	71	378
Mid-year one only	251	62	313
Induction day, year one, and induction day, year two	317	121	438
Induction day, year two only	409	142	551
Total	1,284	396	1,680

continued alongside, and in close relationship with, data collection. Data were used to test continually the emergent concepts and hypotheses and to check their development as the research progressed, while this same testing process informed the fine-tuning of research techniques that was necessary to ensure that subsequent data were those most useful to the study (theoretical sampling). But it was not only the qualitative data which were used to inform the generation of theory. The tendency to associate quantitative data with positivist verificatory research is misleading; both forms of data have a part to play in verification and generation. Quantitative data are but another 'mode of knowing' and can be used in the same way as other evidence in the discovery of categories and their properties.

> In many instances, both forms of data are necessary – not quantitative used to test qualitative, but both used as supplements, as mutual verification and, most important for us, as different forms of data on the same subject which, when compared, will each generate theory.
>
> (Glaser and Strauss, 1968: 18)

The main contribution of the quantitative data to this study, therefore, was to assist the generation of concepts, hypotheses and explanatory theory rather than to verify the outcomes.

The third phase of the study entailed some dissemination of the initial findings to teachers who had participated in the study. In all, twelve teachers assisted in this part of the process at the end of the academic year in which the observations had taken place and each was invited to provide an account of their work with the student groups in question. Teachers were asked to respond to open questions such as, 'How would you describe the progress of the group, to date?' and 'What, on reflection, strike you as particular strengths and weaknesses of members of the class?' They were also asked to describe, as best they could, what they felt to be the particular qualities of their own teaching. The teachers were also provided with accounts of the interpretations that the research team had placed upon the observation, interview and questionnaire data concerning their students and invited to comment upon them. Finally, they were presented with the names of four or five students from their group and asked to identify what they felt to be the major distinguishing qualities of the students concerned. The students had been selected prior to the interview on the basis that, from the observation, interview, evaluation and questionnaire data, they appeared to possess the greatest diversity of characteristics in respect of the categories that were of particular interest to the study. This proved to be one of the most revealing stages of the research, providing as it did for the further illumination, elaboration and validation of the emerging concepts and categories.

The final stage of the research entailed drawing all the relevant data into some coherent explanatory account of teaching and learning in post-16 education. Comparative analysis of raw data had provided the major means of locating key categories, concepts and hypotheses which, in turn, had been subjected to continual critical inspection. However, where the circumstances permitted, statistical analyses (using both parametric and non-parametric techniques) of quantitative data enabled aspects of the emergent theory to be checked. But it was the richness of the qualitative data obtained through broadly focused observation and questioning which served to illuminate the processes involved and, hence, to provide the greatest assistance to the generation of explanatory theory.

A CURRICULUM FOR THE FUTURE

This book is directed ultimately to the identification of appropriate aims, values and organising principles for a post-16 curriculum for the future. The case for a radical reappraisal and reconstruction of the curriculum is grounded in the answers to two key questions. First, 'How do curricula work in practice?' Second, 'In mind of what kind of future should a curriculum for the future be constructed?'

Chapter 2 offers a broad and general account of the present condition of post-16 educational provision in Britain, visiting, in the process, the purposes of education as they are variously perceived. The chapter provides some brief historical insights into how contemporary thinking and practice has come into being and illuminates the British condition further by means of some international comparisons. Britain's changing economic circumstances are examined and some of the implications these hold for the education-work-economy nexus are highlighted, not least the problem of the 'academic–vocational divide'. The chapter also begins to describe the quality of thought invested in recent educational planning, noting its distinctive technical rationalism, and pointing up some of its implications for learning and teaching.

Chapter 3 focuses upon the nature of knowledge and learning opportunities in A-level, BTEC National and Advanced GNVQ courses, drawing from documentary evidence for the purpose.

Chapters 4, 5, and 6 shift the emphasis to the students' experiences and evaluations reported in the form of case studies. Vocational courses are the subject of Chapter 4, A-level chemistry courses of Chapter 5 and A-level history courses of Chapter 6. Each chapter provides insights into life in a small number of classrooms. The purposes of the case study chapters are two-fold: first, to reveal, and thus subject to critical scrutiny and external validation, the analytical categories generated through comparative analysis of the research data and, second, to provide some insight into the similarities and differences between courses operating under similar or different curriculum prescriptions.

Chapters 7, 8 and 9 draw not only from the data and analytical categories generated from the Leverhulme Study but from other sources. They offer a further examination of the economic and social conditions of British educational planning, noting, in particular, the impact of globalisation. The chapters call for a radical reconceptualisation of the problem of learning and, in turn, curriculum and teaching. The concepts of 'studentship' and 'learning career' are, I have argued, central to any such reconceptualisation. While it is certainly the case that careful thought must now be given to new funding arrangements, it is also the case that urgent attention needs to be given to the ways in which curriculum is thought about and to the ways in which curriculum change is achieved in practice. With the necessary flexibility of mind, a curriculum *for* the future is possible. But, first, those minds must be freed from the influence of the infallibilist dogma of the New Right.

2

THE CONTEXT OF EDUCATIONAL PRACTICE

While I do not wish to dwell for too long on matters that have been considered extensively elsewhere, some account of the historical, social and economic context of post-16 education and the impetus for its development and change is necessary if the problem is to be understood in anything more than a simplistic form. My account will, of necessity, be selective and will focus principally upon the driving forces behind curriculum reforms of recent years, upon assumptions underpinning them, and upon the newly changing conditions in which future plans must be conceived.

THE PURPOSES OF EDUCATION

At the very heart of the post-16 debate lie competing views of the purposes of post-compulsory, and even compulsory, education. Since the days of the Mechanics' Institutes, through Technical and FE Colleges, the greatest emphasis has always been upon the preparation of young people and others for work. This is still a major function of the public post-compulsory system. It is part of the tradition of FE, a tradition sustained as much by public as by professional values and beliefs, and in spite of there having been precious little investment by state and industry in vocational education. It was the emphasis upon further education providing a 'preparation for jobs' which underpinned the 'new vocationalism' (Bates *et al.*, 1984; Ranson *et al.*, 1986) of the 1980s. However, in more recent years, the provision of a 'vocational education' has come to be recognised as a more complex matter than that of simply training students in job-specific skills. While it is true to say that General, Liberal and Social Studies appendages to post-war vocational courses were an attempt to provide students with a wider educational base to their studies, it was the BTEC curriculum introduced from the early 1980s which took the first significant steps towards a preparation for work within a broader concept of vocational education. The development of TVEI as an enhancement curriculum, of generic and core skills, and of modular course structures such as GNVQ can be seen as further evidence of some general shift towards a broader, re-focused vocationalism.

The reasons behind these shifts are themselves interesting and result from analyses of the changing needs of the economy, the labour market and, in particular, the nature of work. Post-Fordist and other analyses of current and prospective transformations in Western societies have stressed a requirement for some form of 'flexible' knowledge worker within collaborative, high-trust, high-skill, work relations (Piore and Sabel, 1984; Lacey, 1988; Mathews, 1989; Ball, 1991; Brown and Lauder, 1991, 1992) and it is with some, albeit hasty and superficial, appreciation of these requirements that curriculum development has been stimulated. I say hasty and superficial because, as Young (1993) has noted, a high degree of uncertainty still surrounds the extent of, the directions of, and the full implications of the developments anticipated in the post-Fordist analysis. Indeed, evidence of the anticipated flatter, leaner, hierarchies is not in great abundance, at least in Britain. Moreover, as Avis (1993) has pointed out, the surface features of post-Fordism are largely indistinguishable from those of the 'enterprise culture' and, where curriculum developments do not address fundamental differences between the two, their unresolved contradictions are carried forward into course planning. 'Student-centred learning', 'autonomy', 'entitlement', 'empowerment', 'democracy' and 'citizenship', which figure prominently in recent curriculum developments, are examples of concepts in popular use in post-16 education whose rhetorical value is their power to legitimise and compel common assent to curriculum innovations but whose more sinister function is to obscure the need for critical examination of those innovations (see discussion in Avis *et al.*, 1996: 155–160).

Nonetheless, many of the reforms to have taken place in post-16 education since the early 1980s, despite the problematic nature of their underlying evidence and logic, reflect a clear and visible attempt to shift from a narrowly focused 'preparation for work' towards some notion of preparation 'for life', 'for citizenship', 'for multi-skilled work' and 'for collaborative work relationships'. While the effects of such shifts are most evident in full-time vocational courses, and to some extent in A-level programmes, they have received little or no recognition in NVQ levels 1, 2 and 3. Consequently, the once clear purpose of vocational education has become bifurcated into 'vocational education' based in some broader concepts of vocation and preparation and 'occupational training' whose primary concern is to equip learners with skills for jobs.

Other major purposes of post-16 education might be considered under the headings of 'general' or 'liberal' education. A liberal education stresses the value of self-fulfilment over utility and of the 'educated person' over the expert specialist. Such an education is intrinsically justified, as being of worth in itself and, in post-16 education, it is to be seen as contributing to life-long learning or unfoldment. It is part of an educational tradition which extends back to classical times, which underpinned British secondary and university education up to and throughout the nineteenth century, which

14

has profoundly influenced educational developments of the twentieth century and which has been expressed fully and forcefully in its different ways in the works of liberal humanist educators such as Oakeshott (1962), Hirst (1965, 1969), Peters (1973) and Holt (1978). It is concerned to promote 'ways of experiencing' and, although it is often expressed in terms which bear a strong relationship to subject disciplines, it is not to be regarded in terms of discrete subject perspectives. Subjects, although underpinned by an epistemological logic, are to a degree arbitrary divisions of knowledge made for the purposes of facilitating mass education and for managing the 'knowledge explosion'. A liberal education aims to transcend these divisions, to allow the learner to understand the world in its full complexity.

Curriculum developments throughout the twentieth century represent a movement away from the liberal tradition as subject constituencies have formed to render the curriculum teachable and assessable. The School Certificate, GCEs, CSEs, GCSEs and the mis-titled National Curriculum have simply confirmed the fragmentation of a curriculum for general or liberal education into ten or so elements. What is there, then, in post-16 education which might be described as 'general' or 'liberal', as part of a process of life-long learning and as intrinsically justified? Answers to this question will vary according to their source. There are cases for claiming that TVEI, CPVE, BTEC and GNVQ have been in some small way guided by the principles of a general education, if not a liberal education. But these are weak claims indeed. A-levels, on the other hand, are borne out of the liberal humanist tradition. However, the conflicting expectations that students, teachers, higher education admissions tutors and prospective employers have of A-levels render the prospect of them ever fulfilling the aims of a liberal education remote indeed. The most obvious impediment to A-level in this regard is that any permutation of three subject-specific elements from the universe of knowledge is bound to result in an incomplete curriculum even if judged by the most minimal criteria. There have, during the 1980s and 1990s, been a number of carefully conceived attempts to move A-levels out of their rut (for example, DES *et al.*, 1988a; Finegold *et al.*, 1990; National Commission on Education, 1993, 1994; The Association for Colleges *et al.*, 1994; The Headmasters' Conference, 1994) and it is clear that there is a broad base of support for reform of some type. Sooner rather than later the A-level system will change into a form which will enable or require students to have a broader grounding to their studies. Whether the outcomes will amount to anything resembling provision for a liberal education, however, must be considered doubtful.

The two broad purposes as I have briefly represented them here, despite each contributing to some common good, have their own distinct histories and reflect quite separate sets of interests which have never been satisfactorily reconciled. They represent different traditions, each borne out of and sustained by its own culture. The significance of history and culture in the creation and maintenance of a divided post-compulsory education is crucially important in any analysis of our present state of affairs and for any policy making which might grow from this. But this critical element is so often missing from contemporary policies and proposals for reform which anticipate that change can be engineered simply by bolting-on enhancement programmes to well-established courses or by declaring parity of esteem (see, for example, DES *et al.*, 1991) between 'routes' whose very purposes are grounded in different and even antagonistic cultural interests.

> Beneath its surface, this policy [of declaring parity of esteem between separate pathways] is an instinctive appeal to the *status quo*, to familiarity and, it may be argued, to continuing social differentiation based upon educational background and qualification.
>
> (Richardson, 1993: 27–28)

The 'academic–vocational divide', as it has come to be called, has both legitimated and been legitimated by divided educational and cultural interests over a long history (Hyland, 1994a) and is deeply rooted in our cultural fabric. It will not be swept away simply by the revision of course content, the reformulation of 'routes' or by declarations of 'equivalence' between unequal commodities. The problem, if there is one, has to be addressed at the level of infrastructure, not superstructure. 'Reforms', if they are to effect real change, must provide a full and adequate response to cultural interests and values.

KEY CHARACTERISTICS OF THE POST-16 CURRICULUM

The knowledge base

I have already mentioned the problem of subject specialisation in post-16 education within the context of 'liberal' or 'general' education. But the appropriateness of narrowly focused subject-specific courses is drawn further into question when weighed against requirements stemming from current transformations of modern economies and work. Increasing proportions of the work force are, or will soon become, engaged in multi-skilled work requiring mastery of a range of new technologies and communications skills which subject-specific courses are ill-equipped to provide. Moreover, knowledge is increasing at such an unprecedented rate that the interests of effectiveness and efficiency are likely to be better served by knowledge-retrievers than by knowledge specialist holders whose expertise is quickly outdated and which is not readily adaptable to novel problems. Coupled with the facts that the nature of work is changing at an ever-quickening pace and that adults can now anticipate an average of three major changes of career during their working lives, this amounts to a strong challenge to long-held beliefs that subject specialism is the only platform for expertise. This is not to claim that subjects and specialisms are irrelevant to expertise but to argue that they must be redefined. The 'new expertise' requires not only a broad knowledge base but a 'softening' of subject demarcations to enable learners to work confidently and creatively as knowledge retrievers and knowledge creators. It requires that learners are competent in 'basic skills' of numeracy, literacy, communication and information technology, not merely at the level of technical mastery or proficiency within the prescribed limitations of given tasks but at the level of critical appreciation in order that they may be able and prepared to respond to new and unanticipated challenges. The 'new expertise' also depends heavily upon that primordial quality of the educated person, knowing how to learn, in order that new knowledge can be assimilated, reformulated, applied and evaluated speedily and effectively without dependence upon instruction. With the diminution of heavily demarcated work roles and the expansion of networks and multi-skilled operations, the requirement for collaborative productivity and, in particular, the ability to contribute to the free exchange of knowledge and critique across traditional knowledge and role boundaries, is paramount. This requires a sharp movement away from the heavily individualistic emphasis in both educational and work relations towards a fuller recognition of the potential of collective and collaborative action in both the production and utilisation of knowledge.

Support for such views of our present economic and educational needs has been provided by a variety of political, professional, academic and practitioner groups. There is little dissent from any of the fundamental propositions put forward here. The principle of the broadening of the knowledge base in post-16 education, for instance, has been advanced in some shape or form by such diverse constituencies as all three major political parties, The Association of County Councils, The Royal Society, The Institute of Physics, The Engineering Council, The Secondary Heads Association, The Headmasters' Conference, The Association of Principals of VIth Form Colleges, The Association of University Teachers and many others. And there is no more diverse range of interests than that! However, despite this apparent consensus, no coherent curriculum reform has been brought about, partly because of the political risks attached to reform and partly because of the unresolved contradictions between post-Fordism and the 'enterprise culture' referred to above. It is certainly necessary to look beyond the surface consistencies of proposals for reform and, in particular, present-day working concepts such as 'student-centredness', 'autonomy' and 'empowerment', if the radical changes briefly argued for here are ever to materialise.

One final observation on the matter of subject specialisation concerns Britain's, and specifically England's, position in relation to other nations. While I am not suggesting that curriculum structures of other countries alone should provide the yardsticks by which the English system is judged, the information in Table 2.1 warrants consideration if not concern. If there is any connection between the broad-based post-16 curriculum and a nation's ability to respond to the requirements of contemporary economic and social transformations, it is plain that England is least well placed of all industrialised countries to make such a response. This observation is not new; it provided a significant part of the rationale for the Higginson Committee's proposals (DES *et al.*, 1988a) for five leaner A-levels, for instance. However, those proposals, as others before and since, were rejected as speedily as they were announced, for the reason that they might lower the 'gold standard' of the highly regarded A-level.

The 'academic–vocational divide'

But to what extent has the problem of the 'academic–vocational divide' been addressed in schemes to provide a broad-based post-16 curriculum? Proposals and reforms to emerge in the 1980s and 1990s fall into four categories. First, there are those that have provided for, or sought to provide for, curriculum revision within the existing 'academic' or 'vocational' frameworks. The introduction of AS-levels did offer the prospect of a broad base of study within the 'academic' framework but low uptake by students and uncertainties about the market value of AS have meant that that proposal did not have anything like the impact intended. The International Baccalauréate offered by a very small number of post-16 institutions has

Table 2.1 Students in final year of full-time secondary education

Country	Number of subjects studied
Finland	9+
Hungary	9+
Korea	9+
Poland	9+
Sweden	9+
Japan	7+
Israel	7
Italy	7
Norway	7
Canada	6
Singapore	6
Thailand	6
Australia	5
Hong Kong	5
USA	5
Ghana	3
England	3

Source: Postlethwaite and Wiley (1991). Reproduced with permission.

appealed to only a minority of students, arguably an élite. Interest in the IB has been excited because of the broad base for study that it offers, because of its perceived high academic standing and because of the international recognition that it promises. However, its 'academic' qualities and its broad subject base have counted against it in the minds of that large proportion of students who have always looked forward to post-16 education as the opportunity to discontinue those studies which they least enjoy or in which they have been least successful.

BTEC, CPVE and, latterly, GNVQ courses broadened the basis of study within the 'vocational' framework. These courses must be judged as largely successful in establishing a concept of vocationalism which, as I have already noted, extended beyond the narrowly focused 'skills for jobs' emphasis of some of their predecessors. YTS schemes too, albeit to a very limited extent, attempted to move beyond the 'skills for jobs' emphasis. However, none of these courses or their 'academic' counterparts offered any scope for the proper integration of 'academic' and 'vocational' studies.

The second category of innovations had one principal member: TVEI. Although there is a long history of failed attempts to supplement specialist courses in order to provide a broader base of knowledge and experience, TVEI and the many extension programmes which developed from it included a number of highly successful attempts to enhance established programmes of study. Through TVEI, many A-level courses were broadened to encompass some experience of industry and commerce and the utilisation of course knowledge in those spheres. Some placed emphasis upon life skills and awareness-raising in the form of multi-cultural and equal opportunities education and an introduction to new technologies, guided more by the broader concept of vocationalism adopted by BTEC courses than by the narrowly focused 'skills for jobs' emphasis of the original TVEI design. Many vocational courses were enhanced by TVEI, too, enabling students to broaden their basis of study across a range of experiences extending far beyond the immediate scope of their vocational courses. Some of the lessons of TVEI were carried forward into the likes of entitlement curricula and many institutions have sought formal accreditation for this work to enhance its credibility. However, TVEI and its offshoot programmes made little impression upon the 'academic–vocational divide', not least because the opportunities they offered to students were dependent upon voluntary take-up. The lack of formal certification and, in particular, public acknowledgement of TVEI-related achievements prompted many students to view the TVEI curriculum as a distraction from their core certificated A-level or vocational courses. While TVEI deserves much credit for creating opportunities for bridging the 'academic–vocational divide', and there is much to be learned from its successes, it did not bring about any fundamental change to the 'two track' system. Students', teachers', employers', and parents' expectations of post-16 education, themselves very much grounded in the two traditions and cultures referred to earlier, coupled with an adherence to established structures of post-16 curriculum organisation, effectively ensured that the scope of TVEI was severely limited from the outset.

The third category of innovations to reduce the 'academic–vocational divide' is that of modular course structures. There are numerous cases of modular course developments within existing 'academic' and 'vocational' frameworks such as the innovative but subsequently rejected Wessex A-level project (Rainbow, 1993) and the MEI Structured Mathematics scheme, both of which met with a considerable measure of success in providing a 'flexible' response to students' needs. There have also been a few cases of modular programmes planned to provide some common experience for students progressing to different qualifications, for example a common first or foundation year for A-level and vocational course science students. But greater possibilities for bridging the 'academic–vocational divide' appeared with GNVQ courses in the early 1990s. However, the opportunities afforded by GNVQ for creating an 'academic–vocational mix' depended again upon consumer choice. While some students did elect to combine A-level courses with their GNVQs, many did not. Moreover, doubts must be expressed about the extent to which student programmes created on the basis of GNVQ, and other modular structures for that matter, amounted to integrated and coherent 'academic–vocational' courses of study. In the early years at least, the few GNVQ students who chose to add A-level courses to their programmes did so at least as often for utilitarian purposes as for reasons of enhancing their general education. While popular choices such as A-level sociology by social care students, modern foreign languages by business studies students and information technology by students from a variety of vocational courses might be taken as evidence of a technical bridging of the 'academic–vocational divide' it is not in itself an indication of any harnessing, integration or reconciliation of the purposes and values of different traditions.

My fourth and final category of proposals to abolish the 'academic–vocational divide' includes examples which point to a far more radical reform than those mentioned above. In principle, they argue for a comprehensive post-16 education in which all or most students combine 'academic' and 'vocational' studies. A-levels and GNVQs would be replaced under such proposals by a single qualification and course structure guided by broad aims such as the following:

1 to ensure that all young people undertake a general or broadly based education, including an education for citizenship, up to the age of eighteen;
2 to enable young people to develop a critical awareness of the sciences, social sciences, humanities or arts ('academic');
3 to enable young people to gain experience in the development, applica-

tion and evaluation of knowledge and skills in the contexts of work, community and leisure ('vocational');

4 to ensure that all young people are able to demonstrate mastery of core skills;
5 to provide opportunities for young people to concentrate some proportion of their studies in one or more fields of special interest or need; and
6 to empower young people to learn to seek and achieve self-determination within a context of equality of opportunity.

The Institute for Public Policy Research (Finegold *et al.*, 1990) proposal for a British Baccalauréat was clearly in keeping with the principles of a radical reform of post-16 education such as I have briefly signalled here. Its aims corresponded to a large degree with the six that I have offered and its detail indicated how such an apparently complex and multi-purpose programme of study could be organised and achieved in practice. The British Baccalauréat proposal remains the most complete and coherent plan for radical reform and, unlike many other proposals, made clear reference to *both* the social and economic conditions that had informed its development *and* to the student interests it was designed to serve while providing a vision of post-16 education grounded in moral as well as practical considerations. But, despite attracting widespread interest and support, it has had only minimal impact upon policy.

The Dearing Report on the National Curriculum (SCAA, 1993) might be viewed as a step towards the integration of 'academic' and 'vocational' studies in its recommendation that a variety of optional courses be made available in National Curriculum Key Stage 4. Dearing identified a need for clear opportunities for progression from pre- to post-16 studies and proposed accreditation of vocational and other optional studies in the pre-16 phase. By retaining a statutory core of studies, the Dearing Report provided for some notion of a general education for all, at least up to the age of 16. However, Dearing did not make explicit the means by which curriculum relevance and coherence might be achieved other than to say that his proposals would enable, 'schools . . . to respond to the particular aptitudes and inclinations of their students' and that 'specific decisions on choice of pathways and subjects are best left to students, parents and schools' (SCAA, 1996: 46). Such principles of voluntarism are an indication of the fundamental weaknesses of the Dearing proposals – weaknesses that are shared with many earlier attempts at reform and also, incidentally, Dearing's (SCAA, 1996) report on qualifications in post-16 education. They treat aptitudes, inclinations and needs as unproblematic, assuming that choices at 14-plus can be made in a rational and informed manner by all concerned. They ignore the claim that 14–16 is a significant stage in adolescent growth and development when aptitudes, inclinations and needs are still at a very early stage in their formation. Moreover, they do not take account of the important influence of cultural habitus (see Hodkinson and Sparkes, 1993; excerpts in Bates and Riseborough, 1993; and discussions in Avis *et al.*, 1996) upon adolescent choices.

At worst, Dearing's proposals could merely advance the problems currently surrounding choice at 16-plus by two years without addressing the problem of the 'academic–vocational divide' at all. The greatest likelihood, given the long-established British tradition of separate academic and vocational provision and the culturally grounded expectations and aspirations which have grown from them and which continue to reinforce them, appears to be that the academic, vocational and occupational pathways that Dearing has in mind will serve to reinforce divisions between academic and vocational interests rather than integrate them. The fact that Dearing chose the metaphor, 'bridges', to link his academic, vocational and occupational pathways suggests that his primary interest was in matching students to pathways (or 'routes') in their mid-secondary careers while providing an escape route for those who sought to move or change routes. Bridges enable travellers to get to the other side of some divide; they do not necessarily unify the two or more sides of a divide. Having claimed that Dearing offered no vision of a unified or integrated curriculum for post-14 or post-16 education, I should stress that his proposals did mark out the space within which a more radical reform of 14–19 education might be located.

In 1996, Dearing's *Review of Qualifications for 16–19 Year Olds*, recommended the unification of the School Curriculum and Assessment Authority (SCAA) and the National Council for Vocational Qualifications (NCVQ) into a single statutory body in order to facilitate curriculum reform. Within a few months, government announced a 1997 launch of the Qualifications and National Curriculum Authority (QNCA), fulfilling long-standing predictions (e.g. Maclure, 1991a and 1991b; Ayer, 1994) of the merger of SCAA and NCVQ. On the face of it, the joint efforts of SCAA and NCVQ would appear capable of yielding a coherent and integrated programme of study for 14–19 education. However, serious doubts must be expressed about the extent to which the interests of a general education might be recognised in such a union. As Maclure (1991b) notes, 'the NCVQ belongs at the "training" end of the continuum: its methods and principles are derived directly from the imperatives of training: its culture is a training culture' while SCAA, the driving force behind the National Curriculum, also promotes 'the specification of "outcomes" in the form of attainment targets' and thinking which is 'utilitarian and instrumentalist'. Moreover, given the track records of SCAA and NCVQ, it seems extremely doubtful that any QNCA plan would be based upon a vision of curriculum extending beyond that of syllabus or upon any recognition of the full complexity of the social, cultural, economic and moral conditions into which a radical 14–19 curriculum would have to be implanted. I should add, also, that if past form is to guide assessment of the situation, it is more likely than not that the principle of voluntarism would figure prominently in such a plan. For all of these reasons, I suspect that the formulation of a strategy to confront the 'academic–vocational divide' lies well beyond the scope of the unified efforts of SCAA and NCVQ, even in the form of a QNCA.

I have not yet mentioned NVQs in the context of the 'academic–vocational divide'. It should be remembered that NVQs were developed to secure nationally recognised standards of vocational competence (Hyland, 1993a), to rationalise a plethora of post-16 vocational qualifications, and to grant formal certification to a large proportion of the working and non-working population who were competent but unqualified, particularly in low- and medium-skilled work. The rationalisation process entailed establishing comparability between 'equivalent' or 'near equivalent' courses and achievements while the accreditation process involved giving recognition to competence, regardless of how it had been acquired: the accreditation of prior learning. However, the approach that was adopted in the design of NVQs bore all the hallmarks of a narrow behaviourism not witnessed since the days of Franklin Bobbitt (1918). Occupationally specific curricula were 'stripped to their utilitarian and instrumental purposes, the universe of knowledge fragmented into simplistic behavioural objectives, assessment confined to the readily measurable, achievements narrowed to "outcomes" and the whole dedicated to the pursuit of an ambiguous concept of "competence"' (Bloomer, 1994: 1). Although planned ostensibly for the accreditation of competence, it was not long before NVQs began to impact upon the planning and teaching of courses whose purposes extended far beyond the utilitarian. Many craft and vocational courses became transformed in the process and NVQs attracted strong criticisms for their approach and for their unsuitability to post-14 and post-16 education and to employment (Collins, 1991; Callendar, 1992; Hodkinson, 1992; Green, 1993; Hyland, 1993a, 1993b, 1994b; Smithers, 1993; Steedman and Hawkins, 1994). Some research has even shown that NVQs are less rigorous and reliable in assessing the very basic skills that they were designed to assess than were the practices they replaced (Steedman, 1992). Such transformations in teaching, learning and curriculum as have been triggered by NVQs are the very antithesis of a general education and it is plain that NVQs have little to contribute to a healing of the 'academic–vocational divide'. But this is not to suggest that assessment of competence and the accreditation of prior learning have no place in the post-14 curriculum of the future. It is simply to state that the concept of competence and the processes of accreditation demand far more critical attention than they have been given to date.

On the matter of the 'academic–vocational divide' and the prospects of a comprehensive post-16 curriculum, I have claimed that a radical approach to the problem is urgently needed if Britain is to make an adequate response to the social and economic demands of the twenty-first century. But the kind of changes required cannot be achieved in the short term simply by legislation. Cultural adaptation is crucial to success and that will not come about in the short term. Parity of esteem cannot be legislated for; it has to be achieved in schools and in further and higher education, in the eyes of students, teachers, parents, employers. Bridges between essentially discrete pathways will contribute little if anything at all to a unification of curricula or harmonisation of purposes; in fact they may even heighten differences between pathways rather than diminish them. Nor is it at all helpful to base plans on the principle of voluntarism given the compelling power of culturally located expectations of formal education. The only significant step towards an integrated post-14 or post-16 curriculum is the GNVQ which, at least, has opened up some opportunities for students to combine academic, vocational and occupational studies. But this alone is not sufficient. While GNVQ offers scope for students to incorporate vocational and academic studies in their programmes, it offers no vision of an integrated curriculum. Moreover, its success in combining academic and vocational studies rests squarely upon student choice while its vision is informed by little more than a commitment to the rhetoric of student empowerment and the flawed philosophy of voluntarism.

The 'academic–vocational divide' bears directly upon the central concerns of this book. The perpetual debate about purposes and values of post-16 education is the important backcloth against which students' and teachers' experiences of learning unfold and are evaluated. Their perceptions of academic and vocational studies, of general education, of specialisation and so on are crucial to our understanding of their studentship and teaching. Moreover, it is through the values, expectations and practices of our present students and teachers that the 'academic–vocational divide' is perpetuated. As one A-level student was heard to say to another after the latter had failed to grasp a point, 'You're a right BTEC aren't you!'

Assessment

Knowledge, learning, teaching and assessment are inextricably linked and some features of these linkages will be examined in later chapters. However, it would be a glaring omission from even this brief account of the context of post-16 education were I not to offer at least some such observations at this point.

As I have noted in Chapter 3, views of knowledge and learning have been contested since they were first made objects of serious study. Teaching, too, has been the subject of persistent wranglings, particularly over the last century. Assessment, on the other hand, has been regarded as relatively unproblematic by politicians and, until recently, by teachers and academics. For many years, the predominant form of assessment of A-level students' knowledge, understanding and skills was by terminal examination, entailing essay-style answers to questions based upon given syllabus topics in the arts, humanities and social sciences, or the solution of problems of a known type in mathematics and the sciences. Of course, this is a generalisation and there were certainly some exceptions to this pattern in the 1960s and 1970s. However, it was the 1980s that witnessed a marked increase in the proportions of 'practical' and 'project' work in GCSE, O- and A-level examinations. Teachers and examiners at that time frequently argued that course work, linked or not linked with other methods of assessment, yielded a more valid picture of students' achievements than did terminal examinations alone. Assessments of vocational courses were more varied, typically encompassing practical performance and, particularly for higher level courses, essay-style answers. The 1980s saw significant developments here, too, noticeably with BTEC assignment work and with increasing use of group work and simulated work experience. Not only did educators claim that the newly developing assessment practices in vocational education offered a more complete insight into students' achievements, but that such assessments themselves stimulated and supported the learning process (see, for example, BTEC, 1986a).

The late 1980s saw direct centralist intervention in the practices of assessment. The prime minister, in a policy of retrenchment (Spours, 1993), set a moratorium on GCSE and A-level examinable course work on the grounds that only summative tests and examinations provided the necessary rigour. At the same time, by means of NVQ and, later, GNVQ, NCVQ sought to steer the assessment of vocational courses away from the BTEC pattern to include more specific objectives-led methods. Quite apart from the rhetoric about rigour, standards and accreditation of competence which accompanied them, these interventions were designed to serve the interests of political accountability. The education service, subjected directly to New Right free marketism, was pressed to produce low cost quantified data to allow the 'effectiveness' of institutions and sectors to be judged and rewarded or penalised.

The major observable effects of these moves were four-fold. First, they set constraints upon the use of assessed course work for the promotion and support of student learning in the ways that BTEC courses and some A-level courses were doing. Second, they limited opportunities for students to develop and demonstrate self-reliance, self-confidence and skills in collaboration which course work, and particularly group project work, had allowed. Third, they shifted the focus of assessment towards the most readily measurable 'outcomes' of learning. This required the fragmentation of knowledge and skills into discrete quantifiable elements, in practice often commodified, decontextualised and trivialised, in forms most visible in NVQ and later in GNVQ. Fourth, this form of non-professional or political accountability prompted many post-16 institutions to review their entry and progression criteria following on the work and advice of such bodies as the Audit

Commission and OFSTED (1993) and the A-level Information System (Fitz-Gibbon, 1990; Tymms and Fitz-Gibbon, 1995), thus effecting a marked shift from 'open door' to selective policies. The important point to draw from this is that curriculum design, knowledge, learning and teaching came to be driven, to a greater extent than ever before, by assessment practices whose means were technical and whose rationale lay primarily in political accountability. Learners and teachers in the early 1990s witnessed transformations in knowledge, learning and teaching which were in no way informed by the arguments for the radical reform I have referred to above but which, in many respects, served to impede any such reform. 'Teaching to the test' and 'payment by results' are not merely the slogans of a bygone age; they are the reality of today and tomorrow unless present trends in assessment practices are arrested and redirected.

Routes, trajectories or turning points?

Contemporary literature on the subject of post-14 and post-16 education is apt to assert the need to provide for clear 'routes' for progression, built-in 'flexibility' to enable students to exercise choice, and suitable guidance procedures to back up the whole system. This, as Avis *et al.* (1996) note, is the ideology of individualism and market forces trading under the illusion of empowerment. Indeed, much recent curriculum reform in vocational education has been expressly dedicated to the tasks of clarifying 'routes' and providing for flexibility through modular style programmes of one form or another. It is interesting, too, that this view of priorities has been widely held by interest groups of quite different political, professional or educational persuasions (CBI, 1989, 1993; DES *et al.*, 1991; Maclure, 1991b; Audit Commission/OFSTED, 1993; National Commission on Education, 1993; The Association for Colleges *et al.*, 1994). However, implicit in such approaches are technical rational assumptions about choice making and careership which do not always stand up to scrutiny when weighed against the evidence. Amongst these assumptions are the following:

1 That 14, and particularly 16, are ages when young people have sufficiently well-established identities, aptitudes and inclinations that they should make a commitment to one form of study or another in order to sustain their continued growth and development.
2 That young people of 14 or 16 are sufficiently knowledgeable about their own identities, aptitudes and inclinations that they can successfully utilise this knowledge in the choice-making process.
3 That young people are generally aware of the nature of changing economic, work and social relations and that they can anticipate how their post-16 choices will enhance their personal qualities in such a

manner that will equip them for effective and rewarding participation in work and society.

4 That young people know, or can come to know, those qualities of post-16 courses which have greatest relevance to their own continued growth, fulfilment and prospective success.

5 That post-16 choices should be, and can be, made primarily on the basis of 'matching' young people's aptitudes, interests and needs with the opportunities that courses have to offer.

6 That young people make their post-16 commitments in the knowledge of more or less clearly defined 'routes' to employment.

7 That the needs of young people are best served by assigning them or 'matching' them to 'routes' at the age of 16.

8 That the needs of those young people who are unable to make a commitment to a 'route' are best served by additional information and guidance.

9 That once assigned to a 'route', those who seek to make a major change in their commitment or to withdraw, do so largely as a result of their own inadequacies or through failings in the 'matching' process and, as a consequence, are viewed negatively as 'failures' while their schools, colleges or advisers are deemed inefficient.

Each of the publications cited above in respect of the views of interest groups of different persuasions is explicitly based upon a majority of the nine assumptions and implicitly upon the remainder.

The technical rational model of progression and guidance is highly visible in contemporary policy and practice (Behrens and Brown, 1994) and is grounded in outmoded assumptions about social and economic structures. It is borne out of the economic and social relations of a securely stratified society with clear divisions of labour in which selection and allocation to a particular stratum and occupational field, largely according to meritocratic principles, seriously limits opportunities for later access to other strata or occupations. In its contemporary form, the technical rational model allocates to 'academic', 'vocational' and 'occupational' strata, the main purpose of guidance being to match 'types' of learner, defined ostensibly in terms of ability, aptitude and interest, with strata, routes and trajectories. The effects of the matching process are the reproduction of stratification and an enhancement of career predictability (Banks *et al.*, 1992; Furlong, 1992).

In a socially conservative country such as England it was likely that the new qualifications tracks would operate as a rigid selection system, screening a majority of 16 year olds into one of three groups and so perpetuating the traditional division of status between academic and vocational learning.

(Richardson *et al.*, 1995: 21)

27

There can be little surprise that research (e.g. Roberts *et al.*, 1994) has found that, in practice, young people's opportunities depend heavily upon family, background, gender and residence. But the practice of matching 'types' with trajectories is not only the technically rational means by which iniquities are perpetuated, it is a habit which prevents us from properly addressing our present social and economic needs. The modern economy does not require knowledge or skill specialists with career ambitions framed within the confines of strata or routes; that is 'old think'. Instead, it requires 'flexible knowledge workers', able to transcend in both their thinking and their actions the very strata and routes which the present system serves to perpetuate.

But economic and work relations do not provide the only criteria by which the matter might be assessed. Calls for life-long education and for a 'learning society' are plentiful (Hutchins, 1968; Husén, 1974, 1986; Finegold and Soskice, 1988; Bennett *et al.*, 1992; Ranson, 1992, 1994; C. Ball, 1993; Duke, 1993; Labour Party, 1993) and particularly well judged in the current climate. Few, however, are confined simply to questions of economic development and wealth creation. The 'learning society' entails much more, as noted by the Economic and Social Research Council:

> A learning society would combine excellence with equity and would equip all its citizens with the knowledge, understanding and skills to ensure national economic prosperity and much more besides. The attraction of the term 'the learning society' lies in the implicit promise not only of economic development but of regeneration of our whole public sphere. Citizens of a learning society would, by means of their continuing education and training, be able to engage in critical dialogue and action to improve the quality of life for the whole community and to ensure social integration as well as economic success.
>
> (ESRC, 1994: 2)

Education for social integration and the regeneration of our whole public sphere is an education for citizenship and for active public participation in the community (Carr, 1991). It is a general education for all, focusing as much upon family, leisure and other communal and social interests as upon work. Its emphasis is upon collective participation and collaboration and it will not be too well served by the divisive, individualistic orientations of stratification and routing.

Technical rationality is concerned with the efficiency of means (often confused with quality) and has no place for the concept of value other than in a narrowly utilitarian sense. It is concerned with means over ends and periodically, in the evolution of ideas, it is asserted in forms such as educational league tables or 'competence-based' assessment objectives. Charles Dickens' man of realities, Thomas Gradgrind, is its personification. It seeks to identify certainties of the world in a rule- or law-like form in order that predictions might be made. While searches for certainties in the social world have their limiting features, not least that they may grossly oversimplify that world in the process, full-bodied technical rationality admits no such limitations. The excessive deployment of resources in psychometric testing (FEU, 1994) to support and promote the 'matching' of young people to trajectories is a clear symptom of technical rationality, as are the notions of routes and trajectories themselves.

To return to an earlier point, opportunities structured in terms of strata, routes and trajectories make no allowance for studentship – the critical engagement by students with curriculum and other features of their everyday lives in the processes of making and re-making their roles and identities. Routes and trajectories place students in an essentially passive role and, by so doing, eliminate that most complex of variables, human agency, from the equation. Accounts of, and policy making for, progression are thus simplified down to those of matching qualities of students with those of routes. As Hodkinson in his work on careership has pointed out, they ignore 'turning points'. Anselm Strauss, from whom the concept of 'turning points' is derived, talks of the 'open-ended, tentative, exploratory, hypothetical, problematical, devious, changeable, and only partly unified character of human courses of action' and of 'turning points' in development which 'occur when an individual has to take stock, to re-evaluate, revise, resee and rejudge' (Strauss, 1962: 65 and 71, cited in Avis *et al.*, 1996).

Technical rational solutions to problems of progression exclude any proper recognition of turning points in students' careers. First, they treat the assignment of students to 'correct' or appropriate routes as the primary task. Second, where students are unable or unwilling to make a commitment to some route or other, solutions are sought in additional course and careers information or further guidance. The student is defined as the problem needing assistance (DES *et al.*, 1991; CBI, 1993). Third, as I have already mentioned, they regard students who wish to change their commitment or who fail or wish to withdraw from courses as 'failures' or 'drop-outs' (Audit Commission and OFSTED, 1993). 'Careers advice and guidance . . . should assist young people in choosing the right courses. Too many young people choose the wrong course and drop out very rapidly' (Labour Party, 1996: 12). It is the technical rational account or policy which fails to acknowledge the reality of studentship and turning points but it is the student who is designated the failure. Fourth, in so far as it recognises that 'turning points' exist at all, the technical rational solution is to provide for 'flexibility' by means of 'bridges' and modularity. In practice, bridges are few and far between and, as I have mentioned already, they contribute to the conservation of discrete routes by confining turning point options to choices between alternative routes. Nor does modularity provide any adequate response to the real problems of turning points and studentship. In practice, modular programmes may amount to little more than the extension of free market principles into the education sector in the guise of providing for students'

29

independence of choice. In the process, educators' responsibilities for ensuring coherence and progression are compromised. It is clear that for modularity to make the important impression upon the post-16 curriculum that it might, the thinking behind it needs to move far beyond the 'flexibility for students' argument to include recognition of the problematic nature of turning points and studentship. A set of principles, such as those suggested by Carey, might prove to be an important first step. 'A programme of learning' he suggests:

- should provide entry points based on previous learning experiences and exit points consistent with future aspirations;
- must provide individual students with a balanced, progressive and coherent learning experience;
- must be sufficiently flexible to meet the changing needs and aspirations of students.

(Carey, 1994: 27)

Notions of learning experience, aspiration, balance, progression, coherence and flexibility would certainly require critical examination and definition. The necessary second step would then be to ensure that the principles are reflected in practice – but that is quite another matter, given the political and ideological conditions under which modular courses are promoted and operated.

THE ECONOMY AND WORK

The published statistics on participation in full-time post-16 education have consistently shown the United Kingdom to be in a pitifully low position in comparison with other industrial nations. The 1992 figures, reproduced in Table 2.2 show the UK to have the lowest rates among the 18 OECD countries listed, with the exception of Turkey, for 16-, 17- and 18-year-olds. There has, of course, been an upturn in UK participation since the mid to late 1980s, although by 1996 the figure was still well adrift of that of most other OECD nations. The history of the UK's low participation rate is readily explained by the 'academic–vocational divide', elitist principles of selection and 'ejection *en route*' (Althusser, 1971) and the virtual absence until recently of any provision of full-time vocational education other than on an *ad hoc* basis. The practices of yesterday, as I have already argued, set the limiting conditions for the culture of today. The upturn in participation rates in the late 1980s and 1990s has been the source of much conjecture: the TVEI experience and GCSE courses have been offered as reasons, and no doubt, if the trend continues, the National Curriculum will in time be credited as having made a significant contribution to raising participation in response to government targets. However, the dispassionate observer cannot fail to link the upturn in participation with the decline in youth employment opportunities over the same period.

Table 2.2 Participation in full-time education and training of 16–18-year-olds, 1992

Country	Percentage at 16 years	Percentage at 17 years	Percentage at 18 years
Belgium	97	94	78
Canada	96	81	61
Denmark	92	80	69
Finland	95	86	82
France	92	89	79
Germany	95	93	84
Greece	88	62	45
Ireland	88	77	58
Japan	95	90	not available
Netherlands	97	92	79
New Zealand	88	67	41
Norway	93	87	78
Spain	76	67	54
Sweden	89	87	61
Switzerland	85	82	75
Turkey	39	37	26
United Kingdom	75	57	34
USA	91	75	54

Source: Department for Education *et al.* (1996) *Education Statistics for the United Kingdom, 1995 Edition*, London: HMSO, 20. Crown copyright; reproduced with the permission of the Controller of Her Majesty's Stationery Office.

On the subject of work and the economy, I should like to return to the matter of post-Fordist work relations. Although there is, indeed, doubt about whether Britain is moving in the direction of post-Fordism, the claim that industrialised nations are passing through a transition comparable in scale to that accompanying the discovery of mass production techniques, or even to that of the industrial revolution, is now widely accepted. It is not a recent claim by any means, having been signalled over a generation ago by Alvin Toffler (1970, 1980). The conditions under which the transition is occurring are: the emergence of a global economy with multi-national industries and world markets, a movement of mass production industries away from established industrial nations to Third World states for reasons of cheaper low-skill labour, and the phenomenal growth of new technologies. The 'new internationalism' underpinning current economic transformation is a free market internationalism fostering intense competition between multi-national stakeholders rather than between nations. What, then, is the place of the nation state in this new scheme of things?

Rather than increase the profitability of corporations flying its flag, or enlarge the worldwide holdings of its citizens, a nation's economic role is to improve its citizens' standard of living by enhancing the value of what they contribute to the world economy. The concern over national 'competitiveness' is often misplaced. It is not what we own that counts; it is what we do.

(Reich, 1993: 301)

But what prospects do British citizens have of contributing to the world economy? Britain is less well placed than most industrial nations to respond to newly emerging demands for non-standard unit production and continual demands for product innovation, since it has done comparatively little to date to lay the foundations for the transition that is required. The means of upskilling the labour force and of maximising advantages of advanced technologies are not readily available since a higher proportion of the British productive economy is still firmly locked into the low-skill, mass production end of the manufacturing spectrum than is the case in other industrialised nations (Reich, 1983; Finegold, 1993). But what are the high skills of the high-skill economy?

> The technology of tomorrow requires not millions of lightly lettered men, ready to work in unison at endlessly repetitious jobs, it requires not men who take orders in unblinking fashion, aware that the price of bread is mechanical submission to authority, but men who can make critical judgements, who can weave their way through novel environments, who are quick to spot new relationships in the rapidly changing reality.
>
> (Toffler, 1970: 357)

New work relationships will no longer depend upon clear divisions of labour grounded in technical specialisms but on collaborative work relationships built around the high skill of flexible specialisation (Piore and Sabel, 1984; Phillimore, 1990; Young, 1993). They will entail the integration of skills both horizontally, involving tasks demanding similar levels of competence, and vertically, involving tasks at different levels of competence. Only through such integration can the work force be equipped to respond 'flexibly' to demands for non-standard products and innovation while ensuring maximum benefit from ever-changing technologies. Horizontal integration of skills, as I have mentioned earlier, will require adaptability within high trust, collaborative work relations which transcend traditional job demarcation boundaries. The implications this holds for curriculum development in education and training are clear in principle if not in detail: a broadly based education, a reconceptualisation of the notion of specialism and the knowledge and skill to exploit collaborative working relationships to the mutual advantage of all partners. Vertical integration will demand similar qualities but, in addition, the capability and attitude of mind continually to renegotiate roles and responsibilities with working partners in response to changing demands. Given that personal identity, self-esteem and status are derived from work roles to a considerable extent, it is plain that 'retraining the work force' is far too inadequate a description of the tasks ahead.

A number of researchers and writers in their investigations of post-Fordism have seen fit to distinguish between 'core' and 'peripheral' workers where the former are retained in permanent employment and the latter brought in on a temporary part-time or sub-contracted basis to enable the host industry to maximise its flexibility (Atkinson and Meager, 1990; Phillimore, 1990). Such developments have been quite visible in British industry, commerce and services since the early 1980s. While it is the medium- or high-skill core whose work is most likely to become reformed around principles of horizontal and vertical integration and who will make the greatest claims on education and training, peripheral workers face different prospects. Those peripheral workers or firms who provide specialist high-skill-based 'services' are likely to prove equally demanding of continuing education and training, raising the prospect of a free exchange of labour between core and periphery. However, a substantial proportion of peripheral workers will be low-skilled and unlikely to have ready access to education and training. This 'poor periphery' will endure low security, low wages and progressive marginalisation (Phillimore, 1990) and the prospect of a divided and fragmented society is clearly visible, particularly if treasury responsibilities for post-16 and continuing education and training are transferred to private purses. With the 'poor periphery' in mind, calls for a general education and an education for citizenship in post-16 education appear incomplete. To them must be added, 'political education'.

The needs for a radical review of post-16 education are evident but what is not yet at all clear is who will determine the scale and scope of the review. 'Newly liberated consumers' are clearly viewed by government as central players in the 'market place'. However, a key problem of consumer-led policy is that it provides no assurance that its outcomes will contribute to the common good. In the context of post-16 education, for example, it is difficult to see how consumers – that is, all consumers – will help to bring about the types of radical curriculum reform that are undoubtedly necessary. How will they assess the benefits of the general education, citizenship and other studies so clearly desirable? In so far as they have exercised consumer choice at all in the past, many students have used it to steer well clear of those areas of study for which they could see no immediate utilitarian or intrinsic value. Moreover, just as problematic is the notion that consumers have the necessary knowledge of their own interests and needs upon which to base decisions about what is important to study. But this is not to suggest that students should not be full participants in the planning and development of a curriculum; it is to stress that such developments must not be driven by consumer ignorance.

Similarly, we should be wise to exercise caution in looking to industry for direction. Apart from some enlightened exceptions, the experience that British industry has to offer is essentially that of the very low-skill Fordist work relations that we are trying to escape from. As Moore (1988a) notes, a number of studies (including, for example, Holland, 1977, and Ashton *et al.*, 1983) have demonstrated convincingly that employers attach low priority to educational attributes, particularly within the mid- to low-skill bands. Where they are concerned at all with educational attainment, it is with respect to a 'narrow range of basic skills'.

> Ironically, the attribute on which young people do best relative to older workers is *specific educational qualifications* which actually comes *bottom* of the employers' list of essential attributes, being mentioned by only 2 per cent of employers! In fact, employers give *all* the educational attributes a low priority.
>
> (Moore, 1988a: 270, original emphasis)

Nor can it be taken for granted that the education sector has any unified experience or view on the matter of post-16 education. Many teachers have little experience of industry or commerce and, certainly, limited appreciation of the changing nature of work and work relations stemming from post-Fordist transitions. Some, it might be said, are even antagonistic to certain values of industry and commerce. But teachers have an essential contribution to make. Teachers have expertise in curriculum development, they have direct experience of students and of turning plans into learning opportunities, while some have the breadth of experience and expertise necessary to identify and articulate the organising principles and curriculum detail required for radical reform.

Politicians may be able to offer an informed and balanced overview, representing a wider range of interests, although it would be unfortunate if they seized upon the reform of post-16 education as merely an opportunity to exercise whim or dogma. Clearly, a radical reform that is truly responsive to the needs of a rapidly changing economy and to the wider social changes which accompany it, requires all of these players to make a proper contribution to its achievement. It also requires that an effective working balance is struck between the principles of regulation and voluntarism, for to leave the matter to the free market could be to forfeit the pursuit of the common good.

Finegold and Soskice (1988) argue that a 'low-skills equilibrium' lies at the heart of Britain's educational and economic problems. Britain's relatively poor economic performance is viewed as both product and cause of its educational failings. Equilibrium is maintained by 'a self-reinforcing network of societal and state institutions which interact to stifle the demand for improvements in skill levels' (Finegold and Soskice, 1988: 215). On the one hand, industry is locked into low-skill mass production, unable to make the changes that will allow it to absorb and utilise a more highly skilled work force to good effect; on the other hand, the absence of a high-skill work force has meant that industry has been unable to adapt in response to new economic opportunities and demands. Of course, there has been some movement out of this equilibrium, more noticeable in some sectors than in others. However, transformation has been comparatively slow and by no means smooth. As Finegold and Soskice note, small movements in one sector of education or the economy without corresponding shifts elsewhere 'may result in only small long-term shifts in the equilibrium position'. But the low-skills equilibrium is located within a much broader social and cultural matrix which cannot be disregarded in any formulation of the problem. The concept of 'equilibrium' is helpful in locating the inertia which lies at the heart of the problem but the culturally grounded values, attitudes, beliefs and interests that I have noted earlier in this chapter are as much a part of the low-skills complex as are the educational and political-economic institutions to which Finegold and Soskice refer. We should recognise that inertia is not an industrial-educational problem alone but that its cultural dimension provides, perhaps, the largest 'drag factor' of all. The cultural dimension is of such central importance that analyses of the low-skills equilibrium must be relocated within a broader 'low vision equilibrium', resting upon mutually sustaining economic, educational, political and cultural systems. Only in this way can the *full* complexity of transformation be observed, uncoordinated and piecemeal developments be avoided, and the route to a 'high vision equilibrium' more clearly and confidently articulated.

All of the observations made here in respect of work and the economy have an important bearing upon students' and teachers' experiences and expectations of post-16 education. The nature of work, of education and, particularly, of relationships between the two, is changing on a much larger scale than ever before and teachers' and students' perceptions of themselves, their work and their futures are informed by curious mixtures of 'new' and 'old' values and knowledge. Tensions between newly informed insights and traditional values are visible and need to be acknowledged as such if studentship and teaching are to be adequately understood.

EDUCATION AS A POLITICAL ACT

Changes in educational policy and practice are not simply evolutionary adaptations to changes in public need or to advances in professional wisdom. They are expressions of political will and the instruments of political change, never more so than from the election of the first Thatcher government in 1979. Since that time, the laissez-faire philosophies of the New Right have found full expression in policies of college incorporation and consumer choice, as educational institutions have been relocated in a competitive 'market place'. Market metaphors have accompanied the transformation as knowledge has become commodified: ethos has become 'corporate image', teaching has become curriculum 'delivery', students have turned into 'customers' or, collectively, into 'market niches', and their achievements into 'outcomes'. Even 'student-centredness', the imprecise but long-standing hallmark of humanistic educational practices, has been hijacked to portray the consumer orientation of the new educational world.

But this has been only a one-sided 'free' market. While certain freedoms have been extended to consumers, producers have found their opportunities progressively curtailed. As with the National Curriculum in the schools sector, the post-16 curriculum has increasingly been subjected to central government control. Direct intervention in matters such as assessed course work and, via politically appointed quangos, in curriculum design and accountability mechanisms, has lifted key educational decisions out of the realms of professional judgement, placing them firmly within the domain of political-bureaucratic decision making. The professional aspirations of teachers have rarely been dealt a more serious blow. But what of the criteria upon which political-bureaucratic decisions are based? Here lies the most telling indictment of the political act.

The nature of political control is revealed in the commodification of knowledge and the persistent presentation of educational achievement as the fulfilment of 'performance criteria', themselves arrived at through 'functional analysis'. This shift has been promoted through the work of the National Council for Vocational Qualifications (NCVQ) in its drive towards an ambiguous concept of competence-based education. 'The specificity and putative precision claimed by competence-based schemes have an obvious attraction for those already committed to the value of pre-specified outcomes and input/output efficiency in education' (Hyland, 1992: 32). Through such approaches, the curriculum is rendered more controllable and the educational system more easily accountable. The tight specification of outcomes and assessment criteria limits the scope of educational activity but facilitates the easy 'measurement' of 'unambiguous achievements' that is the essential prerequisite of political accountability and control. However, to transform the curriculum into predetermined objectives in this way is not merely to transform the nature of assessment or accountability, it is to transform the nature of knowledge and learning, too. To emphasise only outcomes is to emphasise only functional and instrumental values of learning. It is also to side-step questions of the moral validity of such approaches and to promote a reductionist concept of education (Bull, 1985). Regulation by specification of outcomes limits, if not prohibits, alternative outcomes to those pre-specified; it stifles creativity and confines recognised educational achievements to the overtly measurable. It affords no recognition of educative processes (Stenhouse, 1975) or of the value of general education.

> by omitting to build upon and extend trainees' capacities in general
> educational subjects – mathematics and English – NVQs fail to
> provide a sound basis for progression in education and for further
> professional development. . . . Young people . . . are being trained in a
> set of narrow competences which will not easily permit either the flex-

ibility or career development in later years which the economy and technical progress increasingly demand.

(Steedman and Hawkins, 1994: 96 and 100)

Such is the price of accountability and control. The criteria governing the development of NVQs reflect the collusion of a naive technicist tradition and the New Right's paramount interest in control. They lack any adequate epistemological foundation and are ill-suited to meeting our present and future economic needs. But they will be enforced:

> The Secretaries of State intend to use . . . reserve powers to regulate all full-time provision offered to senior pupils over the age of 16 and to full-time students in further education colleges. This will be a means of requiring colleges and schools to offer only NVQs to students pursuing vocational options.
>
> (DES *et al.*, 1991: 19)

This is a chilling statement which signals not the political control of education in the public interest but control of knowledge in the political interest.

Political intervention in the curriculum and, particularly, in matters concerning the definition of knowledge and the purposes of education, has obvious implications for teachers. But it also has an important bearing upon studentship. Not only is the post-16 curriculum in a state of transition, it is a transition which is contested. Students have invariably had to make personal adjustments of some kind or other to the demands that post-16 education imposes upon them but, increasingly, public disputation surrounds the long-established benchmarks of the educational world in which those adjustments are made. It is a less stable postmodern world where once 'taken for granted' assumptions about the nature and worth of education are drawn into question and where dynamic tension rather than mutual enhancement may now characterise relationships between teachers, students and curricula. The art of studentship now entails some critical, creative or adaptive response to these tensions.

3

KNOWLEDGE AND THE PRESCRIPTION OF LEARNING OPPORTUNITIES

The central purpose of any education or training is the achievement of some state of greater awareness, or knowing. Whether it is the kind described as conceptual awareness or as competence, the state of knowing is reached through some process of acquiring some form of knowledge. But knowing, in the fullest sense of the term, entails understanding and that, in turn, requires that the learner locates what they know not only within wider conceptual networks but also within the context of its own production. They must know where their knowledge has come from, and how. 'Forgetting this, one is in constant danger of confusing the possession of blobs of so-called knowledge with knowing itself' (Pring, 1987: 286).

The expertise of the educator includes the selection and organisation of knowledge (the object of study) and of learning activities (the means of knowledge acquisition) to provide for the learner's most effective and efficient transition from a state of 'not knowing' to one of 'knowing'. But the art of the educator is not simply the mastery of knowledge and learning activities in order that some formulaic solution to learners' 'needs' can be calculated, for that is to lead to a view of the teacher as technician. The art is to do with the creation of opportunities for learning within the context of course aims and organising principles and the ever-changing dispositions of individuals and whole groups of learners. Opportunities in macro and micro form are created and re-created, moment by moment, by teachers on the basis of personally theorised, though often tacit, views of the relationship between knowledge, learning and the learner(s) in question. Knowledge, learning and the learner in such formulations are not discrete entities but are interdependent; they are constituent categories of teachers' theories of knowledge. In the context of creating learning opportunities in the class-room, none has meaning without reference to the other two. Thus it was that in the Leverhulme Study, teachers' accounts of their practices often treated problems of knowledge and learning as one: the suitability of course knowledge was judged as much by its facility to be learned as by its relevance or import to course aims, and whether various learning activities were worthwhile was gauged, in part, both by the perceived nature of the knowl-

38

edge to be acquired and by the dispositions to those activities of the learners concerned.

Knowledge and learning are seldom presented as interdependent in the established literature. They are more frequently treated as discrete entities to be addressed by two distinct and often isolated communities of scholars: those of philosophers and psychologists. Although individuals of various theoretical persuasions (Kelly, 1955; Esland, 1971) and, notably, the sociology of knowledge movement of the 1970s contributed much to an integrated theory of knowledge and learning, the remnants of a fragmented disciplinary approach to the problem are clearly in evidence. The discrete philosophy, psychology, sociology and history of the post-war teacher education curriculum are both manifestation and perpetuation of the fragmented view. The fact that A-level syllabuses and the National Curriculum prescribe both the content and the aims of learning but normally stop short of any account of the means of knowledge acquisition is a further illustration, while programmes based on GNVQ and NVQ 'outcomes' – and there are plenty of such course programmes – provide the clearest of all indications of a bifurcation of knowledge and learning. Only BTEC, in recent years, has consistently included reference to learning in its curriculum prescriptions.

Despite the apparent shortcomings of fragmented disciplinary approaches to knowledge and learning, I should be foolhardy to attempt my own account without regard to many centuries of scholarship. In the following pages, I offer a very brief overview of theories of knowledge and of prescriptions for the organisation of knowledge in post-16 education, identifying some of the key questions to emerge in the process.

THEORIES OF KNOWLEDGE AND KNOWLEDGE PRODUCTION

The problems of ontology and epistemology have been at the heart of educational debate for over 2000 years as models, theories and counter-theories have contested the nature of knowledge. It is not my purpose here to give any detailed consideration to that debate other than to point out four of its main features which remain problematic in contemporary curriculum planning, teaching and learning in post-16 education.

The first problem, an epistemological problem, that I wish to draw attention to concerns the origins of knowledge. The seventeenth-century philosopher, John Locke, claimed that all knowledge exists in some objective form, independent of the knower. Learning, therefore, was to be viewed straightforwardly as the acquisition of such knowledge. In the eighteenth century, however, Immanuel Kant contested this claim, arguing that human knowledge was not an objective 'human proof' knowledge belonging to some real external world as in the Lockean sense but was, instead, an approximation to reality governed by the perceptual framework of the knower. For

Kant, human knowledge was subjective and learning entailed the creation of that knowledge through the knower's interpretation of experience. Under such a view, learning entails the continued adaptation and re-adaptation of both the learner's interpretations of experiences and the interpretive system of the mind of which they are, in part, a product. However, despite their competing claims concerning the origins of knowledge, Locke and Kant both stressed absolute rationality and individualism.

The second problematic feature centres on distinctions between theoretical and practical knowledge, or conceptual and procedural knowledge. The nature of such distinctions and the relationships between them have occupied the minds of philosophers since classical times. Plato's view was that theoretical knowledge was the basis of most effective practice. A variant of this was advanced by Francis Bacon who, in the seventeenth century, went so far as to claim that metaphysical (theoretical) knowledge was all that was required for the generation of effective practice: 'whosoever knoweth any form, knoweth the utmost possibility of superinducing that nature upon any variety of matter. . . . The ways of sapience are not much liable either to particularity or chance' (Bacon, 1876: 118).

Aristotle, on the other hand, stressed the limitations of theoretical knowledge – necessarily formulated in terms of an abstracted, typical or general case – when it is applied to a particular case. For Aristotle, the unique qualities of the particular case (which constitutes the practical problem) must be taken into account if sound judgement of the problem is to be made. This requires the exercise of 'practical wisdom', entailing the selection, modification and generation of theory on the basis of practical experience.

More recently, others, such as Ryle (1949), Scheffler (1965) and Pring (1976) have articulated their views on basic curriculum organisation through pointing up distinctions between theoretical or propositional knowledge ('knowing that') and practical or procedural knowledge ('knowing how') and by arguing the relationships between them. However, one of the most common ways in which the theory–practice relationship is understood in modern times is as one of mutual exclusion or even opposition. 'On this view, "practice" is everything that "theory" is not' (Carr, 1987: 164). Little wonder, then, that contemporary British primary, secondary and tertiary education have been caught up in the contests between knowledge-centred, child-centred, problem-centred and task-centred or utilitarian curricula!

Third, there has never been strong agreement on the classification of knowledge 'areas' or 'domains'. Relatively recent distinctions for pedagogical purposes have emphasised subject anthologies and disciplines and some (for example, those proposed by Phenix, 1964 and Hirst, 1969) have claimed logical generic 'realms of meaning' or 'ways of knowing' grounded in distinct cognitive functions. The same is implied in Gardner's (1984) claim in respect of 'multiple intelligences'. Alternative views have stressed the essential unity of reality and, hence, knowledge and have argued for problem-based and integrated curricula and against the arbitrariness of subject-based classifications (e.g. Whitehead, 1950; Bruner, 1962). Indeed, Esland, working within the sociology of knowledge, has been moved to describe subjects as 'mystifications which arbitrarily differentiate and objectify the physical and symbolic universes. They thereby constrain the subjective identities of the individuals in a society, and obscure their realization that they are humanly produced' (Esland, 1971: 99).

Others have even laid claim to evidence of new forms of knowledge production, 'characterised by a constant flow back and forth between the fundamental and the applied, between the theoretical and the practical' (Gibbons et al., 1994: 19), all within a transdisciplinary context. I shall return to these claims in later chapters.

My fourth and final problematic feature of the post-16 curriculum is that of the social organisation of knowledge. A distinguishing feature of the sociology of knowledge has been its treatment of taken for granted assumptions about the selection and organisation of knowledge – 'what counts as educational knowledge' – as problematic. In such an approach, knowledge is treated 'as neither absolute, nor arbitrary, but as "available sets of meanings" which in any context do not merely "emerge", but are collectively "given"' (Young, 1971: 3). A key purpose of such a sociology has been to expose the processes through which meanings are socially constructed and become 'given'. This work has taken the form of a critical questioning of the cultural, institutional, class and gendered selection, distribution and legitimation of knowledge.

THE PRESCRIBED CURRICULA OF POST-16 EDUCATION

Contemporary post-16 curricula bear witness to this long history of unresolved debates. Subject-focused A-levels, 'process-oriented' vocational courses and contemporary debates about competence, generic skills, core skills, underpinning knowledge and the 'academic–vocational divide' are not the outcomes of rational curriculum development; rather, they are the historical debris of different ways in which successive generations have thought and talked about the classification of knowledge. Different views of the relationship between theoretical and practical knowledge and the place of experience in relation to theory and practice are evident in syllabus prescriptions, in teachers' accounts of their work and, also, in the ways in which distinctions are frequently made between 'theory' and 'practical' sessions, particularly in the timetables of science and vocational courses. The epistemological dispute about the origins of knowledge is also visible in post-16 education where prescriptions of course content, learning activities (in the notable case of BTEC) and assessment procedures imply a variety of presuppositions about knowledge, learning and knowing. Perhaps more forcefully and more publicly than at any time in the history of mass education, there is now a critical questioning of the status, relevance and legitimacy of the selection and organisation of knowledge in the post-16 curriculum and, most certainly and rightly, of long-established *rites de passage* and access opportunities.

The principal demarcations in post-16 education in practice lie between 'academic', 'vocational' and 'occupational' education or training. Each has its distinctive aims and each recruits its students from within a fairly well focused 'ability band', taking GCSE grade profiles as an indication of ability. What, then, is the nature of the knowledge prescribed for these distinctive courses?

A-level courses

The review of A-level syllabuses revealed considerable variety in the ways in which course content was identified. The most frequently used descriptors were 'knowledge', 'understanding' and 'skills' where the latter referred to competence in investigation, interpretation, communication, application, appreciation, or evaluation. But considerable importance was also attached to plain knowledge of facts and procedures which students were expected to recall or demonstrate with accuracy. Also used were descriptors such as aural perception, technique, organisation, comprehension, experimentation, analysis and critical appraisal. The A-level, it would seem, demanded every conceivable form of knowledge. However, closer inspection revealed marked differences between courses, at least in their prescriptive forms, as the following examples of assessment objectives and mark schedules demonstrates.

From the A-level French syllabus statement of assessment objectives, detailed in Table 3.1, it is apparent that greatest emphasis is placed upon reception and communication skills: reading, writing, listening and

Table 3.1 Extracts from an A-level French syllabus

Assessment objectives	Marks (%)
The examination will test candidates' ability to:	
1. Understand language spoken at normal speed by native speakers	20
2. Understand printed and written texts . . . in a variety of registers, designed for consumption by native speakers	20
3. Communicate effectively in the spoken language to exchange information, ideas and opinions	20
4. Demonstrate knowledge and understanding of aspects of the civilisation and culture . . . where the language is spoken	+
5. Communicate effectively in the written language to convey information, ideas and opinions	20
6. Show appropriate and accurate handling of the written language	+

Note: The two items marked + add up to 20%

speaking. The effectiveness, appropriateness and accuracy of communication is particularly stressed. The term, 'understanding', is used here for two quite distinct purposes. First, it concerns the accurate interpretation of the French language used in written or spoken communication (objectives 1 and 2), an interpretation which can only be made on the basis of an adequate knowledge and understanding of French vocabulary and of the rules, conventions and contexts which govern the usage of the French language. Second, it concerns comprehension of the subject matter communicated and this depends not only upon students' capabilities in literal translation but upon their wider knowledge of aspects of civilisation and culture as detailed in objective 4. However, on the face of it, the syllabus is focused much more upon technical skills (in communication), upon knowledge as fact (of vocabulary and French culture) and upon understanding of rules and conventions of the use of language than upon students' powers of creativity, critique and evaluation. For the most part, it is a 'received understanding' that students are expected to acquire and it is only objective 4 which appears to provide opportunities for students' use of declarative knowledge and their critical engagement with the subject matter.

The assessment objectives for the music syllabus listed in Table 3.2 also attach importance to technical skill, as is evidenced in assessment objectives 1, 2 and 5. Although aural perceptiveness, composition and performance ought not to be seen purely as technical skills, they do entail a significant amount of technical knowledge and skill as indicated in the 'subject content' section of the syllabus, which identifies memory, the capacity to locate errors of pitch and rhythm and the ability to use a 'technical vocabulary' as skills to be tested in connection with objectives 1 and 2. However, objectives 2 and 5 also provide for recognition of interpretive skills and creativity. 'Credit will be given for rhythmic interest and melodic shape appropriate to the character of the words . . . .' Objectives 3 and 4 appear to provide most explicitly for understanding, analysis and critique. However, the papers designed to assess these abilities account for only between one-fifth and one-third of the whole examination. Moreover, it is not made clear in the

Table 3.2 Extracts from an A-level music syllabus

Assessment objectives	Marks (%)
The examination will test a candidate's ability to:	
1. Give evidence of aural perceptiveness	28
2. Demonstrate skills in the techniques of composition	20
3. Demonstrate an ability to understand musical forms, textures and styles, together with the development of instrumentation	20–32
4. Demonstrate an ability to analyse, to comment perceptively on, and to write lucidly about basic aspects of musical style and structure	
5. Perform with technical and interpretive skill	20–32

syllabus whether it is 'received' understanding, analysis and critique which is the focus of study or whether students would be credited for an understanding, analysis and critique grounded in their personal appreciation of music. But this is a problem which besets many syllabuses. Overall, while the music syllabus appears to attach greater importance to conceptual knowledge than does the French syllabus, technical knowledge and skills are still of primary importance.

The physics syllabus (Table 3.3) is far more explicit on the nature of course knowledge, at least in respect of its assessment objectives. From other information provided, it is clear that some 50 per cent of examination marks are given for recall and experimental work and 50 per cent for application, understanding, communication, evaluation and judgement. It is also apparent that objectives (b), (c) and (d) draw from a variety of knowledge including logical, technical, procedural, analytical, interpretive and evaluative, while objective (a) is concerned purely with basic factual or procedural knowledge and (e) with analysis and evaluation. There is a greater emphasis upon interpretive, analytical and evaluative knowledge than upon technical knowledge and skills. Moreover, that 'higher order' knowledge appears to

Table 3.3 Extracts from an A-level physics syllabus

Assessment objectives		Marks (%)
The examination will assess the following abilities:		
(a) *Recall*	Factual knowledge, terminology, definitions, conventions, experimental methods, laws, models	c10
(b) *Experimental*	Techniques; planning and execution of experiments; analysis and presentation of experimental results; simple treatment of limitations and errors	c40
(c) *Application*	Of knowledge to problem solving in familiar and unfamiliar situations, including both numerical and qualitative, theoretical and practical approaches	c16
(d) *Understanding and communication*	Interpretation of data in various forms; translation of data from one form to another; compilation of clear, concise accounts; use of models to explain phenomena	c17
(e) *Evaluation and judgement*	Analysis and assessment of data and situations; decision making on the basis of such analysis and assessment	c17

Table 3.4 Extracts from an A-level sociology syllabus

Assessment objectives	Marks (%)
The examination will assess the candidate's ability to:	
1. Demonstrate a knowledge and understanding of sociological material (including concepts, theories and methods) and of the theoretical and practical considerations influencing sociological enquiry	26
2. Interpret sociological material presented in a variety of forms	c18.5
3. Use sociological material to analyse social issues and personal experience	c18.5
4. Evaluate sociological theories and methods	c18.5
5. Evaluate sociological and non-sociological evidence and arguments	c18.5
6. Present explanations, ideas and arguments in a coherent and logical form	+

Note: + = subsumed in marks above

assume a more significant presence than in the case of the French and music syllabuses considered earlier.

On the face of it, the sociology syllabus (Table 3.4) attaches greatest importance to 'higher order' knowledge. The whole thrust of the course appears to be the promotion of knowledge, understanding, interpretation, usage, analysis and evaluation of concepts, theories and methods, where the emphasis of the latter is at least as much upon a critical awareness of methodology as upon the application of given techniques. I do not wish to overstate the higher order knowledge content here for it is certainly true that for students to achieve any of the higher order knowledge or skills they need to have mastery over much basic factual and procedural knowledge. However, the heavy emphasis upon assessments of performance at the 'higher order' level is inescapable and most certainly greater than that claimed in any of the other three syllabuses considered earlier.

Before further discussion of these examples, I should stress the need for extreme caution in any interpretation of evidence such as this. We should certainly be wary of making sweeping judgements on the limited basis of a few examples and there are, perhaps, three observations on the matter that I should make. First, the syllabuses have different authors and for that reason at least are bound to contain different forms of expression. It could be that styles of expression account for many of the differences between syllabuses that I have noted. However, I must say that I doubt whether this is the case. The syllabus objectives, content, criteria and specimens in each case are too internally consistent for this to be so. The way that knowledge and skills in practical performance in music are described is not remotely paralleled in any other syllabus; the emphasis upon knowledge and skills in the presentation and understanding of written and aural communication in the French syllabus is unique among these four cases; and the emphasis upon critical awareness in the sociology syllabus is unequalled elsewhere. While I do not claim that my characterisation of the differences between these four syllabuses is precise in every detail, the fact that there are important differences between the forms of knowledge prescribed is inescapable. Second, it is important for me to stress that the differences between syllabuses reported here are not necessarily attributable to differences between the subjects concerned. In the case of all of the subjects represented here, there are considerable variations between syllabus options and between examining boards in respect of the forms of knowledge prescribed. Third, in drawing inferences from the exemplar cases selected here, one should note that syllabuses and, particularly, assessment objectives have their own 'built-in' limitations: the reduction of curricula to syllabus format inevitably restricts illumination of the processes of learning, themselves essential to any real understanding of the quality of the knowledge concerned. This is most evident in the frequent use of the term, 'understanding', seldom qualified to show whether the uncritical assimilation of 'received understanding' or students' personal constructions of *an* understanding based upon their critical engagement with their own experiences is intended.

The literature holds many ways of classifying knowledge and, were syllabuses more forthcoming on matters of detail, it would no doubt be possible to make firm distinctions between them on the basis of such classifications. But syllabuses offer only a partial account of knowledge and, for that reason, the distinctions that I make at this stage are on the basis of broad provisional categories.

There are three broad sets of distinctions to be made. First, syllabuses differed markedly in the attention they gave to what I have referred to as 'higher' and 'lower' orders of knowledge. By 'lower orders of knowledge', I mean information or simple skills which link only a limited number of concepts, do not require reference to wider fields of knowledge for their justification and which, in their learning, entail reception, memorisation and rehearsal and, in their application, require only re-presentation in their original learned form. All fifty-one syllabuses from eight boards which I studied for the purpose saw fit to credit some form of lower order knowledge in their examination marking schemes but they differed considerably in the amount of credit which they attached to it. There were no discernible patterns among these data: neither subjects nor boards appeared to account for the variation. On the matter of 'higher order knowledge', syllabuses appeared to vary to an even greater degree than with lower order knowledge. Not only did they differ in the degree to which they credited it, but higher order knowledge was conceived rather differently in different cases. These observations about syllabus accounts of higher and lower order knowledge prompt important questions about the concept of 'A-level' to which I shall return later.

The second set of distinctions that I wish to draw attention to concern relationships between knowledge and its anticipated usage or application. An important criterion, it would seem, is whether knowledge or skills are applied to known, tightly circumscribed problems or to novel and 'open-ended' problems. The term 'application', although frequently used in syllabuses, did not distinguish types of problem according to this criterion, except in a few cases. 'Application' was used to describe any activity, ranging from the enactment of given procedures in a familiar situation to the creation of procedures for the solution of largely unfamiliar problems. In one context, it might have entailed only memorisation and practice while, in another, it might have demanded analysis, synthesis, creativity and evaluation. These observations, too, give rise to questions about the 'A-level-ness' of A-level studies.

The final distinctions that I wish to note are those that are made between the *theoretical* and the *practical*. Some A-level syllabuses made no explicit reference to theoretical and practical knowledge categories although many used the term 'practical work' in such a way as to denote application or performance, notably where the latter had some quite tangible, physical form. In cases where there was explicit reference to theoretical and practical aspects of a course, however, syllabuses varied considerably in their treatments of the theoretical and the practical. Not only did they share no stable view of the essential discreteness–inseparability of the theoretical and the practical but they held different views of which knowledge may give rise to which. Among the syllabuses reviewed, a number used the term 'practical' in no other sense than to mean, 'application of the theoretical'. A similar number used the term to mean, 'experience from which to develop the theoretical'. The lack of any great coherence in the treatment of such matters, again, begs questions about the coherence of the concept, 'A-level'.

This brief excursion into A-level syllabuses has revealed something of the variety of ways in which courses are prescribed. Despite this, 'A-level' is endowed with great uniformity of meaning in the popular imagination. A-levels are frequently referred to as 'academic', requiring intellectual curiosity and entailing extensive written work in ways that imply that all subjects and syllabuses are equally demanding of students' mastery of knowledge and powers of critique. In the 1980s, Prime Minister Thatcher even declared A-levels to be the 'gold standard', revealing presuppositions that there is some internally consistent standard among A-levels and that this standard is sufficiently recognisable to allow discrimination between what is and what is not of that standard. The 'points system' which underpins higher education selection procedures is based upon similar assumptions, especially when employed in its most crude form. But it is such conceptions of A-level, grounded more in the public imagination than in empirical evidence or experience of A-level courses themselves, which define both political and popular realities and which, through their impact upon educational planning and young people's actions, are real in their consequences.

47

Vocational courses: from BTEC National to Advanced GNVQ

At the time that the Leverhulme Study was initiated, many of the vocational courses were operating as BTEC Nationals and it was during the period of the research that most of these came to be replaced by Advanced GNVQs. In this brief review of the knowledge content of vocational courses, I shall concentrate initially upon the BTEC courses before moving to GNVQs.

BTEC Nationals

Unlike A-levels, where prescriptive statements issued primarily from subject- and board-specific syllabuses, BTEC courses were bound by a fairly detailed, over-arching prescription of the distinctive qualities of the BTEC National. Teachers and students frequently asserted the distinctiveness of the 'BTEC way', as did formal course descriptions, and there is little doubt that, in the minds of many of those who experienced them, courses were located within a coherent BTEC philosophy and practice.

BTEC prescriptions were distinguishable by their breadth of reference, covering aspects of curriculum largely untouched by other syllabuses or course specifications. Guidelines included prescriptions of teaching and learning strategies and of the nature and purpose of assignments, matters which in other courses had been left entirely to the judgement of teachers.

> BTEC is . . . concerned with not only *what* is learned but also *how* it is learned; the importance of teaching and learning strategies will there-fore be reflected in BTEC's publications, approval and validation requirements . . .
>
> Course teams must . . . incorporate a range of teaching and learning strategies in their programmes of study. These should include opportunities for students to:
>
> • share in determining what they learn, choose methods that suit them best, and be actively involved in their learning;
> • tackle work-related and/or work-based problems, and make use of real-life experiences;
> • work with others (e.g. in teams) and practise social and interactive skills;
> • speculate and experiment;
> • use appropriate available resources and technology;
> • work to deadlines, and experience and balance conflicting pressures;
> • review and evaluate their work . . .
>
> The strategies advocated here, taken together, entail a learner-oriented approach that should now be typical of all BTEC programmes of study.
>
> (BTEC, 1986b: 1–3)

Assignments involved the application of knowledge and skills to meaningful tasks in work-related situations; they also enabled students to elicit their own knowledge from those situations. They were about learning-by-doing: encouraging students to find things out for themselves and helping them to develop their skills in realistic contexts.

A number of skills and personal qualities that are of great value in working life can be developed only through certain kinds of learning experience. They include:

- self-reliance and independence;
- self-awareness;
- adaptability;
- self-management and problem-solving skills.

These cannot be developed by methods that encourage passivity and acceptance of passed-down knowledge; they require methods that give students the opportunity to exercise independent thought, to plan and organise their own work, and to tackle new situations.

(BTEC, 1986a: 2–3)

Course content was identified in BTEC prescriptions in a variety of ways. Guidelines identified the acquisition of skills and the development of personal qualities as the essential concerns of all courses but did so more by demonstrating how they might be acquired or developed than by giving detailed consideration to the nature of the skills and qualities themselves. The reader was left, to a large extent, to infer the exact nature of the skills and qualities from the given circumstances in which they were to be facilitated. Guidelines also distinguished between core, optional and indicative content, where content was knowledge or 'subject matter', while unit specifications provided greater detail of indicative content linked to objectives. The following example of prescriptive statements or objectives is extracted from the Accommodation Services Unit specification of the BTEC National Hotel, Catering and Institutional Operations course:

1　Recognise the need for effective care and maintenance of building fabric and services.
2　Demonstrate an understanding of the importance of effective energy utilisation and conservation.
3　Appreciate the principles of planning of accommodation, interior design and adaptation of areas for multiple use.
4　Examine a range of services required by guests in a variety of types of residential accommodation and evaluate how these may be met.
5　Appreciate the range and use of leasing and contracting services.
6　Apply appropriate work study techniques to the efficient organisation of the Housekeeping department.

Foremost in the BTEC prescriptions examined for the purpose of this study were the skills and personal qualities referred to above although there was little to indicate the degree of complexity of these skills or the extent to which they were seen to depend upon higher order knowledge. Possibly because of the difficulties of establishing criteria for self-reliance, self-aware-ness, adaptability, self-management and problem-solving skills, BTEC elected to describe their development in the form of general objectives or aims rather than their achievement in the form of specific objectives or 'outcomes' statements.

However, some insight into the knowledge and skills entailed is afforded by BTEC's statements on assignments where reference is made to the appli-cation of knowledge and skills to work-related situations. On the one hand, application and practice of skills 'already learned' suggests a Platonian view of the primacy of theoretical knowledge over practical knowledge. On the other hand, BTEC were heavily critical of 'passed-down knowledge' and went to considerable lengths to assert the value of students finding out for themselves and exercising independent thought when confronting problems of an essentially practical nature. On balance, it is this latter, Aristotelian, view of knowledge which appears to have been most frequently and force-fully asserted by BTEC in its prescriptions of the acquisition of skills. For present purposes, there are two observations to make. First, despite BTEC's great stress upon practical knowledge, its prescriptions provided scope for widely differing views of relationships between practical and theoretical knowledge. Second, BTEC's failure to distinguish between theory–practice and practice–theory relationships, coupled with the ambiguity of its prescriptions, has, in the event, proved to be of crucial importance. Whether intentional or not, it has created the possibility for the theory–practice rela-tionship to be conceived as a dialectical relationship, as theory-in-practice, or *praxis*.

> *Praxis* . . . is informed action which, by reflection on its character and consequences, reflexively changes the 'knowledge-base' which informs it . . . it remakes the conditions of informed action and constantly reviews action and the knowledge which informs it.
>
> (Carr and Kemmis, 1986: 33)

Thus, BTEC's concern with 'learning-by-doing', 'students applying what they have learned' and 'the integration of knowledge and skills from different parts of the course' might be understood not as conflicting aims but as parts of some unified theory of knowledge and learning in which theoretical and practical knowledge are conceived as a duality, not a dualism. Alternatively, it could be that BTEC offered no such unified theory and that those examples of praxis which did occur arose out of what teachers and students were able to bring to bear upon the process of curriculum making in the context of incomplete BTEC prescriptions.

50

While opportunities for the development of personal skills and qualities through *praxis* might have been visible in some BTEC assignment specifications – as in the case of the community assignment in the Nursery Nursing course which asserted the importance of analysis in the achievement of 'flexible, interactive and responsible' child care practice – the specifications of objectives for course units suggested a very different view of knowledge. The verbs, 'understand' and 'appreciate' were most frequently used in a context which suggests that students were expected to acquire a 'received understanding' or a 'given appreciation' rather than to engage critically with the subject matter in order to construct personal understandings or appreciations. 'Understand *essential* . . . structure', 'Appreciate *relevant* . . . ', 'Understand *relevant* factors . . . ', 'Appreciate *the* importance of . . . ', 'Appreciate *the* principles of planning . . . ', 'Appreciate *the* range and use . . . ' all imply that legitimate course knowledge resides in some predetermined and finite information and knowledge base. Other descriptors, such as 'recognise important aspects of . . . ', 'recognise the need for . . . ' , 'apply appropriate work study techniques', 'identify the role of . . . ', 'detail the range of . . . ', 'identify the providers of . . . ' and 'distinguish between different categories of . . . ' appear to confirm that a lower order of knowledge and skill complexity was the essential content of the courses concerned. It is interesting to note the use of the term, 'evaluate', in Objective 4 of the Accommodation Services unit: 'examine a range of services required . . . and evaluate how these may be met'. Given the context, it is difficult to see what was to be evaluated or how evaluation could be carried out at all. In this particular case, it appears that 'evaluate' has been taken to mean 'propose' and that no evaluative skills were required at all.

The clear impression to be gained from BTEC National course prescriptions is one of minimal variation between courses in respect of the skill and knowledge forms concerned. Two distinct forms of knowledge are suggested. The first, from unit specifications, is of a corpus of vocationally specific low order knowledge and simple skills that students were expected to acquire and apply with no necessary critical intervention on their own part. The second, from the over-arching course guidelines, is of knowledge and skills developed by means of some critical engagement of indeterminate order and complexity, by the learner, with knowledge in a practical context.

Advanced GNVQs

The change from BTEC Nationals to Advanced GNVQs was swift, following as it did the publication of the White Paper, *Education and Training for the 21st Century*, in May 1991 (DES *et al.*, 1991). By September 1992, the pilot scheme for some 3,800 young people was in place with short-term plans for the incorporation of all BTEC Nationals into the GNVQ framework. The new qualification was 'designed to provide a broad-based vocational education and offer students an alternative to GCSEs, GCE A-levels and the occupationally specific National Vocational Qualifications (NVQs)' (FEU, 1993: 1).

On the face of it, it would appear that some of the ambiguity surrounding BTEC's notions of knowledge and learning had disappeared and with it, possibly, the 'space' for *praxis*: GNVQ prescriptions tended to a very much tighter and more detailed specification of knowledge content. However, despite this, there was far less evidence of any critical consideration of knowledge or learning than there had been under BTEC. GNVQ was specified, it seemed, with less regard to the *nature* of the knowledge or learning entailed than to 'external' considerations: its utility as a preparation for employment and further and higher education; the relevance of its skills and knowledge application to occupations; its parity with academic qualifications; its relationship with NVQs; its distinctiveness from NVQs; and its utility for classroom-based (as opposed to work-based) learning and performance (Hyland, 1994a). Its function was to 'rationalise existing post-16 general education with a vocational focus by introducing a standardised model for all subject areas and levels' (Oates, 1996: 20).

NCVQ's own account, however, emphasised diversity as opposed to standardisation of the learning experience and, in particular, stressed student responsibility:

> GNVQs have been designed to promote the development of a wide range of cognitive skills, some practical skills, and a body of knowledge and understanding in a broad vocational area. . . . The need to demonstrate these skills to achieve the qualification promotes active learning through projects, assignments, research and investigative activities. Such learning should be supplemented with classroom study, and the use of textbooks or open learning materials, to cover the breadth of knowledge shown by the range statements within each GNVQ unit. . . . An important aspect of the GNVQ curriculum which is a natural consequence of the above learning approach is that students take greater responsibility for their own learning . . .
>
> The outcomes set out in the GNVQ units encourage students to carry out projects, assignments, industry and market surveys, and case studies of industrial or organisational change; to investigate processes and products; to plan and organise operations and events; to design products and services; and so on.
>
> (NCVQ, 1995: 10 and 23)

The launch of GNVQs was accompanied by lavish investment, aggressive public relations and overt sloganising. They were '*doomed* to succeed' (Hyland, op. cit.: 106). But the glossy brochures and advertising videos gave all too little critical attention to GNVQ knowledge and learning. Within only six months of the launch of the pilot scheme, however, it was possible to proclaim the positive qualities of GNVQs in the most confident terms.

> General National Vocational Qualifications (GNVQs) have the poten-
> tial to transform learning for a majority of 16–19-year-olds. . . . They
> maximise opportunities for the individual to achieve by being defined
> in terms of outcomes and providing scope to accumulate credit.
>
> (CBI, 1993: 15–16)

Success was claimed purely on the basis of the GNVQ curriculum prescription: so assured and assertive was the prescription that it was apparently not deemed necessary to await the results of the pilot scheme. 'It was planned and, therefore, it would happen' (Bloomer and Morgan, 1993) – an assumption all too common in the deterministic thought underpinning the 'teacher-proof/learner-proof' curriculum that I have had occasion to criticise elsewhere in this book.

In the event, the introduction of GNVQs was not the huge success that initial publicity claimed it would be. Some two-thirds of students on the 1992 Advanced course pilot scheme did not complete their courses satisfactorily and as many as half had withdrawn mid-course (Abrams, 1994). 'Only half of those who began a GNVQ programme in 1993 had achieved a full award after two years' (SCAA, 1996: 23). Moreover, it emerged that the massive increases in GNVQ enrolments – by far the strongest of NCVQ's claims to success – were not attributable to the qualities of GNVQ courses at all:

> The study found little evidence of centres choosing to offer GNVQs
> because of a definite preference for them over other pre-existing voca-
> tional or pre-vocational awards. GNVQs were chosen because the
> government was perceived to be fully committed to replacing existing
> awards, and making GNVQs the main non GCE-A-level qualification
> for students in post-compulsory education.
>
> (FEU et al., 1994: 5)

From its early days, the Advanced GNVQ was cast in an awkward situation. It was an *ad hoc* innovation for 'assessment-led change' (Oates, 1996: 9). Borne of NCVQ, there were continuous pressures for its compatibility with NVQ. Succeeding, as it did to a large extent, a range of predominantly BTEC National courses, and being taught very often by ex-BTEC teachers, the Advanced course had to contend with the legacy of the distinctive BTEC philosophy of teaching and assignment-based learning – a philosophy which was largely antagonistic to that which had informed the development of NVQs. And if that situation was not difficult enough, it was declared comparable with A-level!

But it is the content and organisation of GNVQ courses which constitute their most distinctive qualities and which reveal, most starkly, the behaviourism upon which the whole model is based. GNVQs are modular courses made up of 'units', each of which is broken down into 'elements' which, in turn, are broken down into 'performance criteria', 'range statements' and associated 'evidence indicators'. The potential for the fragmentation of knowledge through such a method of course prescription is plain to see as the example taken from the Health and Social Care course shows in Table 3.5.

Given that a total of twenty-four elements (114 performance criteria) comprise the Health and Social Care course, the successful integration of course knowledge across units, as referred to under 'Guidance', would, to say the very least, be exacting of any teacher's dedication and ingenuity. While the GNVQ prescription does, indeed, invite teachers to 'relate' the work covered in one unit with that of another, the assessment system appears to give no additional credit to teachers and students who do this and one is left to wonder what degree and quality of integration might take place in practice.

The advanced GNVQ's clearest departures from BTEC National are in its mechanisms for assessment. Not only are the syllabus requirements and assessment criteria specified in far greater detail than under BTEC, but candidates have to complete a short-answer or multiple-choice test at the conclusion of each unit of study. (The specification for the test to accompany Element 1.1 in Table 3.5 is shown in Table 3.6.)

The purpose of tests such as these is 'to give the public confidence in the consistency of assessment for these new qualifications and to provide a checking function to confirm a student's coverage of the range' (BTEC *et al.*, 1995b: 5). It is important to note that it is the need for public accountability, or political confidence, which is driving important curriculum decisions here. Moreover, noting that students would be allowed only two minutes to answer each of the questions in this test, it is possible to gain some insight into the quality of knowledge that they would be able to display in such an exercise.

> While in theory criterion-referenced assessment is welcomed for making transparent what is required, in practice this clarity is elusive. . . . The dilemma is that criteria are never without ambiguity and the temptation is to be drawn into 'a never-ending spiral of specification' (Wolf, 1995). The result of this can be over-detailed assessment and a 'tick-box' mentality which emphasises coverage rather than understanding.
>
> (Stobart, 1996: 2–3)

The claim that, under GNVQ, students assume greater responsibility for their own learning is often projected as fact. However, assumptions that the Advanced GNVQ rests heavily upon student-centred practices are, it seems, hopelessly naive if research into students' experiences of those courses is taken into account. On the subject of teaching, work by Phil Hodkinson and myself (Bloomer and Hodkinson 1996) and by others (e.g. Thompson, 1996) points to frequent reports of students' dependency upon teachers and textbooks and little evidence of vocational progressivism. Where there has been evidence of students exercising control over their own learning – and there have certainly been occasions where it was noticeable – it appeared to owe far more to the idiosyncrasies of teacher or student agency than to the curriculum prescriptions of GNVQ.

Concerns about GNVQ assessment practices fed directly into the Assessment Review Group (Capey, 1995) which found that misgivings about the laborious and cumbersome nature of GNVQ procedures were widely shared among teachers, students and inspectors. Capey pointed to the large number of 'evidence indicators' prescribed for each unit as being central to the problem of assessment manageability and recommended a reduction in the number of such indicators and the adoption of a more 'integrated approach'. In recommending a move from element-based to unit-based assessment, the Review Group felt that,

> this might also lead to more effective learning. . . . [One] implication is that assessors would be making more generalised judgements about performance (see the level descriptions in National Curriculum assessment) when unit-referenced evidence indicators replaced element-referenced indicators.
>
> (Capey, 1995: 24)

Thus, the Review Group proposed a significant relaxing of what appeared to be the most constraining features of the GNVQ framework. Perhaps this would lead, as Capey clearly hoped, to more effective learning.

But the Review Group were also subjected to what they described as 'considerable pressure' from other sources for more demonstrable reliability and consistency of assessments. Doubtless, these pressures stemmed from political concern about public confidence. At the same time, Capey evidently saw the desirability of a form of assessment based upon the integration of skills and knowledge across unit boundaries. Presumably, the Review Group recognised that integration would rarely occur unless it was formally assessed. Capey's dilemma was clear: on the one hand he recognised the educational importance of the integration of experience across unit boundaries; on the other, he was subject to largely non-educationally grounded concerns for accountability. The two interests were not easily reconciled and, in the event, concerns for accountability proved the stronger:

> The review group therefore recommends that: an externally-set assignment that contributes towards grading be produced for one unit or, exceptionally, groups of units for each Advanced and Intermediate GNVQ. The assignment will be internally assessed and externally moderated by the external verifier. . . . Given the resource implications

Table 3.5 An Advanced GNVQ health and social care element description
(Element 1.1)

Element 1.1: Investigate legal rights and responsibilities in relation to equality of opportunity

PERFORMANCE CRITERIA

A student must:

1. Describe why the **principles** which underpin **equality of opportunity legislation** are important to health and social care practitioners

2. Describe the responsibilities of individuals and organisations under **equality of opportunity legislation**

3. Describe **consistencies and inconsistencies** in the rights which individuals have under **equality of opportunity legislation**

4. Explain the **routes** through which individuals may seek redress under **equality of opportunity legislation**

5. Explain the **factors** which influence the formation of **equality of opportunity legislation**

RANGE

Principles: equality of care, individual rights, individual choice

Equality of opportunity legislation relating to: gender, race, disability, pay, employment

Consistencies and inconsistencies: rights under the law, interpretation of the law

Routes: organisational, professional bodies, regulatory bodies, legal systems (local community, national)

Factors: key groups (pressure groups, publicly-funded bodies, political parties, Parliament, European Union), changes in societal values, resource implications, European Court of Human Rights

EVIDENCE INDICATORS

A report, focusing on equality of opportunity legislation relating to one category in the range, which:

- describes why the principles which underpin equality of opportunity legislation are important to health and social care practitioners

- describes the responsibilities of individuals and organisations

- describes consistencies and inconsistencies in equality of opportunity rights between the four UK countries

- explains how individuals may seek redress under the law, providing examples of each of the routes listed in the range

- explains three of the factors which influence the formation of equality of opportunity legislation, giving one example for each.

Notes on the responsibilities of individuals and organisations under equality of opportunity legislation relating to the remaining four categories in the range.

AMPLIFICATION

Principles which underpin legislation (PC1): students should not describe detailed aspects of the legislation, but should explain the key principles and their importance to health and social care practitioners in terms of equality of care and the promotion of individual rights and choice.

Examples of legislation are the Sex Discrimination Acts, the Race Relations Act, the Chronically Sick and Disabled Persons Act, the Equal Pay Act, the Fair Employment Act (NI).

Responsibilities (PC2): students should know the key responsibilities of individuals and organisations, in relation to the principles identified in PC1.

Consistencies and inconsistencies (PC3): it may help students to consider similarities between the rights held by people with disabilities and those held by different ethnic groups under race relations legislation. Inconsistencies can be between parts of the UK, e.g. Fair Employment Act in NI, or between groups, e.g. legal age of consent for heterosexual and homosexual people.

Routes (PC4): students need to understand the variety of routes available for seeking redress; they do not need to know the full details of each.

Organisational (PC4 range): organisational means of seeking redress could include, for example, the range of ways in which clients' complaints are handled in health and social care services, and the rights offered under the Patient's Charter.

Legal systems (PC4 range): could include industrial tribunals in the local community, or the courts nationally.

GUIDANCE

Because equality of opportunity rights and responsibilities, discrimination and ethical issues are important facets of all work in health and social care, teachers and tutors could relate this unit (in terms of both assessment and learning) to all the other mandatory units within this GNVQ. Teachers and tutors could also draw on media coverage of relevant ongoing issues as useful source material for learning and assessment, particularly as the basis for group discussion and debate.

Source: BTEC *et al.*, 1995a, 18. Reproduced with permission of the National Council for Vocational Qualifications.

Table 3.6 An Advanced GNVQ health and social care test specification
(Element 1.1)

FOCUS 1: Principles and responsibilities
Reference: Element 1.1 PC1, PC2

RANGE
a **Principles**: equality of care, individual rights, individual choice
abc **Equality of opportunity legislation** relating to: gender, race, disability, pay, employment

EXTERNAL TEST REQUIREMENTS
a Identify the principles which underpin equality of opportunity legislation (2)
b Identify the ways in which equality of opportunity legislation is applied in health and social care settings (2)
c Describe the responsibilities of individuals and organisations under equality of opportunity legislation (2)

FOCUS 2: Inconsistencies and routes
Reference: Element 1.1 PC3, PC4

RANGE
a **Equality of opportunity legislation** relating to: gender, race, disability, pay, employment
a **Consistencies and inconsistencies**: rights under the law, interpretation of the law
b **Routes**: organisational, professional bodies, regulatory bodies, legal systems (local community, national)

EXTERNAL TEST REQUIREMENTS
a Identify consistencies and inconsistencies in respect of equality of opportunity legislation (2)
b Explain routes through which individuals or organisations may seek redress under the law (2)

FOCUS 3: Formation of legislation
Reference: Element 1.1 PC5

RANGE
ab **Equality of opportunity legislation** relating to: gender, race, disability, pay, employment
ab **Factors**: key groups (pressure groups, publicly-funded bodies, political parties, Parliament, European Union), changes in societal values, resource implications, European Court of Human Rights

EXTERNAL TEST REQUIREMENTS
a Explain the factors influencing the formation of equality of opportunity legislation (2)
b Describe the role of key groups in forming equality of opportunity legislation (2)

Note: The numbers in brackets indicate the number of questions to be set for each item specified
Source: BTEC *et al.*, 1995b, 8–9. Reproduced with permission of the NCVQ.

for the system as a whole the assignment will replace the external test for the units involved. It is anticipated that it will be a unit identified as taken later in the course which may itself harness knowledge and skills from earlier units . . . thus providing a 'synoptic' quality to the assessment. Where this unit draws directly on the learning from other units it may not be necessary to test these.

(Capey, 1995: 28–29)

Capey's main recommendations for more manageable assessment procedures and for more externally set assessments were 'consolidated' in the form of Dearing's *Review of Qualifications for 16–19 Year Olds* (SCAA, 1996: 26). However, the case for assessments which promoted the integration of skills and knowledge across unit boundaries appears to have become lost in the process. Dearing offers nothing – apart from an endorsement of the Capey recommendation that the focus of assessment be shifted from elements to units – that provides for a greater unification of knowledge and skills. He offers little hope that the student experience of GNVQ will change significantly from those outcomes-dominated, teacher-centred, student-receptive experiences reported elsewhere (Bloomer and Hodkinson, 1996).

Reflecting on the qualities of the BTEC National course prescriptions described earlier, there are a number of points to note about the transformation from BTEC National to Advanced GNVQ courses in respect of course knowledge and the creation of learning opportunities. First, while BTEC National courses were subjected to a distinctive 'BTEC philosophy' grounded in beliefs and values concerning course knowledge, learning, teaching and assessment, the emphasis in the Advanced GNVQ is upon the tight prescription of standardised learning *outcomes* rather than upon the processes, activities or experiences which constitute learning itself. Second, GNVQ knowledge is subject to far more detailed specification than that of BTEC and, while GNVQ appears to have the stronger grounds for claiming consistency of outcomes, it also appears to afford a greater likelihood that knowledge will be fragmented in the experience of students. Third, GNVQ literature gives little critical attention to the business of teaching. Indeed, it would be absurd were it to do so given its lack of any serious consideration of learning. However, the metaphor, 'delivery', is used very frequently by NCVQ and by others party to GNVQ courses. From such terminology can be detected the dominant underpinning concepts of knowledge and learning at play in GNVQ design and implementation. Fourth, there can be little doubt that the change from BTEC to GNVQ has brought about a dramatic change in the purposes and practices of assessment. Under BTEC, considerable emphasis was placed upon 'assignments for learning', upon assessment being integral to, rather than an adjunct of, learning. Under GNVQ, the dominant justification is plainly political as assessment has been directed to the service of accountability within a crude comparability model.

59

REFLECTIONS ON PRESCRIBED KNOWLEDGE AND LEARNING IN THE POST-16 CURRICULUM

In so far as it has been possible to penetrate the post-16 curriculum in this brief discussion of course knowledge and learning opportunities, it is apparent that there are some important differences between the *pre*scriptive curricula of A-level, BTEC National and Advanced GNVQ.

A-levels are primarily knowledge-based courses. While there are occasional references to practical work, fieldwork and experimentation, it is theoretical knowledge located within academic specialisms which is most highly valued. 'Factual' information, technical skills, application and creativity are also valued but in a manner which places them in a subordinate relationship to theoretical knowledge. While practical knowledge is given recognition in A-level syllabuses, this is at least as much because practical application offers an opportunity for testing theoretical knowledge as because practical knowledge is valued in its own right. But the A-level emphasis upon theoretical knowledge does not, of itself, imply any particular view or theory of learning. Indeed, a reading of A-level syllabuses confirms that the declared ends (students' acquisition of theoretical knowledge) might be achieved in a variety of ways, combining strategies derived from any of a number of theories of learning. However, it would be an incomplete and possibly misleading account of A-level knowledge and learning which ignored assessment practices and their potential impact upon the curriculum. By far the greatest proportion of assessment at A-level is by terminal examination. The two- or three-hour papers that are most commonly used are invariably broken down into smaller sections, while other papers require one-word or short answers which delimit opportunities for students to demonstrate their knowledge in its full complexity. The time limit on examinations compels students to state knowledge as concisely as possible rather than to deliberate lengthily upon the problematic nature of some specific knowledge. Creativity and novelty, whether of a demonstrably practical or theoretical form, can become stifled, since, while credit can be given to successful risk taking, much less is given to failed risk taking and often none at all is given for the act of risk taking itself. Taken together, these observations suggest that the 'safest' preparation for examinations is for students to stockpile dependable, 'correct' course knowledge, to rehearse that knowledge and to dispatch it in its most unambiguous form. The cost of this is that 'non-essential' course knowledge is discarded, that complex or contentious knowledge is simplified and that creativity is abandoned because of its risks. But a not insignificant proportion of A-level assessment is based on course work in which students might be allowed to exercise choice over topic and medium of presentation, in which they can confront problems in an holistic and complex form and which, being less directly subject to time constraints, may afford greater opportunities for risk taking and creativity than do examinations. Of course, all of this is somewhat conjectural and the full impact of assessment methods upon course knowledge and learning cannot be inferred from syllabus prescriptions alone. However, if received wisdom about curriculum backwash is to be taken seriously (see, for example, DES/Welsh Office, 1988b: para. 16; Gipps, 1990: 34), it is distinctly probable that the assessment procedures adopted, whether external examinations or course work, will affect course knowledge, learning and teaching in the ways I have suggested here.

The principal criterion for distinguishing the BTEC National from other courses was BTEC's commitment to the particular learning strategies described above. Priority was attached to enabling students to engage with problems in their full complexity in order that they might develop their own knowledge and skills. But there was also a knowledge base specified in BTEC courses and there were periodic tests of this knowledge. The knowledge base, sometimes ambiguous and certainly varied, as I have mentioned, was not finite in the way that A-level syllabus knowledge is. It was not located within an academic specialism. It was more eclectic and was justified both by its vocational relevance and its appropriateness to the needs of the learner. The notion of 'indicative content' provides some illustration of BTEC's commitment to a curriculum whose learning and teaching methods were broadly specified but whose content was negotiable, to allow tutors the freedom to respond to the needs of learners, to opportunities available within institutions or localities and to requirements stemming from unique or changing employment conditions. In the BTEC case, course knowledge was selected according to its relevance to problems and to students rather than because of its presence in the syllabus. The BTEC National was, however, highly prescriptive on the matter of problem-based learning and its arrangements for assessment reflected this. In fact, BTEC assignments were specifically designed to overcome the limitations of terminal examinations and would appear to have afforded greater opportunities for students to exercise choice, to confront problems in their holistic and complex forms and to take the necessary risks demanded for creativity, than do A-levels. Whether or not the assessment methods complemented BTEC's commitment to problem-based learning strategies and what impact they had upon course knowledge and teaching cannot, of course, be taken for granted but, as questions, they will remain clearly in focus in the analyses of specific course cases which follow.

The major distinctions between BTEC National courses and Advanced GNVQs have already been made earlier in this chapter and I will not labour them at too great a length here. Like BTEC, GNVQ is justified in terms of its vocational relevance and it, too, has prescribed that a range of learning activities be undertaken by students. However, it is far less prescriptive of learning strategies and processes than was the BTEC National. To be sure, GNVQ syllabuses make repeated references to students assuming responsibility for their learning but, in fact, make less explicit provision for this than under the BTEC National. There is more evidence of a fragmentation of course knowledge under GNVQ, with specifications broken down into 'units', 'elements' and 'performance criteria', and less compelling evidence of a commitment to the exploration of holistic knowledge in context. The knowledge base of GNVQ is more tightly specified than that of BTEC while one of the most striking differences is the GNVQ emphasis upon 'outcomes' in contrast with BTEC-style 'processes'. In short, there appears to be far less freedom for tutors to exercise their discretion over course content under GNVQ. Advanced GNVQ assignments appear to reflect many of these qualities: recent research suggests that they are regarded less by teachers and students as opportunities for experimentation and risk taking and more as hurdles to be overcome through the application of ritualised procedures. Finally, the major difference between BTEC Nationals and Advanced GNVQs almost certainly lies in their assessment practices. There can be little doubt that the driving force behind GNVQ assessment is that of accountability. The greater emphasis upon strict criterion referenced testing of the easily measurable, as in the end-of-unit short-answer tests, is highly indicative of GNVQ's paramount commitment to external rather than internal referencing.

This chapter has been largely concerned with the nature of *pre*scriptive[1] accounts of course knowledge and learning and with distinguishing the principal qualities of each within 'academic' and 'vocational' courses. In summary, the three types of curriculum prescription examined here might be described as essentially 'content-based' (A-level), 'process-based' (BTEC National) and 'outcome-based' (Advanced GNVQ). The following three chapters each focus upon teachers' and students' experiences and evaluations of courses which, at least at the *pre*scriptive level, are different in 'type'. The *de*scriptive accounts reported here provide an important opportunity for the appraisal of the potential and limitations of contemporary methods of curriculum prescription.

4

KNOWLEDGE AND LEARNING IN PRACTICE
Vocational courses

In the next three chapters, students' and teachers' experiences of a number of different courses are examined in some detail. The purpose is not to attempt a detailed account of the particular courses concerned since that would not be possible given the limited access afforded through the Leverhulme Study. Rather, by examining the various descriptive curricula in play in a few exemplar cases, the aim is to illuminate further the qualities of learning and knowledge in practice with a view to deepening understanding of the curriculum-knowledge-learning matrix.

I should point out here that the insights reported in the next three chapters are informed by course documentation and by the classroom observations and interviews with teachers and students which were conducted on each of two separate visits to each group. There was rarely more than a six-week interval between visits and in a minority of cases only a single visit took place. Thus, the insights afforded by this process of data collection are limited: the observation data are based upon only one or two 'snapshots' taken at particular points in the development of a course and should not be taken as indications of typical class meetings throughout that course. On the other hand, the administration of the questionnaires was not confined to any such time scale, while the interviews encouraged students and teachers to reflect both upon prior experiences and upon phenomena external to the courses. It is on the basis of these latter data in particular, and upon the rigorous comparative analysis of all data, that claims about the critical and salient qualities of courses and persons have been made here.

CHRIS YARDLEY'S BUSINESS AND FINANCE GROUP

The cases reported in this chapter are all BTEC National and Advanced GNVQ courses. The first is Christine Yardley's second year business and finance group which, during the first half of the observed session, had been fully occupied in a role-play exercise. The roles had been assigned to six students by their tutor at a previous class meeting and the students had had ample opportunity to research their roles. The role-play required the players to conduct a meeting to address the problem of river pollution, the roles being chairperson, councillor (town A), councillor (town B) and representatives from industry, the Tourist Board and Friends of the Earth. The 'meeting' was observed by the tutor and two students, the latter having been supplied with an assessment sheet listing the course skills that the role-players were expected to demonstrate. At the conclusion of the role-play, Chris dismissed the students to the refectory for twenty-five minutes while she met with the two observers, Kevin and Claire, in order to decide upon the grades that should be awarded to each student.

CHRIS   Who was it that you were observing?

CLAIRE   Emma, Kay and Donna. (She proceeds to acclaim Emma's performance.)

CHRIS   Yes, I was very pleased with her. I suspect she's gone away with exactly what she wanted.

CLAIRE   Kay researched well but she was very nervous.

CHRIS   How much did she contribute to the meeting?

CLAIRE   (Some disagreement with Kevin.) . . . she should have got involved with the costs and been more assertive.

CHRIS   What about Donna?

CLAIRE   (Gives her views.)

CHRIS   (Looks to Kevin.)

KEVIN   I was watching Tony, Andy and Simon. Tony (the Chair of the meeting) was a bit quiet at times.

CHRIS   Was he in control? Did he allow someone else to take over the meeting?

KEVIN   (Agrees reluctantly.)

CHRIS   On the whole, that Chair lost control completely.

KEVIN   (Commenting on Simon, the Tourist Board representative) The compensation idea was good. So was Andy.

CHRIS   How well did the meeting go?

KEVIN   They didn't really decide who was doing what?

CHRIS   ('Shaping' Kevin's answer) They needed a clear summing up. (She draws Claire back into the discussion.) What about grades, then? Do you think you should give them all the same grades, then, on skills?

(Kevin and Claire disagree with uniform grading and they proceed to discuss each student in turn, starting with Simon.)

CLAIRE   I put 'pass'.

KEVIN   'Pass plus'.

CHRIS   I put 'merit'. I'm open to your ideas.

(After discussion, it was agreed that 'pass plus' be awarded to Simon, a 'pass' to Kay and a 'distinction' to Emma.)

CHRIS Donna bent over backwards to be reasonable. Did she manage
her role?

(Claire and Kevin agree that while Donna did manage her role, her performance was little more than adequate.)

CHRIS I gave her 'merit'. She stayed in role. She was flippant at times
but with Andy supporting, she did a reasonable role.

(Claire and Kevin disagree.)

CHRIS So I'm too generous, am I?

(They agree on 'pass plus' for Donna and proceed to consider Andy.)

CLAIRE 'Merit'!
CHRIS I thought he did an excellent job. 'Distinction'!
KEVIN I think 'merit plus'. (A 'merit plus' for Andy was agreed.)

(Later, after the whole class had been recalled . . .)

CHRIS We have discussed you fully. We have given you grades – not
group ones, it did not work out that way at all. (She reads out the
agreed assessments for each student.)
ANDY (To Simon) What did you set out to get?
SIMON Merit!
ANDY We were ripped off, then!
CHRIS Time has run out. Are you satisfied and happy?

(The students indicate by 'Mmm', 'Yes', or nodding their heads that they are.)

The role-play described here was, on the face of it, an exemplar of 'active learning' and of the provision of opportunities for students to generate and test their personal knowledge, understanding and skills. It reflected, too, the tutor's idealised curriculum where students developed insights and skills through 'listening to each other' and 'considering each other's point of view'; and where the outstanding student possessed, 'an ability to listen; ability to question; a good ability to communicate; a willingness to do extra research and work on an independent basis'.

In Chris's view, 'it's very much down to them'. Her students were to take their own risks in learning and exercise their own judgements on the selection of knowledge and its method of presentation. Indeed, in the observed session, she saw herself as 'a bystander, virtually. I allowed the students to take over the lesson and I observed. Towards the end of the lesson I could feed back to the students on what had taken place'.

But what of the students' experiences of learning?

How did you learn?

By watching people. Also, I had an assessment sheet in front of me with all the skills on it. I went by that as well – if people stuck to their roles and how much they contributed.

What, for you, were the most helpful parts of the session?

Soon I'll be doing a meeting like this. Because I was an observer today, I could observe the points which will help me when I do a meeting. It definitely helped being an observer first. I feel happier doing the meeting now. I can see what standard I have to reach for that mark.

(Claire, role-play observer, interview)

Claire's account indicates that her analysis and judgement were clearly focused by the criteria contained in the assessment sheet. She used the assessment sheet criteria in preference to any that she might have generated on the basis of her own experience as an observer. Thus, it seemed, opportunities for her own critical reflection were constrained as she engaged in the routine task of applying given criteria to a given event. However, it is also evident that her anticipated performance in a similar role-play activity later in the course exerted an influence upon her view of things. 'I could observe the points which will help me when I do a meeting', she said, suggesting that her appreciation of the role-play was filtered, even distorted, by the presence of her own instrumental needs. But to imply that she simply selected out of the role-play those aspects of performance that she might mimic in her own would be to lose sight of the potential that such aspects held as stimulants to her own reflection. In Claire's case, though, there was little to indicate that she had exploited such potential.

Many of the other students' accounts also stressed that learning on this particular occasion had been achieved through the observation or practice of technical and personal skills and most claimed that this had been helpful to their own skill development. While many stressed the relevance of others' viewpoints, such remarks inevitably concerned the skills of 'listening to' and 'arguing against' others' viewpoints within the context of the role-played meeting. Some, however, did not appear to value the role-play as much as others.

What kinds of learning activity help you learn most effectively?

Not working in groups! I hate working in groups – individual work is something which I enjoy. You can go away and achieve the best standard for yourself . . .

(Andy, interview)

This is the first indication by any student of dissent from a 'student-centred' philosophy of teaching and learning, although Andy was not alone in admitting as much. However, he did not display any anxiety about group work in the observed role-play exercise and was, in fact, awarded a 'merit plus' for his efforts. Although apparently resistant to any notion of group work, he had somehow managed to achieve a good measure of success in this and other group activities throughout the course. He had complied for his own strategic purposes, 'because if you don't do each assessment, like the simulation this morning, you don't pass' and success will 'hopefully enable me to secure some backing from the bank'. But Andy's and others' strategic compliance was not confined to learning activities alone as was noticeable in his and Simon's acquiescence to being 'ripped off'.

Andy's, Simon's and other students' accounts of what they had learned, why they had learned it and how they had learned revealed a considerable diversity of students' preferences and evaluations. While some were in strong accord with the course commitment to group work, others were not and it is evident that the studentship of these young people entailed an innovative adaptation which accepted the course goals while rejecting some of the prescribed means (see Merton, 1968: 194). But these students, though rejecting the given means, invariably suppressed their concerns, projecting the outward appearance of conformity.

The business and finance students all claimed to have learned how to do something as the result of their participation in the role-play but it is not clear what they had learned. Role-plays and simulations have the capacity to offer students insights, both emotionally and intellectually, into the complexity of their own lives and those of others and, in turn, to a deeper understanding of the same. They also offer opportunities for students to practise the performance of certain skills. In so far as the observed role-play assisted students in the development of more effective performance, it is not apparent whether this was achieved through students' deeper insights into the dynamics of human relations, through their performance of technical skills or through some combination of the two. From the course syllabus prescriptions for learning and from Chris's expectations of her students' learning, it is clear that the intention of both was for students to assume responsibility for constructing their own performances, drawing as they deemed fit from prior course knowledge, the exercise assessment criteria and their own experiences of their previous performances. While the teacher was largely responsible for providing the prior course knowledge and the assessment criteria, she provided little instruction to students on how they might utilise or evaluate their experiences of previous performances or, indeed, on how they might turn personal qualities to greater advantage. Chris provided students with the 'space' in which they could formulate new personal knowledge, hoping and expecting that this would manifest itself in improved performance. Whether all students achieved such a practical knowledge is a matter for some doubt. Judging from their own accounts, it appears that in occupying the 'space' provided by Chris, some were concerned only to meet the requirements of the assessment sheet criteria (see Claire's account, above) while others had some greater concern for the development of their emotional and intellectual insights. (Andy, below, for example, presents his account much more in terms of gaining control over himself than in terms of mastering technical skills.) Students perceived the demands of the role-play exercise in different ways and, as a result, each set about creating a different stock of personal knowledge and skills in order to meet those demands. The knowledge gained varied qualitatively from one student to the next as did their selections of opportunities for learning. For some, studentship entailed a heavy reliance upon instruction and concentration upon the mastery of technical skills and their application in the quest for unequivocal course knowledge. Others were more accepting of problematic knowledge, attaching greater importance both to their own experiences as sources of knowledge and to the development of personal critical awareness as the purpose of learning. In Andy's case, personal experience was of crucial importance in explaining not only the benefits he claimed to derive from learning but how he evaluated and selected from the learning opportunities available to him.

What did you learn in today's session?

Not a lot, really, because we covered a lot of it last year. It has helped that I didn't come straight from school – that I worked before. I've been put in situations like that at work. It's easier for me than for people who've been just taught it at college. . . . When you've been placed in a situation in reality, it's a lot easier to cope in a simulation.

What, would you say, were the most helpful parts of the session?

When you are having to argue your point and keep your cool instead of just blowing a fuse. You've got to restrain yourself, keep your temper and keep plugging away for what you want.

Andy's comments, here, on the subject of his prior experience and its relationship to the role-play exercise provide further insights into his strategic compliance, referred to earlier. Despite the fact that he claimed to possess already much of the knowledge and skill which was to be gained from the role-play exercise, he made a full contribution to it and, despite saying that he gained little benefit from it, he did not condemn it. He complied, it appears, for two main reasons: first, he wanted to be graded favourably and, second, he could at least see the benefits that the role-play might have had for other students. His prior experiences enabled him to recognise the exercise as authentic: it was a fair simulation of a 'reality' in which success was achieved through a combination of self-control and perseverance. The exercise was authentic to Claire, too, but for entirely different reasons: it successfully exhibited strong and weak performances of the technical skills on her assessment sheet and, thus, provided her with helpful insights into her own preparations for a similar event in the following weeks.

Chris's business and finance group exhibited many visible signs of success. Moreover, the tutor's described and idealised curricula were largely complementary and reflected to a high degree the course prescription. Chris's personal curriculum values stressed learner independence and critical engagement in the generation of course knowledge. She sought to promote positive dispositions to interactive learning and group work and favoured a 'non-directive' approach to teaching. However, there was more evidence in the case of Chris's group of what teacher and students brought to bear upon the process of curriculum making. The impact of Chris's own teacherly values – her 'pedagogical position', her 'person as teacher' and 'professional self' – will become more evident as other cases are reviewed. The significance of students in the process of curriculum making, however, is amply demonstrated in the cases of Claire and Andy. The different ways in which these two students 'acted upon' the learning opportunities available to them gave rise to two very different descriptive curricula.

This first example offers initial insight into apparently harmonious, productive student–teacher relationships achieved well within the terms of formalised course prescriptions. But such consistency between the values embedded in prescriptions and those which teachers and students brought to their courses was not apparent in every case. In the following example of a first year nursery nursing course, a different story unfolds.

PAULINE THOMAS'S NURSERY NURSING GROUP

In keeping with the BTEC philosophy referred to in Chapter 3, the unit aims of the nursery nursing course stressed the importance of an inquiring, investigative approach, while the teaching and learning strategies section advocated practices that closely resembled those employed in Chris's business and finance course.

> A variety of methods should be used and emphasis must be placed upon student-centred learning. Resource materials should be freely available to students and form part of an approach that seeks to promote common skills practice and development, particularly in information seeking and analysis, and communication in oral, visual and written form.
>
> Individual and group work, presentations and discussions will assist.
>
> (BTEC, 1991: 2)

'Brainstorming' was firmly established in the nursery nursing students' vocabulary and it was apparent from interviews with them that an activity known by that name regularly occurred in their class meetings. Thus it was that five minutes into one of the observed sessions, Pauline, the tutor, announced to her seventeen students that they were about to have a brainstorm on weaning. The announcement was followed by Pauline picking up some chalk and the students picking up their pens and pencils. All were poised to write . . . something.

PAULINE   Right! What's weaning?

LAURA   Introduction of solid food.

PAULINE   To whom?

LAURA   The child.

SARAH   To the baby.

PAULINE   Do you know what time it starts?

JEAN   When it gets its teeth.

PAULINE   That's a bit vague. It's about four to six months. The Department of Health recommends that the introduction of solids should not start before four months. Notice that it is a recommendation, not a law. Lots of things are behind the statement. Why is there an earliest time to introduce food? (Pause.) What would happen if you introduced it before then?

SARAH   The digestion system's not ready?

PAULINE   Anything else you can think of? (Pause.) Well, one danger is obesity. Babies get too fat and there are other reasons – not just the digestive system but the kidneys get overloaded if the waste products are too strong to be got rid of. That's why added salt is to be avoided. (Pause.) From a parent's point of view, why do parents start weaning before four months? Any ideas about that?

ANNA   They don't know about it.

PAULINE   I'll put 'ignorance of recommendation' down.

LAURA   It's easier for them to mash food they're eating up.

PAULINE   I don't know about that.

TESSA   Milk might not fill the baby up.

PAULINE   (Does not respond to Tessa.) Any others? (No response.) Well, tradition is another one. 'Is he on solids yet?' is something people ask about babies. (Pause.) The key might be that the baby is not satisfied, especially at three months. Think back to human growth and development. Think what a three-month-old baby is able to do. Any ideas? (No response.) A three-month-old baby is much more active, awake for longer during the day, turns their head from side to side if laid on their fronts. They can hold on to things. (Pause.) Do you know what they recommend you start with? (No answer.) Bland cereal food, baby rice. Anyone know why baby rice is the chosen food?

CHLOE   Goodness in it?

PAULINE   Not really. The reason is there is no gluten in it. Why

70

shouldn't young babies have gluten? (No answer.) Those who've heard about gluten, what do you know about it? (No answer.) Well, coeliac disease is due to an allergy: an allergic reaction to gluten. (Pauline then announces a 'practical session'.) So we'll look at the practical side, then come back to some theory. (She leaves the room to collect some materials.)

LAURA   What does bland mean?
SARAH   Well, if I said you were bland, it would mean you're ordinary, boring.

Despite the fact that in her account of her teaching and of her students' learning, Pauline argued strongly against 'spoon-feeding' – which she saw to be a feature of GCSE courses – and stressed the importance of students' 'self-sufficiency in terms of their own learning', the over-riding impression to be gained from the 'brainstorm' was that of Pauline manipulating the students into a state of dependency. Their contributions were rarely accepted and it was apparent that the tutor had some preconceived agenda of essential course knowledge which she expected students' contributions to fit. To say that Pauline 'shaped' students' contributions would be something of an under-statement; she barely gave them any recognition at all. Only Sarah received acknowledgement for the value of her contribution and it is perhaps not surprising that as the session progressed, students withdrew from the exer-cise. The impression conveyed to the observer was that over the course of these few minutes, student energy had become swiftly diverted from the contribution of ideas on the basis of their own knowledge and experience to the conscientious recording of the 'correct' knowledge dispensed by their teacher. This much was confirmed by the students' recollections of the session:

Firstly, we did a brainstorm and then Pauline went through and explained our answers.

We did a group brainstorm about what we knew already and then our tutor said what was right and wrong.

We had a discussion on what we thought were the advantages and disadvantages. Then we were given a handout on the subject.

(Student evaluation schedules)

Moreover, when describing their own learning, students tended to stress a passive, receptive role:

Pauline standing at the front and telling us with some practicle (*sic*) in it.

Through listening to our tutor and through practical work.

Through discussion and observation.

(Student evaluation schedules)

However, these observations should not be taken as criticisms since the students considered the most helpful parts of the session to be:

Pauline at the front. More information to be obtained.

Listening to Pauline. She can give us more information than we can find out for ourselves.

Practical and demonstration. Theory can be boring and by being given typed sheets it's very easy not to read them.

(Student evaluation schedules)

Although 'brainstorm' and 'discussion' were used by students to describe what was plainly a question and answer episode, and 'practical' was used as a label for demonstration accompanied by exposition, there is no mistaking that the essential thrust of this session was the transmission of knowledge from the teacher to the students. Moreover, a clear majority of students expected and valued the efficiency of such transmission – and had very thick files of notes to prove it! Through greater familiarity with the course it became apparent that a common sequence of learning activities adopted was: (1) some form of group work, (2) question and answer or exposition called 'brainstorming', and (3) demonstration or opportunity for application, all running in tandem with an investigative assignment. From the observed session, however, it was apparent that any knowledge generated through group work or gained from some out-of-class experience became subjugated by the teacher's views of essential course knowledge in the 'brainstorming' phase.

While the 'brainstorming' and, indeed, a number of other activities which took place in the nursery nursing course, are not entirely consistent with the formal course prescriptions of teaching and learning strategies, there is no doubting the harmony between the learning opportunities created by the teacher and the expectations held by the students. The students sought 'correct' knowledge; they had considerable faith in their teacher's ability to supply it; and the teacher supplied it. But how did this situation come about?

The proposition that Pauline manipulated her students into a dependence upon her as the font of all knowledge is, indeed, plausible. In the 'brainstorm' exercise, the effect of her responses to students was to filter out many of those contributions which students made on the basis of their own prior knowledge and experience and to change others into some 'correct' form. Pauline's actions in this case provided a marked contrast to those of Chris who appeared very much more receptive to students' contributions. Pauline's own account adds some weight to the suggestion that she was driven primarily by a concern to transmit what she perceived to be the essential course knowledge. At the end of the observed session, she stressed that her main concern was, 'getting over information, procedure'. Moreover, when commenting upon differences between first and second year courses, she observed that, 'They're different in terms that the second years are much better at integrating elements of the course. . . . The first year are far less sophisticated; they haven't got the information to do that.'

Thus, Pauline's view appeared to be that it was necessary for students to acquire essential course knowledge before they could engage profitably in any work of a 'student-centred' or 'problem-solving' form later in their course – a view shared, incidentally, by many other vocational and A-level tutors. This, in so far as it is true, clearly sets Pauline apart from the formalised prescriptions of her course and their emphasis upon students eliciting knowledge and understanding on the basis of personal practical experience – 'information seeking, analysis and communication'. Her students were *given* the 'correct' knowledge and expected to *apply* it to practical problems.

But it is equally plausible that Pauline was merely responding to the expectations of her students. Perhaps it was the students who were the dependent learners, offering passive resistance to any attempt to encourage them in the discovery or creation of new knowledge. However, there are two major reasons why it is unlikely that this was so. First, the evidence from the observed sessions provides quite a number of illustrations of students attempting to volunteer their own ideas but failing to have their contributions incorporated into their teacher's account of essential course knowledge. Moreover, there were no examples of the teacher exhorting the students to proffer contributions and failing to get a response except in cases such as that reported earlier where the students retreated from question and answer opportunities having failed to make any impression with their initial offerings. Second, in their responses to the student questionnaires administered during the first day of their course, Pauline's students uniformly expressed stronger expectations of, and preferences for, exploratory learning activities than did almost all of the students on other vocational or A-level courses.

The overall impression gained from this single insight into the nursery nursing course is one of the students being largely reconciled to accepting their teacher as the source of all legitimate course knowledge. This interpretation is supported by evidence from other events in the observed sessions. Despite the fact that Pauline claimed to stress the value of 'student-centred' learning, as did her course guidelines, the students' dependence upon 'teacher-centred' knowledge was plain to see. There was no evidence from the observed sessions of any willingness to entertain knowledge as problematic. Rather, it was presented by the teacher as information, implicitly treated as objective and true and seldom contested. It was overtly utilitarian, a tightly prescribed knowledge frequently justified by both teacher and students as directly applicable to the work of the nursery nurse. This was technical knowledge of definitions, rules and procedures which, in one sense, was suited to enabling students to operate effectively in the work place but which was not enabling them to address any of the wider contextual or moral issues in which nursery nursing practice is located. The relationship of course knowledge to student experience was also very clear: knowledge preceded experience and was to be applied to the practical rather than elicited from it.

While there was a general contentment among students on the nursery nursing course to pursue a passive information-seeking studentship, there was also evidence of some differences between students in the learning activities they valued. Some objected to 'copying off the board' on the grounds that it was time consuming and did not, in itself, assist learning. A few showed signs of restlessness and were conspicuous by their non-participation in the 'brainstorming' while others showed signs of frustration that their keenness to participate was largely unrewarded. The course had been running for only five months and yet, to the observer, it appeared that the teacher–student and the student–student harmony witnessed in the business and finance course considered earlier was not so evident in this case. There was emerging a diversity of tolerance, not evident in students' written evaluations or in their interview comments but visible through their engagement – or lack of engagement – with the learning activities observed. Perhaps, for some, their strategic compliance was becoming tested with the prospect of more divergent forms of studentship to follow in due course.

It is quite apparent that the nursery nursing course was qualitatively different from Chris's business and finance course. Although Pauline spoke with some conviction about the value of student independence in learning, it was clear that such ideals were not manifest in practice. There was evident tension between her descriptive and idealised curricula. While it is possible to attribute this to the fact that she was working with a first year group and, therefore, had to suspend some of her own curriculum principles in order that the students could acquire the prerequisite attitudes and skills for more autonomous learning in the second year of the course, there was much to suggest the greater plausibility of other lines of explanation. There were strong indications that Pauline's contribution to the situation was to stress the fact-like, non-problematic, commodified nature of course knowledge and to promote an uncritical, receptive and dependent notion of student learning *in spite of* indications from at least some of her students that they were able, prepared and keen to engage in interactive learning activities.[1] Indeed, she was 'teacher as instructor' and suppressed such opportunities.

In Pauline's nursery nursing course, the impact of the views of knowledge, learning and teaching which the teacher brought to bear upon the course was strong and clear to see. The impact of the students upon curriculum making is less clear. On the one hand, many students displayed evidence of a passive, receptive dependency. Their studentship was tightly geared to obtaining the most direct access to what they perceived to be essential factual information. Personal knowledge, critique and evaluation counted for little, it seemed, in their pursuit of non-problematic truths. It might even be suggested that these students were instrumental in confirming their tutor's views of course knowledge, learning and teaching and that it was their studentship which gave shape to the events which took place. On the other hand, there were signs that some students were becoming frustrated through being denied opportunities to utilise their own experiences and to exercise their own constructions of knowledge within the course. But these were early days – the course had a further sixteen months to run and plenty of time for the further unfoldment of these students' learning careers. The important points to draw from this case are the strong impact of the tutor upon the process of curriculum making, the divergence among students in their impact upon the process and the relatively weak presence of the formal prescriptions of curriculum in this case compared with Chris Yardley's group considered earlier. We should note, in particular, the qualitatively different descriptive curricula to emerge in this case compared with those of other courses operating under similar external prescriptions.

KEITH DELVE'S ENGINEERING GROUP

The second year engineering class provides a further insight into the processes of curriculum making. In contrast to the nursery nurses, the engineering students in their responses to the questionnaires administered on the day they entered their course expressed stronger expectations of, and personal preferences for, *receptive* learning activities than did most other post-16 students.

Keith Delve, the tutor, voiced three main concerns about the course and the students. First, he felt that the course structure was too inflexible, the compulsory elements not allowing for much student choice of options or much diversity among the options. Second, he claimed that many of his colleagues taught in what he described as a 'didactic' or 'traditional' fashion. Third, he pointed to the fact that the vast majority of students were male and that, with only a few exceptions, they possessed an immature approach to learning and low self-motivation. Keith was strongly committed to the 'BTEC philosophy of learning and teaching' but felt hampered, largely owing to the concerns just noted, in his attempts to fulfil its potential. Early in the interview, he made his position clear by outlining the changes which he would like to make to the existing course.

> I'd have much less didactic teaching. I'd have one-third student-led activities in an environment such as Trevor [a colleague] and I have. I'd prefer much more access – greater flexibility in choice of options. I'd introduce a wider variety of non-engineering skills: more European experiences, more work experience and more women. I'd change the way in which the course is delivered and have more in-service training to bring about less traditional teaching. . . . I'd have more experiential

75

learning: learning by doing, building up significant knowledge, and building on the knowledge they already have.

The content of Keith's idealised curriculum was determined as much by its relevance to the students' general education as to their engineering preparation although quite how he imagined women might be regarded as a non-engineering skill, it is difficult to say! But what distinguished Keith most clearly from virtually all of the teachers interviewed in the study was his seemingly passionate commitment to student independence in learning – to 'exploratory learning' and 'facilitator teaching'.

What's the main purpose of today's session?

For them to develop ideas and put them into practice. It's a micro area of the course where it gives students the opportunity to work for themselves. It is non-didactic. The emphasis is on them. I'm here as a facilitator. . . . We don't have such a short lead on them. We let them go on project work and tutorials but in maths, electrical engineering and maybe science it is more didactic, classroom-based. We're building on skills in practical sessions – learning by doing.

How do you expect the students will learn today?

Learning by doing. To make things happen: they make decisions for themselves. They are creating the situation and the tutor observes what they are doing. . . . It's an exploratory lesson from the teacher's point of view: one in which you don't rely on teaching skills but on your own experience. . . . They'll learn from their mistakes, their lack of planning. They correct ideas in their mind, then carry them out.

How do you help students to solve problems that you know the answer to?

Well, I don't give immediate responses unless it's dangerous. I don't necessarily give them the solution; I let them work it through.

Keith's account of teaching and learning resonates strongly with those provided in BTEC course prescriptions although it must be said that the guidelines for the engineering course do not stress the virtues of exploratory or interactive learning activities as heavily as those for other courses. But it is one thing for a teacher to lay claim to certain values and beliefs and another for them to be reflected consistently in practice. What actually happened in Keith's class meetings?

It is not possible to reproduce an extract from one of Keith's sessions as has been possible with the other cases considered here. His only communication with the whole group was at the beginning of the session when he relayed information concerning visits, higher education and work experience. After that it was, 'Right, you can get on with your projects now'. The students each pursued their individual design projects and periodically approached the tutor, in ones or twos, for assistance. Invariably, Keith responded to student inquiries with questions: 'How does that fit in there? I don't understand.' 'What's your next stage?' 'What do you think?' 'What would happen if . . . ?' or 'Why have you chosen a box section?'

True to his word, it appeared, Keith avoided providing his students with any direct instruction or 'correct' answers, choosing instead to contrive situations where students would employ reasoning and trial and error in order to make decisions 'for themselves'. This was 'learning by doing'. But how did the students describe their experiences? First, Cliff:

Please describe in your own words what you have learned.

Accessibility of stock material for projects. Changing project design to accommodate. How to appreciate other points of view.

Could you describe how you learned?

By talking with lecturer.

Which part(s) of the session were most helpful to you in your learning?

The exchange of ideas and information, knowledge with project lecturer.

(Student evaluation schedule – Cliff)

Cliff suggests that he regarded himself as the decision maker as Keith intended he should be. He talks of changing his design in response to new circumstances and of exchanging ideas, 'points of view', with the teacher. The knowledge appears to have been a problematic knowledge, there being no clear-cut 'right' or 'wrong' answer to the problem. Rather, the solution was achieved by Cliff after he had weighed up the implications of observations offered by his teacher. While Cliff had deepened his insight into the nature of a problem, Bryan, in contrast, had learned something quite specific:

Please describe in your own words what you have learned.

I have learnt that to substitute AC in a voltage doubler circuit I would need to build an oscillator.

Could you describe how you learned?

I did some research in the library and asked the teacher.

Which part(s) of the session were most helpful to you in your learning?

Finding out my information from the library and having the freedom to do so. . . . I had to use my initiative to derive the information. . . . I feel I maximised the time and derived some important information.

(Student evaluation schedule – Bryan)

Like Cliff, Bryan confirms that he was the decision maker. The need for specific knowledge had arisen out of his project and in describing his quest, Bryan conveys the clear impression that he was in control of the search. He did not present his problem to Keith but used his own 'initiative' in a strategy which he describes as research. What is more, he appears to regard his research as a positive learning experience. Rob tells a similar story although his search was not triggered by a need for some specific knowledge or information but by the fact that his design would not function as it should have done and he could not tell why.

Please describe in your own words what you have learned.

Power amplifier and audio equalisation circuits construction.

Could you describe how you learned?

By researching in service manuals.

Which part(s) of the session were most helpful to you in your learning?

By getting stuck and not being able to progress. . . . Because I learnt how to solve a problem the wrong way.

(Student evaluation schedule – Rob)

Rob used trial and error techniques, not being sure exactly what he was looking for. He searched the manuals for clues as to what he might have overlooked and then experimented on the basis of what he had picked up. This process involved 'getting stuck', 'not being able to progress', 'researching' and solving. His learning to 'solve a problem the wrong way' is a reference to his experimentation during which he managed to get his design to function but not as effectively as he desired. Like Cliff and Bryan, Rob maintained a high degree of control over his learning: he decided how he was going to solve his problem and what he was prepared to accept as a satisfactory solution. Steve and a number of other students, on the other hand, tell quite a different story:

Please describe in your own words what you have learned.

The technician is very helpful. We do not need a CPS212 clip – it is too complicated to use. We can use an OR gate.

Could you describe how you learned?

From the technician.

Which part(s) of the session were most helpful to you in your learning?

Talking to the technician and reading from an electrical catalogue. The technician is full of information.

(Student evaluation schedule – Steve)

Steve was not alone in taking the short cut or in recognising that the technician had considerable experience of supporting student projects, working with a variety of different tutors. Many students commented on the fact that the technician was a valuable resource while some, including Steve, recognised that he was also a reliable source of answers. Thus, Steve did not trouble Keith too often with his project problems. Instead, he took them straight to the technician who provided instant workable solutions, saving Steve the trouble of having to conjure with Keith's questions.

To some of Keith's students, class meetings did appear to entail 'learning by doing' and personal decision making. For others, though, 'doing' meant gaining access to necessary information by the shortest available route, in much the manner adopted by many of the nursery nursing students. An evident divergence of studentship had emerged in Keith's group: although at the commencement of their course, the engineering students were unified in their preference for receptive learning activities, by the second year they had become more diverse in their outlooks on knowledge and learning. Whether this was attributable to the particular conditions of the course, to the 'natural' development of the students, or to both, it is not possible to state confidently at this stage.

On the basis of the observed sessions and interviews, it was plain that the students' descriptive curricula were many and varied: they were learning essentially different things, albeit under common descriptions such as 'assignment-based learning', 'problem solving', 'practical project work' and 'learning by doing'. Some did elicit theoretical knowledge from practical experience while others were content simply to obtain the information that enabled their designs to function. For some, knowledge was created through their interpretations of experience while, for others, information from some external source was deemed adequate, even superior. Some students saw fit to draw significantly upon their 'non-engineering knowledge' in their project work, notably on matters of aesthetics and household practicalities, while the attentions of others were much more visibly confined.

Keith's curriculum values were quite distinctive and there are clear signs that the views of knowledge and learning which he introduced to the situation had a significant bearing upon his construction and presentation of learning opportunities. He attached importance to student independence in learning: to students' generation of their own knowledge through their deliberation upon practical experience. He also held a clear view of his role as teacher and that was to stress its non-directive, non-intrusive nature.

However, Keith's descriptive and idealised curricula were evidently in tension despite the fact that the latter was very much in keeping with the basic principles of his externally prescribed curriculum. His idealised curriculum was at odds with the values and time-honoured practices of his colleagues and his departmental structures and culture. It was also in conflict with the values and the practices of some of his students.

The diversity of studentship among Keith's engineering group was highly visible. However, what should not pass without comment is that, despite the conflicting views and preferences existing among the group (and their tutor), they were nonetheless able to function productively and harmoniously. Either the tutor was ignorant of what some of his students were actually doing or he was prepared to suspend his own deeply held convictions in the interests of their shared, greater educational good. At the same time, it seems quite probable that there was some strategic compliance among the students.

The distinctiveness of the engineering course group lies in the lack of uniformity among students' views of learning and knowledge, despite their apparently common experience and their uniformly positive initial predisposition towards receptive learning activities. While the significance of teachers as curriculum makers has been demonstrated in all of the examples considered here, the engineering group confirms the importance of students as curriculum makers.

JEAN WALL'S BUSINESS AND FINANCE GROUP

A further example of divergence of students' views of knowledge and learning was Jean Wall's business and finance course. This was a second year group which, on the occasion of the observation, was revising SWOT (strengths, weaknesses, opportunities, threats) analysis in preparation for a course assignment. The session proceeded through four main phases: (1) exposition by Jean on the main features of SWOT analysis; (2) student individual and paired work to generate ideas in response to a problem presented by Jean; (3) feedback from individuals and pairs to the whole group with Jean eliciting ideas and recording points on the board; and (4) students working in groups, preparing for a new course assignment. The third, 'feedback', phase soon developed into a question and answer session with many of the qualities of Pauline's 'brainstorms', discussed earlier. Throughout, there was little voluntary participation by the students and it appeared that the teacher felt less comfortable when eliciting and responding to students' contributions than when presenting her own knowledge by exposition. Moreover, many of the students were not only unresponsive but uncooperative throughout. Some were plainly disenchanted with the whole morning's activity.

The students' accounts of this session revealed the greatest divergence of evaluations provided by any group so far. Of the nineteen students, six claimed that Jean's exposition was most helpful and that the individual, paired and group work was less helpful:

Which part(s) of the session were most helpful to you in your learning?

At the beginning of the lecture when the lecturer was teaching. The lecturer went through it on the board.

Which part(s) of the session were least helpful to you in your learning?

The rest of the lecture, working on my own.

(Student evaluation schedule)

A further six students claimed that individual, paired or group work was the most helpful:

Which part(s) of the session were most helpful to you in your learning?

When we are allowed to work on our own and establish our own work rate, etc. I find it easier without having to listen to endless lectures.

Which part(s) of the session were least helpful to you in your learning?

Waffling by the lecturer. We need more in-depth talks, not skimming.

(Student evaluation schedule)

The remaining seven students did not see fit to distinguish so clearly between learning activities in this way and some went so far as to stress the value of a combination of different activities:

I try to use every part of lectures in a positive way and feel there is something to be gained from most situations.

(Student evaluation schedule)

The observed behaviour and written accounts provided by Jean's group confirm that while only one or two were negatively disposed to most of the opportunities made available to them, over half of the remainder discriminated clearly between different learning opportunities to the point of withdrawing their involvement from the activities which they valued least. Nicki and Jo talked persistently throughout Jean's attempts at exposition and took very few notes, if any. Jon and Graham were dedicated note takers but spent virtually the whole of the time that they were assigned to individual and paired work talking about Camp America, successfully bluffing their way through the 'feedback' session. The students' tolerance of learning activities which they preferred least was evidently low and the strategic compliance mentioned earlier in respect of Chris's and Keith's groups was barely visible at all. The students, apparently, felt little compunction about their failure to assist the maintenance of even an illusion of harmony and some, such as Nicki, were quite public in expressing their dissent through persistently talking and, on a couple of occasions, swearing well within the hearing of the entire class.

In so far as it is possible to generalise from the cases considered thus far, advancement from first to second year courses was characterised both by a progression from essential or basic course knowledge or information to practical project work of some form or other and, often, by the emergence of a visible and assertive studentship. But the forms which studentship took and

81

the conditions under which it became manifest were by no means uniform. In a few cases, it was barely visible at all and the students appeared to be content to respond positively to a variety of opportunities and challenges. At the very least, they were prepared to exercise tolerance in the face of expectations which may not have matched their preferences. While Chris's students also displayed evidence of divergence in their preferences for learning activities and in their studentship, they presented no challenge to their tutor's expectations, electing for strategic compliance instead. Pauline's was a first year group whose members, while displaying some signs of different preferences and values, were essentially compliant, even passive, in their acceptance of the conditions created for them. The students in Keith's second year engineering group were as diverse as any in terms of their attitudes to learning. However, any objections that individuals might have held towards 'learning by doing' did not reveal themselves in open dissent. Rather, they were able to develop and utilise strategies of their own in order to achieve the shared aims of the course. They were innovative, albeit to a degree which may not have been recognised by their tutor, but their course provided them with the freedom in which they could act innovatively without displaying any public dissent from their tutor's expectations. Jean's students, however, did express their dissent.

The impression created by Jean is one of high compatibility between her described and idealised curricula. As with most of the other tutors considered here, Jean gave voice to the 'BTEC philosophy of teaching and learning' and was liberal in her use of 'student-centred' rhetoric. 'It's the process, really, today that matters', she asserted when describing student learning in the observed session. Her own contribution, she claimed, was 'to facilitate their learning . . . I really think today is almost experiential learning to some extent'. 'We expect them to take far more responsibility for their own learning', she stressed, as she continued to rationalise what had happened in the observed session in terms of the popular clichés of 'student-centred learning'. However, as with Pauline, the looseness of the rhetoric which Jean employed for the purpose of describing teaching and learning is quite apparent. That rhetoric served not to clarify the nature of the practices concerned by enabling their particular features to be distinguished, but to help sustain a 'surface of agreement' (Goffman, 1971) among those who directly or indirectly participated in them.

Jean described herself as a 'facilitator' who provided student learning with 'some of the structure'. However, a number of her students, including some whom she regarded as being among the most successful, offered a contrasting account. Sam went so far as to distinguish learning from non-learning, in a way which was quite at odds with the view that Jean was apparently keen to promote:

I like it when I'm sat here and the teacher's up there and she's writing

82

on the board; she's actually lecturing to us. I prefer that because I come away and think, 'Yes, I've learned this'. When we've got practical work, which was like choosing the business premises, we were just discussing amongst ourselves; we weren't actually learning.

(Student interview – Sam)

Paul's account of his experiences of learning on the course also stood at odds with the impression conveyed by his tutor.

I think we learn most of our work off the board. It's never *really* tricky but it's complex so you have to take loads of notes – and then you get on to assignments.

(Student interview – Paul)

Neither Sam's or Paul's descriptive curricula sit comfortably alongside Jean's descriptions either of what did happen or what ought to have been happening.

Jean's descriptive and idealised curricula were marked by inconsistencies. On the one hand, she claimed to enact the BTEC philosophy embedded in her course prescription and to value the generation of course knowledge by students on the basis of their critical examination of their own practical experiences. She proclaimed the virtues of interactive learning activities and student autonomy. On the other hand, however, observations of her group meetings revealed that these values were not reflected in practice as fully as her claims suggested they were. But whether or not Jean truly believed that she was acting in a manner consistent with her declared values is not a matter of the greatest consequence for the moment.

There are two matters of importance here. First, we should note how the rhetoric of student-centred learning used by Jean and many of her colleagues served to disguise rather than illuminate the true nature of their practices. Second, we should note that the divergence of studentship among the students in Jean's group includes considerable variation in the degree to which the students were prepared and able to exercise tolerance. While students in Chris's, Pauline's and Keith's groups tended towards strategic compliance in their adaptations, some members of Jean's group provided the most visible indications of retreatism, innovation and even rebellion. (Further discussion of these and other forms of studentship appears in Chapter 7.) All in all, this is the strongest indication so far of the power of student agency in the process of curriculum making.

PAM KEANE'S AND JOHN VANSTONE'S GROUPS

Pam and John were tutors of first and second year courses, respectively, and in both cases the learning careers of the students concerned appeared to fit the general patterns already identified above. Pam's business and finance group, for instance, were as varied in their preferences for particular learning activities as were any other first year group, but the students did not overtly reject any of the opportunities presented to them by their teacher. Instead, they complied with her wishes. As has been noted in other groups, the students laid great store on the handouts provided by their teacher. Indeed, it was confirmed by many students that the handouts formed the comprehensive and authoritative knowledge base of the course. A common view of course knowledge was that it was 'objective'; it was an 'exact' knowledge, a view reinforced by the teacher's organisation and presentation of course knowledge. It was also a commodified knowledge, with the tutor concerned to 'get through' and 'get the information over efficiently'. The students responded positively as collectors of knowledge, each judging their success by the amount and intelligibility of their notes. Teacher and students were positively disposed to one another and all, it appeared, viewed the course as successful. At the same time, all felt able to subscribe to formal course prescriptions and to the rhetoric of 'student-centred learning' despite, in practice, promoting and participating in a reality that was quite different.

John's leisure group were not untypical of most of the other second year groups encountered in the study in many important respects. John freely espoused a 'student-centred' philosophy: 'I direct them to sources to find out the answers for themselves.' He believed that students benefited most from assuming responsibility for the choice of both topic and method of inquiry, 'because they're able to develop their own interests in what they're researching and put it into a realistic and relevant context'. Moreover, the observed sessions did contain many examples of John acting in a manner entirely consistent with the views he claimed to hold. Like a number of his fellow tutors, he frequently utilised discussion, 'brainstorming' and group work while resisting temptations to exposition. On the other hand, while he often responded to students' queries with questions or by re-presenting their problems to them in a different light, he was also inclined to provide the specific answers that many of his students sought.

Which part(s) of the session were most helpful to you in your learning?

The lecturer answering my questions. We had to get on with our own work and all we had to do was to ask questions and get them answered. The questions answered were extremely clear and extensive.

The tutor pointing me in the right direction for part of my project. Otherwise, I would of (*sic*) done it wrong.

(Student evaluation schedules)

Indeed, the students varied somewhat in their appraisals of the learning opportunities made available to them. Some, a minority, valued the opportunities for exploratory and interactive learning.

I like discussions – debates. I love that – you can really get your teeth into it and stand up for what you believe.

I like to do things myself because [if there's] something you don't understand you can talk about it – then understand. If you take down notes, you never read them. They go into your file and you never look at them – rarely look at handouts either.

(Student interviews)

By far the majority took a different view, however.

I didn't learn anything today. I prefer to sit down and have a 'proper' lecture rather than [be] left to my own device in college.

Which part(s) of the session were least helpful to you in your learning?

The group discussion. We just larked about . . .

The group work.

Our own class discussions.

Which part(s) of the session were most helpful to you in your learning?

When explanations were given on areas that would have confused the class. Lectures can be boring but when a clear explanation is given it makes things more interesting.

John's easy/comprehensible explanations of details. John is an expert in this field and I trust what he says.

Note taking for future reference. I can look back and see what I have covered.

(Student evaluation schedules)

It is pertinent to note here that in their responses to the questionnaires administered on the day they entered their course, the leisure students, like the engineers, expressed stronger expectations of, and preferences for, *receptive* learning activities than did most other post-16 students. While, by the second year of their course, there was a greater divergence among students' preferences, a majority had not changed their preferences in the slightest. They wanted and expected lectures, notes and answers, regardless of their teacher's best attempts to encourage them otherwise.

Compared with one or two of the earlier cases, John's group was not marked by any overt dissent among students. Their tolerance prevailed, it appeared, because John had been able to provide a variety of different learning opportunities but had not tried to insist upon all students engaging fully in each. Consequently, those who chatted among themselves when they were supposed to be engaged in purposeful group discussion had not been reprimanded, unlike in Jean's group. But those students had not gone unrewarded since, later in the session, they received the necessary notes and answers to render their learning effective. Interestingly, for these students, their dependency upon their teacher as the sole authoritative source of knowledge had been fostered in the very environment that had been created to promote 'independent learning'. The power of studentship was seldom more vividly illustrated. For other students, the greater rewards lay in discussions and 'debates' and, in these students, a quite different form of studentship was apparent. However, given that they were sufficiently rewarded by their preferred activities, their tolerance of other activities ensued, too. Harmony, it appeared, had prevailed, although this should not be allowed to obscure the many varied learning careers that were evidently in progress in this course or the quite disparate forms of knowledge to which each career was attached.

SUMMARY

This chapter has focused upon a range of vocational courses, their students and teachers. Comparative analysis of a total of thirteen cases has yielded a number of empirical generalisations, each serving to illuminate some aspect of relationships between knowledge, learning, teaching and curriculum. In summary, five main points emerge from this analysis.

First, the prescriptive curriculum was found to be widely reflected in the rhetoric employed by teachers in their accounts of their work but was not always evident in their practice. Despite being bound by a common curriculum prescription, teachers varied considerably in the ways in which they 'acted upon' that prescription. The prescribed curriculum, it would appear, has a limited effect upon practice; the process of curriculum making hinges as much upon the values and views of knowledge, learning, teaching, human nature and educational purposes which teachers bring to bear upon their work.

Second, upon entry, vocational course students stated only marginally greater preferences for interactive learning opportunities than did intending A-level students. In many groups, students' preferences were quite diverse although the engineering and leisure students stated a marked preference for receptive learning activities, and the social care and nursery nursing students strong preferences for interactive learning opportunities. Thus, it would appear, claims that A-level and vocational courses attract students with different dispositions to learning are ill-informed.

Third, first year courses were most commonly focused on students' acquisition of basic course knowledge while activities which enabled them to utilise knowledge and to draw upon their own experiences or practical knowledge were concentrated in the second year. While there were examples of second year courses which sought to promote students' personal explorations and constructions of knowledge in project-style activities, there were others where opportunities were largely restricted to the application of previously rehearsed basic course knowledge. Neither the common patterning evident in first year course provision or the diversity of practice evident in second year courses are consistent with the curriculum prescriptions concerned.

Fourth, coincident with students' progression from first to second year courses were changes in their studentship. In first year courses, there was little evidence of students rejecting the learning opportunities made available to them; for the most part they complied with their teachers' expectations. By the second year, there was evidence of a greater diversity in students' dispositions to learning. There were also clear indications of a rejection by some students of some of the learning activities made available to them. Some retreated from group participatory activities while revealing a heavy dependence upon their teachers' authoritative knowledge and their own stock of notes. Others, a minority, came to find receptive learning activities tiresome and frequently sought to render course knowledge problematic by introducing personal values and experiences into their class meetings.

Many students more or less complied with the demands of different learning activities, either for the reason that they felt the activities to be sufficiently rewarding or because they had faith that rewards would be forthcoming at some stage. In other cases, strategic compliance was evident as students appeared to suspend objections they might have held, believing that not to do so could have prejudiced their teachers and fellow students against them. There were others, the 'innovators', who, rejecting certain learning activities, quickly found some alternative route to the knowledge that they required in the form they required it. There was also a small number of students whose rejection of particular activities was voiced in open dissent. Whether students complied with expectations, responded innovatively or dissented, appeared to turn heavily upon their teachers' tolerance of their studentship and upon the students' preparedness and ability to recognise in their teacher a person willing and able to meet their needs as learners. Moreover, those tutors who were unaware of, turned a 'blind eye' to, or colluded with 'innovation', encountered a far lower incidence of open dissent than those who insisted upon students adopting prescribed strategies in every detail.

Finally, despite their rhetoric, BTEC National and Advanced GNVQ courses were just as likely to foster receptive learning as the interactive learning to which they were expressly dedicated. Equally, they were as likely to provide for students' acquisition of a theoretical and absolutist knowledge as they were for their utilisation of personally constructed and practical knowledge. Whether and how they did so was determined essentially by teacher and student agency.

5

KNOWLEDGE AND LEARNING IN PRACTICE
A-level chemistry courses

A-level chemistry courses provide the focus for this chapter. As in the case of the vocational courses in Chapter 4, a number of examples of learning and teaching are described and analysed in order to illuminate the curriculum in practice.

RICHARD CONDER'S GROUP

RICHARD   So out of this you want a pure product. I want you to suggest how to do this. . . . If I hold up the bottle, what do you see?
ELLEN   Two layers.
RICHARD   How will I do it? It's principles of techniques.
ELLEN   Separate the layers?
RICHARD   How?
CHRIS   Heat it?
RICHARD   No.
JESS   Use a test pipette to suck it off?
RICHARD   A bit tedious. Any suggestions? This is very easy.
LISA   Decant it off?
RICHARD   A bit difficult as it'll mix when poured. What are you going to use? Think! Think! Think!
RACHAEL   Separating funnel?
RICHARD   Yes!

This style of questioning occurred frequently throughout Richard's first year A-level chemistry group sessions and was, he claimed, effective in prompting student thought.

> They learn by thinking about it themselves, by trying to sort the problem out. I want them to think what the impurities are, where they've come from and what is the best way to get rid of them. If they think through for themselves, hopefully they can sort out problems they meet in the laboratory. It may drag a little, like pulling teeth out, but if I do it that way, hopefully they'll remember in future.

But the students, it seemed, were not always as keen to participate as Richard would have liked.

> They won't volunteer quick answers. I have to draw answers from them. . . . They don't like committing themselves if they're unsure whether they're right or wrong. They're hesitant in coming out with it.

Richard was evidently keen that his students should remember and reproduce knowledge without hesitation. His view of the successful learner, taken together with the question and answer sequences which figured so frequently throughout his sessions, reveals fairly clearly the behaviourist principles which underpinned his practice. The fact that he frequently asserted the importance of students 'thinking about it themselves' must be understood not so much as 'creating' or even 'deducing for themselves' but as 'recalling for themselves'. Every example of Richard's questioning was a request for students to recall some specific information that he had previously presented to them. In fact, a common sequence of events throughout Richard's sessions was:

1 Teacher presentation of some basic propositional or procedural knowledge by exposition.
2 Teacher demonstration of proposition or procedure.
3 Student application of knowledge to practical problem (often a replication of the teacher's demonstration).
4 Student recall of experience of application in terms of the original propositional or procedural knowledge (in response to teacher questioning).
5 Student recall of propositional or procedural knowledge originally presented (in response to teacher questioning).

Further evidence of the behaviourism that informed Richard's work was to be found not only in the high incidence of repetition, practice and reinforcement which occurred in his sessions but also in his selection and organisation of classroom knowledge. Knowledge was organised into small discrete units, each to be learned in small incremental stages. Once sufficient knowledge had been acquired, it was then possible for learners to attempt to forge links between hitherto independent 'units'. Indeed, Richard's planning of the whole two-year course was based upon the same principles.

> What I mean is that there's a lot of foundation work to do in the first year, chemical equations and calculations and new techniques . . . you've got to get the factual content in. For example, chemical equations and calculations – there's a lot done in the first year – you have to concentrate on that. Also, a lot of new practical work and new techniques. Really, the first year is the foundation of A-level study. . . . There's much more emphasis on answering A-level examination questions, three per week

throughout the second year: two structured questions and one essay question. Structured answers are written on the question paper, so it's about knowing how to present the content in the answer.

On the qualities of the 'outstanding student', Richard volunteered:

Hard work. Natural ability. It is the ability to pick it up – for example, equations and mathematics. Twenty per cent is practical, so manual dexterity is important. The ability to apply chemical knowledge to a passage and be able to work the thing out for themselves. A basic understanding is the main thing. The aim is to increase understanding as we go along – a gradual process so that at the end of the year they're ready for the exam.

Many of the key elements of behaviourism are revealed in these short extracts from Richard's account. Course knowledge is described as 'factual content' and 'new techniques', each requiring that the learner accept a 'given' version rather than construct their own version through reasoning or experimentation. 'Natural ability' to 'pick it up' is set forth as a primary condition for effective learning while 'knowing how' to offer up that knowledge in an examination is something to be achieved through knowing given procedures and through practice. The perceived requirements of the examination exert a powerful influence upon both knowledge and learning with being 'able to work the thing out for themselves' and 'the ability to apply chemical knowledge' meaning, simply, recall and application. Throughout, there is no indication that Richard treated knowledge as problematic or subjective or that learning entailed anything more than the reception, memorisation and re-presentation of knowledge and skills in their original 'pure' form.

Richard's views of knowledge and learning were unambiguous and were reflected in his teaching practice, as observed: his described and idealised curricula were highly consistent. However, his treatment of knowledge and learning, at least as witnessed in this first year group, did not correspond entirely with those set out in the statement of aims and assessment objectives in his course syllabus. While stressing the need for basic knowledge and 'skills in laboratory procedures and techniques', the aims also claimed that the course should 'foster imaginative and critical thinking', 'develop students' abilities to acquire knowledge by means of practical investigation [and] to form hypotheses and to design experiments to test them'. There was little evidence of these in Richard's first year course or even in his own accounts of his second year course. Moreover, while the assessment objectives attached due importance to 'knowledge' ('the ability to recall and communicate information . . . '), 'comprehension' ('the ability to interpret familiar information . . . ') and 'application' ('the ability of candidates to use and communicate their knowledge and understanding in situations which, to

90

some extent, are unfamiliar or to deal with familiar situations by unfamiliar methods') – which were all quite visible in Richard's work – they also asserted the importance of a fourth 'ability': analysis, evaluation and synthesis. But there was barely any evidence from Richard's account or from his observed practice that he sought to promote such critical qualities. Perhaps that was what he was alluding to when he spoke of 'knowing how to present the content'. If so, he would appear to have been treating analytic, evaluative and synthesised 'outcomes' as achievable by the deployment of given, rehearsable procedures rather than by reflective critique and, quite possibly, was being entirely realistic in holding such a view, given his experience of how students had fared in previous examinations. Alternatively, it could have been that analysis, evaluation and synthesis were to figure more prominently in the second year of the course and that Richard's accounts were framed for the interviewer's benefit in terms congruent with the observed first year course. In any event, Richard had consciously decided that his overall strategy was one of progression from basic incremental (factual or procedural) knowledge to more complex knowledge of some form or other.

On the matter of knowledge sources, Richard did stress the value of non-syllabus knowledge:

> I try to expand the course to make it relevant. Each week, we look at the science and technology magazines and also we look at five topics outside the syllabus. We visit museums as well. . . . I teach the content of the course and try and extend it wherever possible. I feel that chemistry is one of the most relevant subjects as, wherever you look, you've got chemistry all around you.

The boundaries to admissible course knowledge were determined by Richard's criterion of 'relevance' to the lives of his students. However, that 'relevance' was itself framed within the boundaries of chemical knowledge. Richard saw fit to try to extend his students' experiences beyond the scope of the syllabus but not beyond what he perceived to be the scope of the subject.

The students' accounts of their learning mirrored, to a large extent, those of their teacher. When describing how they had learned in the observed session, they frequently referred to Richard as the source of knowledge and to their own responsibilities for dependent note taking, memorising and application.

> It was described to us by our lecturer. We made notes and drew diagrams.

> Our lecturer taught us how to use the apparatus last week then gave us instructions on how to carry out the experiment today.

> Our lecturer went through the apparatus so it was clear in our heads. The books also provided diagrams to help.
>
> (Student evaluation schedules)

Moreover, Richard's central role in this process was not only recognised by the students but his expositions were often referred to as being among the most helpful parts of the sessions.

> Richard describing how to do the experiment at the beginning because then we know how to do the experiment so we are able to observe more and work efficiently.
>
> Going through equations of what we will see happening at the beginning of the lecture. The explanations, step by step, of what happens in each experiment helps to grasp the concepts of the subject.
>
> Note taking more than the practical but the practical emphasises the theory so they work well together. I find it easier to concentrate on the theory.
>
> (Student evaluation schedules)

But many students also valued their practical work as being among the most helpful:

> Set up the experiment by ourselves and see the reaction is actually what happened. Because it helps to understand more than if it is just told by the lecturer.
>
> Carrying out the experiment and learning from the mistakes so that next time it can be done better.
>
> The testing of the product and the setting up of the apparatus. Gives me practice on setting apparatus up. Gives me a reference for the tests I can do to unknown substances in the future.
>
> (Student evaluation schedules)

The students' accounts convey a very strong sense of their dependency upon their tutor and even in respect of practical work it is apparent that their concerns were more with the accurate replication of demonstrated procedures than with their own experimentation. From these accounts, it is apparent that there was a high correspondence between students' and teacher's expectations, providing further confirmation of the consistency between Richard's described curriculum and his personal curriculum values. They shared a common coherent view of knowledge and learning and there is little evident dissent from the way things were done. Indeed, when asked to identify any parts of the session that they had found unhelpful, most of the students did not nominate anything as being unhelpful while those who did identify something suggested only 'washing up', 'clearing away', 'waiting for the practical' and, perhaps the most telling of all, 'parts of the practicle (*sic*, again!) that did not work'!

Questions arise from these observations, though, concerning the origins of these particular views of chemical knowledge and learning. Is the consistency of expectations a product of the particular teacher–student relationships that Richard and the group had cultivated during their time together? Does the explanation somehow lie in the nature of the subject? That is to say, does chemical knowledge exist only in the forms described and utilised by Richard and his students and can it be learned only by means of the strategies that they adopted? Does the explanation lie in the nature of science or, as much student and teacher folk-lore would have it, in the culture of scientists? Answers to these questions will become more clear as further cases are considered but, for the present, it is worth noting that all groups of chemistry students reported a significantly stronger personal preference for receptive learning activities[1] upon entry to their courses than did A-level students in general. That is to say that students' and their teachers' expectations and personal preferences were established long before they came together for the purpose of A-level chemistry. The harmonious and productive relationships in this group had arisen out of the students accepting their tutor as authority, both as the primary source of essential course knowledge and as the pedagogue demonstrably capable of meeting their learning needs.

Many of the students offered extrinsic reasons for their choices of course, frequently citing higher education as their intended stepping stone to a specific career or to work of some kind in the 'medical' or other 'scientific field'. Richard viewed the main purposes of the course in much the same light. Earlier cohorts of his students had proved remarkably successful in achieving such goals, with 86 per cent progressing to higher education over the previous eight years. That the rehearsal of procedures for meeting examination requirements assumed such importance for both tutor and students is to be understood in this context. Moreover, the utilitarian values displayed by the students and, to a large extent, by their teacher at the onset of their course is a key to understanding the social conditions within which subsequent learning was to take place and, in particular, the behaviourist beliefs and practices displayed in the thoughts and actions of tutor and students. Chemistry was a means to an end, not an end in itself and, consequently, the intrinsic and problematic character of the subject was of less concern than were the 'facts' and procedures which could be relied upon to produce examination answers. Practical work was, therefore, seen to perform two main functions:

1 to provide confirmation that the theory was 'right';
2 to provide opportunities for students to practise techniques to perfection.

Practical work did not provide for experimentation, for enabling students to elicit knowledge from practical experience. Or if it did, the students gave little indication at this mid-point of their first year course that practical work afforded such opportunities. Learning theoretical knowledge entailed the absorption of 'facts' and was tested and consolidated through its demonstration in a practical context. Learning procedural knowledge entailed an absorption of basic information to be perfected through practice: trial and error learning 'from the mistakes so that next time it can be done better'.

Chemical knowledge was not a subjective knowledge, it was essentially an objective, absolute and 'correct' theoretical and procedural knowledge which could be demonstrated through its application in a practical context. Therefore, students' ideas were deemed by them to be either 'right' or 'wrong' and it is easy to understand their reluctance to engage as fully as they might in Richard's question and answer sequences. No value was attached to the 'educated guess' or to the 'critical observation or query'. These were 'distractions' in the eyes of most students since they so frequently led only to 'wrong answers'. Richard was plainly aware of this and sought to engage his students more fully, prompting them to take the risk of an informed guess even when they were not entirely confident. But this was a bit of a struggle for Richard and it remains to be seen whether his students' views of knowledge and its acquisition changed at all over the second year of the course.

Finally on the subject of Richard's course, I should like to turn to the notion of studentship. Richard's views of course knowledge and learning were, as I have remarked, coherent. Moreover, with the exception of his conviction that they should engage more actively in his question and answer sessions, his students shared his views to a large extent. Even the students' low levels of participation in discussion and answering did not prove damaging to this particular partnership since Richard, it seemed, was prepared to suspend his concerns about participation, at least for the time being, presumably in the interests of the greater good of all concerned. Tutor and students also shared common views of the key purposes of their course. Within this context, students uniformly viewed their tutor as meeting in full their requirements as learners. There was no reason for the students to embark upon alternative learning careers to those which their tutor prescribed for them and which they themselves had actively sought. Their transition into post-16 education had been relatively smooth: new routines had been confirmed within existing habitus (see discussions in Avis *et al.*, 1996). However, there were signs of a heavy dependence of students upon their tutor as the source of essential course knowledge and many were not well disposed towards those learning activities which required them to view knowledge as problematic or to assume personal responsibility for critique or evaluation. Thus, their predominantly conforming studentship was essentially one of dependent acquiescence, but whether this would prove sufficient to enable them to meet the requirements of 'analysis, evaluation and synthesis' as spelled out in the course syllabus remains to be seen.

While the course of studentship ran smoothly for most members of Richard's group, there were signs that a few students were not entirely comfortable in the passive and receptive student role. One such case was Sarah whose 'studentship was innovative in so far as she sought novel and eclectic sources to assist the development of her personal chemical knowledge' (Avis *et al.*, 1996: 154), who did not settle easily into receptive learning activities and who was described by Richard as 'airy fairy' (ibid.: 153). However, any resistance that Sarah might have offered to Richard's methods was nullified by her respect for, and liking of, him as a person. Sarah was not alone in recognising in Richard a person who 'has the students' interests at heart'. Such perceptions of Richard contributed significantly to the harmonious and productive relationships between teacher and students and, in turn, to the coherence of this A-level course.

DEREK PEPPERILL'S GROUP

The same was not true of Derek Pepperill's A-level chemistry group. In response to the questions inviting them to identify the least helpful parts of the session, some members of the group focused only upon their teacher's contribution:

> Mr Pepperill. He's a patronising old git who won't teach new methods until he has covered out of date material first. (Male)

> The teacher was least helpful. When I asked him a question, he expected me to know what I was doing. If that was the case, I wouldn't be asking a question. He was very impatient and made me feel stupid for asking. (Female)

> The teacher because he's a sexist pig. He prefers the boys in chemistry and doesn't ask my friend and I any questions because he thinks we don't know the answers. We are NOT BIMBOS. (Female)
>
> (Student evaluation schedules)

The circumstances in which these students' views had been formed were all too apparent in the observed session where, despite the fact that more than half of the group were female, Derek directed every one of over twenty questions to male students. Although Derek and his students appeared to subscribe to a common view of knowledge and of learning – that is of an essentially 'objective' knowledge and receptive learning – it was quite apparent that their expectations of teacher–student relationships were highly conflictual. Unlike in Richard's case, many of Derek's students saw little reason for tempering their negative appraisals of their teacher and, given the rare opportunity of a researcher's interview and questionnaire, these otherwise compliant students gave vent to their feelings in full.

While some of Derek's male students adapted easily to their new routines, the studentship of the majority entailed strategic compliance or retreatism. But such adaptations were made necessary because students could not engage satisfactorily with their teacher's expectations of, and behaviour towards, them as persons; they were not brought about, as was the case in a number of examples described in the last chapter, because students' views of knowledge conflicted with those of their teacher.

HENRY STAPLETON'S GROUP

A more vivid example of conflicting perceptions and expectations is to be found in Henry Stapleton's group of second year A-level chemistry students.

(Mandy makes to pose a question.)

HENRY   Red herring number one coming up. What's that, Mandy?

MANDY   (Having quickly revised her decision to ask a question.) My brain's hurting.

HENRY   Oh dear! (He turns to face the class.) This is the moment when most people decide they should have chosen German. (Kate attracts Henry's attention. He turns to the class.) Are you ready for red herring number two? What was your question, Kate?

KATE   What's the difference between primary and secondary amines?

HENRY   (Answers Kate's question with the aid of a chalk board. After a minute, he turns to Jason.) Jason, if I went back to last year, could you give me a definition of a base?

JASON   Don't think so.

HENRY   So, if I gave you five minutes to look at your notes, could you?

JASON   I think so.

(The session progresses to a discussion of the equipment to be used in the ensuing practical work.)

HENRY   Chris, I think we'd want two pipettes, don't you?

CHRIS   Couldn't we use a flask?

HENRY   At your age, young man, I'd have thought you'd want an accurate experiment, not just sloshing chemicals about!

Throughout Henry's classes, there was a discernible reluctance among students to engage in verbal communication with their tutor. They reported Henry's frequent use of sarcasm and were not in the least well disposed to what they saw to be his primary motivating technique: the use of humiliation. How, though, did Henry describe himself?

I don't regard myself as a chemistry teacher primarily. I see myself as a brain stirrer, teaching a way of thinking and unlocking the mysteries of a subject called chemistry. They're more apprentices in the mysteries of chemistry. I'm a catalyst, I think. I'm the channel of communication between the body of knowledge called chemistry and them. A catalyst to make them think. I'm not a feed pipe – definitely not – I'm more than that.

To Henry, what the students perceived as sarcasm was 'brain stirring' – to make them think. He was, in his own mind, the trigger which unleashed the spirit of human inquiry. But, then, on the subject of human learning, he claimed:

> I try to create an atmosphere in the lesson where knowledge is absorbed. . . . I don't expect them to absorb more than 10 per cent in a lesson. Most of it [absorption] comes with the *use* of the lesson material. I hope that if I come back to a point, they'll absorb it a bit better. I use a lot of repetition in lessons. I go over and over, forwards and backwards.

On the one hand, Henry claimed to be a catalyst, not a feed pipe, promoting the exploration of chemistry's mysteries. On the other, he spoke with equal conviction about ploughing the field of chemical knowledge over and over, forwards and backwards, on the assumption that, presumably, more and more will come to be learned. His accounts of repetition and absorption resonate strongly with the 'shit at the fan' principle of teaching: at the first throw, some 10 per cent of the important substance will stick; keep throwing and the layers will somehow build up into a cohesive whole. Henry added, when describing the chemical knowledge underpinning his teaching:

> I regard the syllabus as the minimum. . . . I draw on everything I know. I draw on my whole knowledge to illustrate points and tell stories.

The coherence of Henry's views of knowledge and learning is difficult to discern on the basis of these insights alone. He appeared to take the view that knowledge originates *both* from within an established body of chemical wisdom for which he is the gatekeeper *and* from his students' own thinking about the mysteries of chemistry. Of course, there is nothing unreasonable or contradictory in that. On the matter of learning, he stressed that the students were *both* active (thinking) and passive (absorbing). Again, this is not at all unreasonable and may well be indicative of a coherent view of knowledge and learning. But it is Henry's further remarks about students' thought processes which illuminate his own position most clearly.

> They have to be taught to think and write. It's a great hurdle. They find it difficult getting organised and they find learning difficult. They expect it all to make sense immediately and they find it difficult when it does not make sense immediately.

97

Taught to think? How do you achieve this?

I give them exercises to find out how the brain works. They need to know this before they can use their brains. I like to see them thinking sideways. . . . They need to manipulate new learning facts into either new or expected patterns.

If you ask a question and you don't get the response you're looking for, what do you do?

One: generally go around the class. Two: sometimes I tell them. Three: I leave it in the air.

Why leave it in the air?

Because I think there should be something in the air at the end of a lesson; something they're worried about. Because I'm trying to make them think. They might sit down and look it up, etc. In other words, it's the thinking processes in their heads that should carry on.

Much appeared to turn on Henry's expectation that students 'manipulate new learning facts into either new or expected patterns'. Henry was the primary source, possibly the sole source, of factual chemical knowledge, which he imparted at his 10 per cent efficiency rate. His function beyond that, as teacher, as catalyst or brain stirrer, was to recreate the 'mysteries' of chemistry. He did this partly by discharging knowledge at a rate which he believed to be faster than his students' 'absorption rates' and partly by deliberately providing incomplete accounts – by leaving something 'in the air'. This is 'brain stirring' or the promotion of lateral thought ('thinking sideways'). Thus, his claim that students manipulate new facts makes sense: he provided the facts in a form which required the students to disentangle them, search out any missing information and assemble them into coherent explanatory accounts. Of course, Henry's views of learning did not fit any single theoretical account of the matter. On the one hand, he discharged 'factual' knowledge incrementally, providing reinforcement by means of numerous specific questions and by repetition. His approach here was distinctly behaviourist except for the fact that he intentionally gave out more information than he believed his students could ever process ('absorb'). On the other hand, he strove to promote his students' deeper understanding of complex knowledge through a 'problem solving' approach, expecting the students to manipulate their own patterns or understandings.

From the observations, it was apparent that Henry's students did encounter the very learning opportunities he described. He did make rapid-fire statements of chemical facts; he did plough 'backwards and forwards' across the same basic information; and he did appear to leave quite a lot of things 'in the air'. Henry's account of his teaching was, it appeared, entirely consistent with what he actually did. But how did his students experience it?

Some students' comments confirmed the impressions conveyed by Henry in his remarks about 'brainstirring', though not necessarily in the manner he would have appreciated:

> You probably noticed he's completely off his rocker. There's continuous note taking; it's a mess – he jumps around from bit to bit. You have to spend time at home writing them up and making sense of them. It's very different to all my other tutors. You have to keep on the ball the whole time. You don't get set reading, etc.
>
> (Student interview)

Others alluded to their own responsibilities for thinking and manipulating the basic information which Henry provided, although there is a strong suggestion here that the students viewed the experience more in terms of incompetent teaching than in terms of 'brainstirring'.

> You've got to be able to teach yourself. Some outstanding students take three hard A-levels and get good results, regardless of the teachers they have.
>
> (Student evaluation schedule)

Many of Henry's students testified to what they perceived were gaps in the information which he provided.

> In many lectures you write notes including many of the things which you don't understand but are expected to use.
>
> Learning the reactions without learning a general formula. Is the reac-
> · tion an exception or a general rule?
>
> Experimentation is explained with very little detail of what you *actually* have to do.
>
> (Student evaluation schedules)

Some gave examples of how they had managed to clarify their situation while others described the strategies which they pursued in order to do so.

> The results of the experiment were helpful because then the aim of the practical became clear.
>
> Working with other people is helpful. It's good to work in a group, you can support each other.
>
> (Student evaluation schedules)

All in all, these students projected the view that learning was essentially a matter of constructing their own chemical knowledge. However, they did not appear to think that the process had been stimulated by Henry's catalytic teaching or by the learning opportunities which he had created for them. None ventured that they had had their brains 'stirred' or had acquired new thinking skills as a result of the problems that Henry had set. Nor had they recognised the benefits of developing their own understanding from a basis of partial knowledge. Rather, they expressed frustration and resignation at having to cope with a teacher they deemed inadequate for their purposes and whose main contribution was to mystify both the content and processes of their learning. Ironically, their creative and critical thought had been stimulated by what the students saw to be incompetent teaching: such learning as had taken place had taken place *in spite of*, rather than as the result of, Henry's teaching.

Unlike Richard's students, described earlier, Henry's group varied considerably in the value they attached to different learning activities. On the matter of repetitive activities, for instance, there were opposing views:

> The repetition was most helpful. More examples on the topic. I learn better by repetition.

> Repeating the experiment to make sure we obtained the correct results [was least helpful]. It's very time consuming and boring second time round.
>
> (Student evaluation schedules)

Dictation, a regular feature of Henry's sessions, was regarded positively by some of these A-level chemistry students as a useful way of compiling necessary notes. Others, however, thought not, since dictation did not allow them to think while taking their notes and, it appeared, Henry made no provision for thought during the dictation process.

> It's continuous non-stop talking without going over the information. There's no time to solidify the information.

> I prefer written dictation notes so that you can use them to refer to when doing an experiment. Every new topic you need a base to work from. It's a hassle to take notes and be on the ball at the same time.
>
> (Student evaluation schedules)

Nonetheless, many students stressed the importance of notes, regardless of how they acquired them. Notes were essential if they were to begin to understand what it was that they were supposed to be learning. Notes were the clues – the essential tools for locating missing knowledge and for demystifying Henry's expositions.

> I learn more from notes but practical work backs the theory up.

> [Most helpful to me were] my own notes made at an earlier date. My own notes were most useful; they are not filled with colourful metaphors for chemicals which confuse us all during lessons. Our lecturer is verging on insanity and confuses us immensely.
>
> (Student evaluation schedules)

What Henry's students proffered that they needed was factual knowledge and 'given' explanations in an unambiguous form. Compared with other A-level students, and in common with other chemistry students, Henry's group stated a marked preference for receptive learning activities and showed little enthusiasm for interactive learning activities.

Unrewarded, as they perceived themselves to be, the students coped with the situation by use of a number of strategies. Peer support, both in and out of class, was mentioned by some students as being most helpful in enabling them to make sense of what their teacher or, more importantly for many, their A-level course, expected from them. Small groups of threes or fours would meet up regularly to pool and try to make sense of their fragmented experiences. The course textbook and the insights offered by those students who were regarded by others as particularly able provided authoritative sources as students set about piecing their course together.

But it was not only chemical knowledge which Henry Stapleton's students found to be problematic. Henry was a problem too. The students had little positive regard for the ways in which he related to them. 'Merlin' was one of the more benign descriptors that was applied to him; others stressed his sarcasm, pomposity and his indifference to students as people. 'Off his rocker', 'verging on insanity', 'non-stop talking' and 'jumping from bit to bit' have already provided some indication of the students' perceptions. But they also pointed to the frequency with which Henry disparaged their genuine intellectual and practical inquiries.

CARA   How do we measure it? By pipette?

HENRY   How else? Are you going to use your hands?

For Henry, this was good humoured banter, a precondition of 'brain-stirring'; for the students, it was humiliating and unhelpful. While many retreated from any such engagement with Henry, some resorted to challenging their tutor by turning the tables on him. This was only just over half way through a two year course and some students were displaying behaviours which, under any other conditions, would be described as insolent.

Despite his intentions to the contrary, Henry's presentation of interactive learning opportunities – if that is, indeed, what they were – made little positive impact upon his students' dispositions to learning. The students were faced with a situation in which chemistry was made incomprehensible and they resorted to such means as were available to them to make sense of the situation and to create their own learning opportunities. In their studentship, they looked beyond the scope of the opportunities provided for them by their teacher and, in particular, to strategies that had served them well elsewhere. While there was an evident dependence upon teachers and textbooks for essential course knowledge among both Henry's and Richard's students, Henry's group 'acted upon' their prescribed curriculum in very different ways to Richard's. There was little evidence of strategic compliance since, in the experience of the students, there was little to be gained from such a response. Only one student could be described as conforming and he, incidentally, failed the final examination for the course. Others resorted to combinations of retreatism, rebellion and, above all, innovation. However, the scope of their innovatory practices was severely bounded by their own concepts of knowledge and learning.

On the face of it, Henry, Richard and Derek had much in common. Their views of knowledge and learning coincided to a marked degree, as did those of their students, while their courses were planned along more or less similar lines. However, they were very different in the impact they had upon their students' learning. In Richard's case, strategic compliance was most evident, in Derek's less so, and in Henry's hardly at all. These three cases alone indicate the variety of ways in which teaching can bear upon learning and, of course, how students' dispositions to knowledge, learning and to their teacher can have profound effects upon their descriptive curricula.

ROBIN TOYE'S GROUP

On the basis of the cases considered up to this point, Robin Toye would appear to be the A-level chemistry student's ideal teacher. He distinguished explicitly between 'correct' and 'incorrect' chemical knowledge and between what was on the syllabus and what was not. His teaching of his second year group was structured principally around an unambiguous presentation of 'correct' syllabus knowledge very much in keeping with the expectations and learning preferences of his own and other chemistry students. He was also preoccupied with constraints of time – the need to 'get through the syllabus' – and frequently offered this to his students as the reason for halting their work on one topic and redirecting them to something new. Robin's work with his students was, as a result, characterised by little encouragement of student questioning, few opportunities for students to exercise judgement, to formulate opinion or to summarise their experiences in their own words and, at times, an over-riding concern that students should 'just do', 'just accept' or 'just learn' the fact, principle or procedure in question.

ROBIN I want you to explain in your own words why ECu=0, so you'll be saying something like . . . (he proceeds to give the students an explanation). I want you to find out what the E of copper is. Do it in rough as you might get it wrong. My advice to you is . . . (he then provides the students with detailed instructions on how to find the E of copper).

(The students proceed to calculate the E of copper.)

ROBIN   How are we getting on, Jane? 0.34? That can't be right. (He
then completes the calculation, writing each step on the board, as
the students copy down his handiwork.) Does that come out, Jane?
Has anyone else got that value? (A few hands are raised in reply.)
Quite a popular value so it must be right. Right Jane?

JANE   I've got it now.

ROBIN   Right, problem solved. Anyone else not got it?

DAVID   I haven't.

ROBIN   Right, we have a problem with logistics of time. Just write the
value down and perhaps have another go and we can discuss it in
tutorials.

There are numerous further examples to be drawn from what he said and did
in the observed sessions which indicate Robin's views of knowledge and
learning:

> Then explain why it leads to a decrease in ΔH and if you cannot, just
> say it does and think about it.

> You just look the value up and that's what it is.

> (After going through questions set for students' homework.) I think
> that's all the points arising from the questions. Any questions? No?
> Good!

> Let's not prolong this, you should have written . . .

> I remember how confused the students were last time I did this. Let's
> not prolong this, just do what Stephen did.

Robin's own interview responses reveal quite clearly his assumptions that his
students' learning of A-level chemistry is best achieved through their passive
absorption of the non-problematic version which it is his responsibility to
provide.

> When they fall behind with work, I must admit I lecture rather than
> teach. . . . My old chemistry teacher told me, 'Never tell a student
> what you can ask them'. But if you do that all the time, facts get frag-
> mented and information lost. . . . I'll do anything if it doesn't take a
> lot of time. Time hampers learning, hampers teaching. Learning goes
> on inside and outside of the classroom. You [i.e. the students] need to
> spend more time out of the classroom to gain the learning experience.

For Robin, class meetings were primarily for the purpose of imparting essential syllabus information, while it was the students' responsibility to
consolidate that information outside class meetings. How, then, did the
students regard their acquisition of chemical knowledge?

The first point to note is the diversity of responses by students. Many offered a positive appraisal of Robin's attempts to meet their needs and, in doing so, indicated that their views of chemical knowledge and learning had much in common with those of their teacher.

I like it here. It's regimental – marked down. You can refer to notes.

Regimental?

Yes. It aids my method of learning. It's logical and ordered which makes it good for revision notes.

(Student interview)

The students pointed specifically to the benefits of receptive learning activities, to notes, and to the important functions of 'examples' in the simplification and communication of knowledge and understanding, as indicated by the following accounts of what they found to be most helpful to their learning.

All really. Good notes for revision.

The lecture and board work. Board work shows clear examples and gives me time to transfer them to my notes.

Copying from the blackboard. Also, repetitive exercises induce (*sic*) knowledge.

(Student evaluation schedules)

Some even went so far as to claim that interactive learning activities, or any departures from the prescribed content of the syllabus, detracted from their opportunities to learn. Among the activities considered to be least helpful were:

Class discussion and participation. Slow learning as a result.

When we had to make our own notes. We often miss out important points and get confused.

When the lecturer gets sidetracked. It is difficult to concentrate.

(Student evaluation schedules)

However, there were some criticisms of the tutor's tightly structured expositions. As with almost all of the A-level chemistry students referred to in this chapter so far, Robin's class was highly critical of the speed with which they were expected to record the information he presented.

The speed of the teaching. I can't take in what I'm writing down AND listen to the teacher.

The rapidity of some parts. I need time to take things in sometimes and digest learning.

Hours of lecturing can send students to sleep. A short demonstration is more interesting.

(Student evaluation schedules)

But while the vast majority of students gave clear signs of a passive, dependent studentship, a few indicated not only that they had misgivings about the common lecture/note taking format of class meetings but that they found greatest benefit when able to test out their newly forming knowledge and understanding in some way. For these few students, the most helpful learning activities were considered to be:

The lecturer asking us questions because we pay more attention and need to think for ourselves.

When we had to think and describe things for ourselves. It makes it easier to understand than to just write down what someone else says.

(Student evaluation schedules)

There were some indications that students were divided in their views of what were the most helpful learning activities. However, there was, alongside these, a general view among students that Robin was able to meet their requirements. They had no reasons to raise any serious objections to his teaching as Derek's and Henry's students had done. But that is not to suggest that all were coping with the demands of their course equally well. When asked what they had learned in the observed sessions, two of Robin's students replied as follows:

That chemistry is mind blowing. And that I don't understand a word of what is going on.

I'm not too sure. But I will read the notes at home and, with the aid of a textbook, try to understand it at a higher level.

(Student evaluation schedules)

The important point to note in the case of these two students is that nowhere in their evaluations did they attribute responsibility for their apparent failings to their teacher. In the first case, the student viewed the nature of the subject as the cause of her difficulties while the second saw it as his responsibility to gain an understanding of what had gone before by means of further personal study.

Robin's described and idealised curricula were highly consistent and, to a very large degree, shared by the students. This contributed much to the stability and productivity of the class and, in these circumstances, it did not seem to matter to teacher or students that key aims of the prescribed curriculum in respect of the promotion of imaginative and critical thought were not fulfilled. Robin was content that students treated subject knowledge as essentially objective and learning as simply a process of uncritical

assimilation. Propositional, theoretical and procedural knowledge and explanations were all dispensed as objective facts, as correct or incorrect
information, while the quest for understanding was exhibited by only a
small number of students, and then not very forcefully. In the main,
students exhibited a dependence upon their teacher for essential course
knowledge and displayed few signs of willingness to assume responsibility
for their own generation of knowledge. Their studentship was predominantly conformist or retreatist. It is in this context that their remarks about
'regimentation', the value of 'good notes' and clear examples and their criticism of 'sidetracking' and of Robin's pacing of his presentations of
information must be understood. The students expected their teacher to
select, organise, present and reinforce knowledge for their 'consumption';
they did not expect to have to 'process' that knowledge other than by assimilation and retention. Most rejected opportunities for critical or evaluative
thought, preferring to concentrate their energies in receptive rather than
interactive learning activities. Their expectations were rooted in behaviourist
assumptions about learning and, in so far as Robin's teaching strategies met
his students' expectations, his own views can be seen to be grounded in the
same behaviourism.

Robin was expected to be 'teacher as instructor', a role that he found easy
and natural to fill. But the consistency of outlook shared by teacher and
students was not confined to matters of knowledge, learning and teaching; it
extended to shared views of ability and, even, human nature. Specifically, an
inability to learn in any given context was attributable to some deficiency in
innate learning ability, a view readily maintained alongside one which
treated knowledge as objective fact rather than subjective construction.
Moreover, it must be said that the structural and cultural location of Robin's
chemistry course (and, it transpired, of most of the courses considered in this
chapter) was such that it was supportive of the views of curriculum
expounded by Robin and his students.

Again, the important parts played by teacher and students in curriculum
making are clear to see. The consistency of their expectations did much to
determine the nature of the teaching and learning which ensued, even
though this was not entirely consistent with claims contained within the
prescribed syllabus. The end result was markedly different from that for
Henry Stapleton's group for reasons that are now quite apparent. Indeed,
with these insights in mind, it is interesting to reflect on Richard Conder's
first year group, whose students appeared to hold similar expectations to
those in Robin's group but whose tutor was attempting to encourage them
to more autonomous and critical learning. Would Richard succeed in any
great measure in bringing about significant change in his students' dispositions to knowledge and learning? Would passive studentship prove the
stronger? Would there emerge over time a rich diversity of students' dispositions and practices, as in John's group, described in Chapter 4, and, if so,

would Richard be able to meet all their needs and expectations? Or would the tensions between tutor and student views of the idealised curriculum prove so strong that stability and order would break down, as in Henry Stapleton's group?

KEN STADDON'S GROUP

Compared with the other cases considered so far, a number of Ken Staddon's first year A-level students revealed a greater critical awareness of learning and knowledge.

> If I write things down, I learn from my own writing but discussion makes you think and argue several points of view. You're given facts but they're not necessarily true. You can decide which is best for you – what sounds right.

Facts are not true?

> In chemistry, like, models of atoms, cloud theory – well, they're wrong. It was believed that they were the best model at the time but they're wrong. They have been proved wrong and you go on to a new model. You don't expect them to be true any more.
>
> (Student interview)

Such a view which ascribes value to interactive learning activities and which regards chemical knowledge as 'provisional' and theory as theory (as distinct from fact) is rare indeed among A-level chemistry students, and certainly among those in the first year of their course. While few of Ken's students expressed such views of learning and knowledge so cogently, almost all of their accounts were consistent with the above claims about learning and knowledge. None exhibited the strong dependency upon teacher and text-book as the sole authoritative sources of knowledge, as was witnessed in other groups. In fact, a good number expressly stated that direct instruction was not the most helpful learning activity.

> The practical part [was the most helpful] because I find it easier to learn through doing the experiment rather than having it explained.

> It [the least helpful] would have been lengthy note taking but there wasn't any; it's repetitive, I spend more time on writing than on learning.
>
> (Student evaluation schedules)

However, Ken's own perspective on knowledge and learning provides something of a contrast to those of his students and can be used to illuminate the students' experiences. Ken confirmed that basic factual knowledge and technical skills are an essential element of the course and that, to a degree, students must obtain a command of these before they can proceed to deeper understanding of the subject.

> It's true of chemistry and other subjects, but particularly true of chemistry: you need to know the knowledge. Get the knowledge on board as early as possible. Don't leave it all to the end.

> There are facts – recall things. You've got to recall specific facts that you need to know. For example, basic properties of groups in the periodic tables. There's a lot of other stuff but they're not able to do that. My experience is that they concentrate on the concept but the bit they don't like to do is to learn things.

For Ken, the use of the term, 'learning', was confined to the memorisation of factual knowledge, Indeed, this was not the first time that this restricted usage of the term was found among chemistry teachers, as was revealed in Derek's account of changes to his course syllabus:

> I think that over the last four or five years the syllabus has changed. There used to be things like metals which was just learning, pure learning. . . . There's more understanding and application now but you can't get away from learning, especially with organics.

> (Derek Pepperill)

Many chemistry teachers, it appeared, made such a distinction. However, Ken's students, unlike Robin's group, for instance, were not overly keen on the 'learning' side of things; the problematic nature of chemical knowledge held some greater attraction. Ken was well aware of this: 'the bit they don't like to do is learn things'.

However, while Ken laid considerable stress on the absorption ('learning') of basic factual information and technical skills, he also communicated a stronger concern than, say, Robin did that his students should be able to manipulate such knowledge for scientific ends. It was this manipulation which promoted students' understanding (a term which Ken used frequently) and that was essentially something for which the students held a key responsibility.

> It [the course] gives them a good understanding of basic chemistry and some practical skills. I suppose it helps them to think logically, in a more scientific way. . . . Chemistry A-level's field of knowledge is by far the largest, larger than any science. If they don't take it on board, they struggle. They think they can learn it all in the term before the exam but they can't. They need time to take it on board – a bit at a time. Concepts of physical chemistry need to be applied to a knowledge base. It's something you need to take on now [i.e. early in the first year of the course] so that when you do physical concepts, you've got something to relate it to.

108

Thus, basic information and skills, deemed 'objective knowledge', were to be absorbed through processes of 'learning' while conceptual or elaborated knowledge was to be acquired through the subjective experience of trans-posing and manipulating such knowledge and relating it to new problems. It is noticeable, also, that while Ken's teaching did stress the importance of recall of basic information, he also allowed greater 'space' than did some earlier cases for his first year students to engage in processes of manipulation across knowledge 'boundaries'. This was revealed in the nature of his ques-tioning, where requests for recall were low in incidence compared with other classes and where the frequency of his requests for reasoned explanation and prediction was high. It is also to be noted that he frequently responded to students' queries with questions of his own, not unlike Keith, the engi-neering tutor referred to in the last chapter.

The dominant form of studentship in Ken's group was conformity: on the one hand, the students had either found that their initial expectations had been met or they had become socialised successfully into new schematic perceptions; on the other hand, their tutor had adapted successfully to his students' expectations. There were no obvious examples of strategic compli-ance, retreatism or rebellion – none, it appeared, had any reason for rejecting either the goals or the various means of their course. There were, however, as I have mentioned, cases of innovation where some students periodically sought to bring a more critical focus to bear upon chemical knowledge, by questioning that knowledge which their tutor expected they would simply 'learn'. But this desire to make chemical knowledge problematic was entirely in keeping with the tutor's expectations and became a cause for concern only when students were not found to be meeting the requirement that they should 'learn'.

Although I have only dealt very briefly here with the case of Ken Staddon's group, it is apparent that the descriptive curricula in that group were qualitatively different from those of the other chemistry courses described so far. These differences are plainly attributable to the curriculum values which teachers and students brought to bear upon the prescribed curriculum. It is also apparent that there was a variety of views of knowledge and learning among the students in Ken's group and that these were likely to make for diverse forms of studentship in the ensuing months. But these were early days and it would be foolhardy to attempt to predict the descrip-tive curricula yet to be generated through this particular teacher–student chemistry. However, the signs are that they would have been quite different from those of the four courses reported earlier.

ERIC FIELD'S GROUP

The final A-level chemistry group to be considered here offers something of a contrast to those described above. The extent to which the teacher, Eric

Field, sought to elicit course knowledge from his students' experiences and to stimulate their own reasoning of chemical problems was far greater than in the earlier cases. Eric frequently used questions of the 'tell me something about' and 'why?' varieties as opposed to the 'tell me what' type so common elsewhere. He attached great importance to the use of examples from students' everyday experiences and to encouraging them to formulate their own understandings of the scientific phenomena which they routinely encountered. There was, indeed, a detailed syllabus for the course but Eric's attentions, it appeared, were focused less upon the prescribed content and more upon the declared aims.

The aims are to

provide, through well designed studies of experimental and practical chemistry, a worthwhile educational experience for all students, whether or not they go on to study science beyond this level and, in particular, to enable them to acquire sufficient understanding and knowledge to:

1 become confident citizens in a technological world, able to take or develop an informed interest in matters of scientific import;
2 recognise the usefulness, and limitations, of scientific method and to appreciate its applicability in other disciplines and in everyday life;
3 be suitably prepared for studies beyond A-level in pure sciences, in applied sciences or in science-dependent vocational courses.

But it would be a mistake to suppose that Eric's practice was simply the product of his curriculum prescription. The aims of those syllabuses to which the earlier teachers were working were very similar to the above.

For reasons that are not attributable to his syllabus aims, Eric's views of knowledge and learning contrasted markedly with those of other chemistry teachers reported here. Chemical knowledge was a provisional knowledge and students were periodically exhorted to communicate their understanding in a manner which stressed the theoretical rather than factual nature of scientific knowledge. In a manner consistent with such views of knowledge, Eric persistently encouraged his students to hypothesise and to subject their thinking to critical inspection by the group. It was noticeable that, in comparison with other chemistry teachers, he delayed giving answers to students' questions, preferring to use their questions to stimulate their own personal hypotheses and general critical awareness of chemistry. He was not, it seemed, as preoccupied as others with 'getting through' essential basic course knowledge or 'facts' as a necessary foundation for chemical-scientific inquiry.

But while, in the student questionnaire, Eric's group reported a significantly lower *incidence* of receptive learning activities in their A-level class meetings than did any of the chemistry groups observed, they expressed only a marginally stronger *preference* for interactive learning activities than did students in those other groups. How, then, did they respond to the learning opportunities which Eric presented to them?

> To be honest, the amount of factual work wasn't too heavy, but the amount of understanding and concepts involved I personally believe is astronomical. . . . He tends to ask questions to get us to think in order to get round answering him.

> [I learn] by listening to the teacher's explanations and making my own notes of the points I believe to be relative. Also, you are asked questions individually which invites you to think and to provide your own opinions.
>
> (Student evaluation schedules)

It is apparent that some students, at least, not only recognised the purposes of Eric's questioning but were ready to accept some responsibility for the generation of their own chemical knowledge. Others, while seeming to confirm the value of Eric's questioning, gave an indication that questioning and discussion were a primary purpose of class meetings and that the acquisition of basic knowledge was a task which they were responsible for *in advance of* each class meeting. While the other classes considered here tended to use class meetings for the dissemination and acquisition of basic knowledge and to require students to pursue further reading and inquiries in their own time, the responsibilities seemed to be reversed in Eric's class.

Which part(s) of the session were most helpful to you in your learning?

> The class discussion involving questions being asked. We tend to show off in class and try to answer as many questions as we possibly can. Therefore, we thought in class and had prepared before the lesson started. We prepared for the lesson so we get more familiar when we get round to the same problems. This way we can understand and remember more.
>
> (Student evaluation schedule)

Quite a number of Eric's students seized upon the relevance of discussion topics to everyday experience when identifying what they felt had been the most helpful features of the observed session.

> It's much easier to understand things when they're related to everyday life. Also, discussion helps you to understand concepts and enables you to remember and apply them.
>
> (Student evaluation schedule)

However, similar experiences were construed by others to be a distraction:

111

Which part(s) of the session were least helpful to you in your learning?

Talk not relevant to the subject, i.e. the teacher's motorbike. It allowed me to switch off.

(Student evaluation schedule – Melanie)

The side-tracking wasn't very helpful, but I find that if little stories are told in between explanations I remember the lesson more! Side-tracking, as I said, is funny, but it wastes time and you don't learn as much.

(Student evaluation schedule)

There is an indication in these latter accounts that the students concerned were preoccupied by the desire, evident in many of the students in the other classes considered here, to elicit only 'essential' course knowledge. The relevance criterion, it seemed, was being used to discriminate between what was perceived to be prescribed syllabus knowledge on the one hand, and non-syllabus, experientially based knowledge on the other. The claim that knowledge grounded in extra-syllabus experiences provided opportunities for a critical examination of syllabus knowledge or for a deeper understanding of chemistry was, it appeared, either rejected by these students or deemed irrelevant to their own learning. One of these two students volunteered the following observations about knowledge and learning.

My interest is in science rather than English and French. It's a factual thing whereas English is more, well, you can say what you like sort of thing. . . . I learn best by just listening and writing down notes that are useful and important.

(Student interview – Melanie)

Although many of the students in Eric's group appeared to have come to view chemical knowledge as provisional and to have adapted to, and accorded value to, interactive learning activities such as questioning, discussion and eliciting knowledge from personal experiences, some had not adapted in this way. Just as in Richard's group, where students held strong expectations of, and preferences for, receptive learning activities and where there was a minority of students seeking interactive learning opportunities, so the opposite appeared to be the case in Eric's group: interactive learning opportunities were more commonplace and a minority of students preferred receptive learning opportunities.

On the basis of the interviews, questionnaires and observations, it is apparent that there was consistency between Eric's described and idealised curricula. His views of curriculum knowledge were to stress weak subject boundaries, while his views of learning emphasised the importance of learner independence in critical engagement with knowledge sources and of learners' positive dispositions to interactive learning activities. As a teacher, he viewed himself as a catalyst whose purpose was to support students in

112

their own constructions of course knowledge, if not their generation of a unique, personal science.

What is apparent from Eric's group is that, despite sharing a curriculum prescription with many of the other courses described here, the emergent descriptive curricula of his students were qualitatively different from those of most of the other cases. This is readily understood in terms of the views of knowledge and learning which the tutor brought to bear upon the process of curriculum making. But there was also diversity among students' evaluations of the learning opportunities made available to them. A few demonstrated their dependence upon teacher or textbook knowledge, an intolerance of non-syllabus knowledge, and a preference for receptive learning opportunities, while others were more inclined to expound the value of personal constructions of knowledge and interactive learning activities. They were only just over half way through the first year of their course and yet it was apparent that some students' dispositions to knowledge and learning had undergone a significant transformation from those they reported at the commencement of the course, while others, it seemed, had not. But despite this variation in students' dispositions to knowledge and learning, there were no signs or reports of students challenging the way in which their course was organised and presented. Unlike the students in Henry's and Derek's groups, Eric's students were conformist or strategically compliant for the most part, with one or two exhibiting signs of retreatism. As I have noted with a number of the groups reported here, Eric's students had sufficient reason to suspend their own concerns, presumably in the interest of what they perceived would be their greater educational good.

SUMMARY

The six A-level groups considered here were selected from the total of twelve observed and questioned on the simple grounds that they offered the greatest richness of data. Two notable omissions from the selection are those of two groups following a 'Wessex' A-level course where, if I might risk over-generalisation, the dominant views of knowledge and learning were comparable with those of Eric Field and his students, described above.

On the basis of the accounts presented, it is apparent that the label, 'A-level chemistry', hides a very wide range of educational practices and experiences of learning. Indeed, there are examples where the knowledge, learning and teaching taking place within a chemistry class bears a stronger resemblance to those of some of the vocational courses described in Chapter 4 than to those of other chemistry courses. The comparative analysis of all twelve cases from the research served to confirm these and other observations. There were six main points to emerge.

First, chemistry teachers were not united in a single subject-view of knowledge and learning. However, a majority were inclined to emphasise 'knowledge as fact' and 'learning as reception and memorisation' in their accounts of their courses and, in the observed sessions, to confirm those views as being reflected in their practices. For some of these teachers, the reasons for maintaining such views may be found in the perceived restrictions of syllabuses and time allocations. Despite this, many of those interviewed claimed to be trying to steer their students away from a view of scientific knowledge as fact and encouraging them to take greater responsibility for the construction of their own chemical knowledge and more critical perspectives on the subject, as explicitly stated in prescribed course aims. In practice, however, it was apparent that few succeeded in doing this in any great measure and some made no noticeable attempts in this direction at all.

Second, chemistry students expressed a significantly stronger preference for receptive learning activities and a lesser preference for interactive learning activities upon entry to their courses than did students on any other course. In some of the groups observed, tutors held expectations of knowledge and learning which were consistent with those of most of their students. However, in many of the groups, there were some students whose expectations did not coincide with those of their tutors and who resorted to a variety of modes of adaptation. This variety is not only revealing of the significance of student agency in curriculum making, it is a further reminder of the limited scope which both external prescription and teacher planning have for obtaining control over student learning.

Third, the most common practice in the organisation of A-level chemistry courses was for teachers to concentrate their attentions upon the 'basic factual knowledge' of the subject in the first year of the course and to provide for experimentation and more exploratory activities, in so far as they occurred at all, in the second. The rationale, commonly expressed, was that students 'needed the basic knowledge which GCSE did not provide' before they could usefully benefit from activities which demanded the exercise of discretion and judgement. This is a claim already met in regard to vocational courses. However, the one exception from this pattern – Eric Field – placed far greater stress throughout *both* years of his course upon students learning from their exercise of judgement. In Eric's case, 'basic factual knowledge' was distributed throughout the entire course, not concentrated in the first year, and his students were encouraged to seek such basic knowledge at the time they needed it, in order to perform experiments or engage in class discussion and questioning.

In the majority of cases reviewed in this chapter, however, there must be doubts as to whether students seriously engaged in experimentation. The structure of sessions, the preponderance of demonstration prior to 'experimentation' and the students' accounts of their 'experiments' combine to provide a strong indication that it was application of previously acquired

114

knowledge and skills which took place in practical sessions more often than genuine experimentation.

Fourth, despite the frequently voiced claim that chemistry was a 'hard' subject, it appeared that 'hardness' was more readily associated with the quantity of memorisation than with the conceptual or logical complexities of the subject. Interestingly, the 'hardness' claim was associated more commonly with those groups whose courses focused heavily upon 'basic factual knowledge' in their first year. Certainly, the predominant anxiety expressed by students was not about the difficulties of reasoning through abstract conceptual problems; it was nearly always about the *amount* of abstracted information which had to be learned.

Fifth, compared with students on other courses, A-level chemistry students were much more inclined than others to attribute responsibility for their learning to themselves. Such a tendency rests comfortably with the views of knowledge and learning most apparent among chemistry students.

Finally, although there were cases of rebellion and retreatism among the A-level chemistry students, the dominant mode of studentship was conformity. Strategic compliance was evident in a few cases, while some students adopted innovatory practices. Whether adaptation was through strategic compliance, innovation, retreatism or even rebellion, it was almost always maintained privately and the *outward* appearance of all of the courses, with the notable exception of some of Messrs Pepperill and Stapleton's students, was of uniformity and compliance.

I shall return to the points raised here in Chapter 7 when the processes of studentship will be fully elaborated. In the next chapter, my concern is with teachers and students of A-level history whose experiences, it must be said, contrast starkly with those of the cases considered in the last two chapters.

6

KNOWLEDGE AND LEARNING IN PRACTICE
A-level history courses

The last two chapters have shown that there are a number of parallels to be drawn between vocational courses and A-level courses in respect of course knowledge and learning activities. To be sure, there are visible differences between course groups but these would appear to be as readily attributable to the idiosyncratic practices of individual teachers as they would to the qualities of particular course prescriptions. In order to gain further insight into students' experiences of knowledge and learning, this final chapter of cases focuses upon history, a subject selected in order that it might yield contrasting experiences to those of the vocational and chemistry courses.

MARIA IRWIN'S GROUP

Maria was the tutor to a second year A-level history group and from her initial interview it was apparent that she had clear views of the nature of her subject and of the demands that A-level placed upon herself and her students.

> It's a content laden subject. It is imperative to give them information, videos, documents, diagrams, etc., and time is of the essence.

What will the students learn in today's session?

> They'll continue to learn how to extract information from a text. . . . They're quite hopeless as a rule. They find it difficult to sift the salient facts out of prose. I think it's a lack of practice and they're not literate in the sense that they don't read. Their reading is too mechanistic for the purposes of the exercise. Their vocabulary is not good and they don't fully understand the language. I mean, one part of the homework was based on one particular word. They haven't got the general knowledge the examiners assume. I think the examiners are divorced from the reality of what 16- to 19-year-olds know.

Whose responsibility is that general knowledge?

> Well, I do try and explain. I mean, I can't allow red herrings but I do

try and explain to enhance their knowledge. But then, again, you're restricted by time. You know, independence in the second year is prevented by the threat of exams. Independent learning *is* time consuming.

For Maria, A-level historical knowledge is seriously time-constrained. Not only in her interview but frequently during her lessons she stressed the urgency of 'getting through' course knowledge within the limited time available. Giving students essential information or 'content' was the central concern around which class meetings were planned and yet she was plainly aware of the desirability of a more critical and reflective approach to course knowledge. She described the 'good student' as one who could 'see connections and is articulate enough to put the connections on paper'. Moreover, she claimed historical understanding could be best achieved when 'connections' were made with a general knowledge. However, in Maria's experience, her students not only lacked such a general knowledge but lacked the reading and interpretive skills necessary to make 'connections'. While she expressed some willingness to assist them in making good their 'deficits', it is quite apparent that time constraints were all-important in framing her opportunities for action.

It was no great surprise that Maria's class meetings provided a strong reflection of her main concerns. Her sense of urgency was evident in the four principal activities which took place in the two sessions observed: dictation, exposition, question and answer sequences and brief periods of discussion. Its impact upon students was unmistakable.

In what ways will today's session be of value to you?

Gives my speed writing skills a run out and practice makes perfect for exam day.

Which part(s) of the session were least helpful to you . . . ?

Speed of lesson was very fast and I feel we need to take things slower to take them in (and down on paper). Maria can talk faster than I can write.

Where my notes are poor and so I don't understand it. Maria speaking too fast.

When the difficult parts of the notes were said quickly. Because it doesn't give time to understand the information given and for it to 'sink in'.

(Student evaluation schedules)

These observations resonate with those made by a large number of the chemistry students.

It was equally apparent that, try as she might have done to encourage her students in making 'connections' between given historical events and other knowledge, the paramount effect of Maria's efforts was to focus their concerns upon 'factual' historical information.

Could you describe how you learned?

Word for word by rote.

Through answering questions from facts taken from the book.

(Student evaluation schedules)

The question and answer sequences, whether initiated by teacher or students, frequently focused upon specific answers and even when Maria sought to provide or elicit explanations of events, students' questions were invariably about factual detail. It was also apparent that many students were content to receive explanations *as facts* in themselves and were demonstrably unprepared to subject them to critical inspection. However, from their accounts of how they learned, many appeared to regard their receptive role as quite adequate for the purpose.

Could you describe how you learned?

By listening to the lecturer and taking notes.

Maria talked and I took notes, listened to discussions and questions by the students.

It's all about listening. Concentrating for the full sixty minutes is a taxer. But you only get out what you put in and that's the inner purpose which drives me and spurs me on.

(Student evaluation schedules)

Students' widespread acceptance of receptive learning activities[1] of one form or another was confirmed as they identified the particular activities which had been of greatest assistance to them:

Which part(s) of the session were most helpful to you?

Maria and the book. Maria formed the questions while she read the book. Therefore, it's easier to read the book and answer the questions.

When humour and examples are used to illustrate a point – also repetition.

Reading notes and answering questions were most helpful because I managed to retain information.

Could you describe how you learned?

With the questions you can tell if you've got a sneaky tutor but Maria wrote out the questions in the order the answers came up in the book

118

which makes it easy to read, learn and write at the same time.
(Student evaluation schedules)

However, while discussion was a minority activity, some students clearly suggested a preference for this and other interactive learning activities.

Could you describe how you learned?

With discussion, you tend to get interesting points from Maria and people round the room who've seen documentaries and throw bits in. Few people generate debate but I enjoy debates because I'm a loud mouth anyway.

I like it when you're asked questions, being put on the spot. I tend to fall asleep taking notes − I don't like note taking. You need to be forced to think for yourself, asked questions.

Other people's ideas. Also where it goes into more detail on any aspects.

Which part(s) of the session were most helpful to you?

Discussion, question and answer. During note taking I tend to switch off and my brain leaks out of my ears. So I prefer discussion sessions.

And the least helpful?

Straight note taking.
(Student evaluation schedules)

The majority view among students stressed knowledge as information with little apparent awareness of, or enthusiasm for, contested knowledge. Only a minority, it seemed, were to any extent moved to engage with multiple perspectives or argument. In their learning, the majority endorsed those activities which required their relatively uncritical reception of historical information. They felt no need to search beyond what they regarded as authoritative sources of historical knowledge and their concerns with informational detail, retention and repetition conjure up a vivid impression of uncriticality. Only a few were able to show any enthusiasm for a critical engagement with knowledge sources beyond teacher and textbook. It was this attitude to knowledge and learning which Maria criticised in her remarks about the students' 'mechanistic' approaches to reading.

How this situation came about is not at all clear. It is evident that Maria had some part to play in so far as it was through her that students had come to experience time constraints and their impact upon learning opportunities. But whether Maria was the 'cause' of this scenario must be held in some doubt since, in her own words, she valued students who were able to make 'connections' and who could utilise a general knowledge in the process of deepening their personal understanding. She claimed that she did not want to foster the passive reception of information but believed that the limitations of time coupled with students' deficiencies in reading skills and general knowledge effectively delineated the conditions within which she could exercise her own judgement as a teacher. An alternative, yet equally plausible, account might stress the significant power of students' expectations in determining the situation. If the students had shown resistance to interactive learning activities, it is easy to see how Maria might have come to adapt her teaching to suit their apparent needs. However, there is very little evidence that the preferences which these students held for specific learning activities differed from those of other history students or, indeed, from those of A-level students at large.

There is evident tension between Maria's described and idealised curricula. Not only was she very much aware of this but, frequently, in her class meetings, she revealed it to her students as the source of her frustrations. The students, on the other hand, brought a variety of expectations and dispositions to bear upon the processes of curriculum making and acted upon the opportunities which their tutor created for them in different ways. Maria, it seemed, despite occasionally cajoling her students into some form of argument or berating them for their lack of general knowledge, was not only tolerant of what they did not do or did not know but behaved in ways which actually encouraged her students to persist with the very attitudes to knowledge and learning that she criticised. Thus, most of her students could be found to be conforming – either to the norms to which Maria had become resigned or to the values embedded in the idealised curriculum which she had, effectively, accepted as unattainable given the conditions under which she worked. Among the minority of students who asserted the value of interactive learning activities were some whose adaptations to the predominantly passive activities of Maria's classes could be described as strategically compliant, retreatist or innovative. 'Switching off' during note taking, for example, allowed students to maintain an outward appearance of conformity, while their occasional attempts to promote, extend or divert discussions might be regarded as innovative.

Again, it is clear to see that the descriptive curricula of this course owed a great deal to the values and dispositions which tutor and students brought to bear upon their situation. They were not simply prescribed. Nor, it is apparent, are curricula free from contextual constraints. The fact that Maria was a part-time tutor hoping for full-time employment was not, perhaps, entirely unrelated to her anxieties about 'getting through' the syllabus. She confided in her interview that examination results, syllabus coverage, and the extent and accuracy of students' notes were three of the most visible aspects of her work upon which external scrutineers might base their judgements. She was, she agreed, extremely conscious of the need to maintain an outward appearance of competence under these particular criteria.

LIZ POPE'S GROUP

Maria's colleague, Liz, also taught a second year A-level history course using the same syllabus. There, however, the similarity would appear to end.

How do you expect the students will learn today?

A combination of lecture, reading, discussion – they interrupt – it's very organic. You can go off at a tangent and not be where you thought you were. I don't mind that, I just make sure I've covered the syllabus by the end of the year. You don't have a structure – sometimes it goes well, sometimes it goes like a lead balloon.

What sort of questions do you ask?

I don't very often ask for recall. I don't try and examine them. I elicit ideas and get them to develop their own arguments. They make really good points but they don't always develop their ideas.

Evidently, Liz's account of essential historical knowledge and skills placed far greater emphasis upon students' personal constructions of a subjective knowledge than, it seemed, did Maria's. Although this might not be an entirely accurate distinction to make between Liz's and Maria's views of knowledge, it certainly reflects important differences between the forms of knowledge which they sought to promote in their classrooms. While Maria was heavily preoccupied with constraints of time, Liz was seemingly unconcerned about that matter. As far as Liz was concerned, providing experience in the exploration of knowledge and in the construction of historical arguments and explanations were her primary aims in planning and teaching; the syllabus content was, most certainly, a secondary consideration. Indeed, Liz went so far as to claim that her approach was entirely consistent with provisions made within the syllabus and its examination.

> They're thrown very much in at the deep end and do a lot for themselves. It threatens them a lot. . . . The syllabus fosters not dependence but fosters research and reading. Independent judgement is marked generously even if it's not absolutely correct.

The observations of Liz's class meetings confirmed that what she claimed to be aiming to do was visible in practice. The observer's notes at the time recorded that

> The aim of the lesson was for them to solve a problem and form a view on whether the reign of Mary was doomed. The students were encouraged to interrupt, question and offer opinions on the subject matter.

Many of the students, it appeared, accorded value to Liz's stress on discussion and other exploratory activities.

121

Could you describe how you learned?

From ideas raised firstly by the class and Liz and from Liz purely prodding ideas from us.

Which part(s) of the session were most helpful to you?

Different people's points of view, as this often can help me or give me ideas to work on.

The class discussion was most helpful [as] it gives the opportunity to share/discuss different ideas and theories. Although some contributions aren't particularly useful because they lack proper thought/evidence.

Class discussion and formulating my own ideas. I feel that doing research and your own intellectual thinking about a topic stimulates interest and enthusiasm.

(Student evaluation schedules)

A majority of Liz's students responded to our questions in a manner which confirmed that they regarded themselves as 'knowledge makers'. While most acknowledged that the acquisition of information was necessary, they saw its purpose as providing a catalyst for the development of their personal understanding. These students exhibited a greater sense of personal responsibility for the formulation of insights and explanations and tended to regard this as their primary objective as history students. Most of Maria's students, on the other hand, viewed the acquisition of information as the primary objective and, in so far as they accorded value to interactive learning activities at all, did so more often for the purposes of confirming and exemplifying that information in some objective sense than for the purpose of rendering it problematic. While there were a number of students in Liz's group who claimed to have acquired a critical historical knowledge and also to have established important 'connections' between that and a more general knowledge, it would not be true to say that all of the group had achieved this, or even that they valued it. Some, in fact, were not in the least enthused about those activities geared to promoting critical or reflective thought.

Which parts of the session were most helpful to you?

The most valuable part of the session was the lecturer and the notes taken from the board. The photo-copied sheets provide information which can be used for future reference. The lecture provided detailed information on the topic.

And which parts of the session did you find least helpful?

The debates with conflicting ideas and stupid suggestions. Some ideas were based on people's opinions without reference to evidence.

Which learning activities do you prefer?

Direct lecturing and making notes. I like being told because I don't like reading and interpreting for myself. It's the most efficient way because you can sit in exams and blabber it all out – that's my psychology.

Which part(s) of the session were most helpful to you?

The reading and being lectured because I was able to take notes for future reference, for essays, etc.

(Student evaluation schedules)

As Liz herself put it,

Some long for a bit of dictation. They want to take home quite a lot of back-up study sheets and handouts.

It would be quite misleading to portray Liz's and Maria's class meetings as manifestly different, as simply the consequences of the teachers' distinctive concerns about knowledge and learning. Liz employed a similar range of learning activities to those of her colleague, albeit with a far greater amount of time given over to discussion and a noticeably greater encouragement of students' personal interests and constructions of knowledge. The important difference between the two was that most of Maria's work, even the discussions, was perceived by students as being primarily for the purpose of information acquisition, while in Liz's case the whole was perceived by many students as being for the purpose of promoting a personal critical awareness.

The predominant view among Liz's students emphasised the subjective origins of knowledge. Consistent with this was a generally shared understanding that learning entailed the generation of such knowledge through students' engagement with a variety of knowledge sources including primary evidence, a variety of interpretive claims and, not least, interpretations advanced by student peers. Except in a minority of cases, learning did not take the form of a search for a single unambiguous truth; rather, it was the progressive exploration of evidence and argument for the illumination of the contested nature of historical knowledge. But such views of knowledge and learning did not discount the importance of the acquisition of historical information. Rather, they provided the all-important context in which the relevance of information was to be understood. Students commonly accepted that reading and exposition, or 'lecturing and note taking' as they frequently described it, were important and helpful in their own learning of essential historical information. But such learning was important only in so far as it was a necessary precondition for their critical engagement with historical knowledge. It was not, in itself, the primary object of their studies, as appeared to be the case with many of Maria's students.

Liz's students were largely conformist: teacher and students held common expectations in respect of knowledge, learning and teacher–student relationships. There was little evidence of strategic compliance or retreatism except among those few students who declared a definite preference for receptive learning activities. Even here, though, the use of exposition and student reading for purposes of acquiring information, as discussed earlier, appeared to be sufficient to satisfy these students. While some such students' adaptations to their course might be described as strategically compliant, in so far as they did engage in group discussions, a small number could be described as retreatist in view of their noticeable lack of participation. However, nowhere among Liz's group could studentship be described as rebellious or even innovative.

Reflecting for a moment on Liz's and Maria's groups, it was apparent that in both courses the teacher and a majority of students held common expectations in respect of knowledge, learning and student–teacher relationships. Subscription to such common expectations provided stability and coherence to the courses concerned and perhaps explains the absence of overt dissent in either group. In both cases, however, there was a significant minority of students whose expectations were not consistent with those which predominated, although such students were, it appeared, able to gain satisfaction of their own needs by responding selectively to the variety of learning opportunities made available to them. Although such studentship was not explicitly provided for in their teachers' planning, it was accommodated without much difficulty, and possibly without notice, in practice. However, while it can be argued that the coherence and stability of both Liz's and Maria's courses were grounded in the predominantly shared expectations of teachers and students and in the extent to which divergent expectations could be accommodated in the manner described above, it is inescapable that the normative expectations were different in each case, despite the fact that both groups functioned under the ostensibly similar conditions of a common syllabus and departmental structure and culture.

BERNARD LEWIS'S GROUP

The third and final case that I shall consider here is that of a first year A-level history group taught by Bernard Lewis. On the face of it, Bernard's views of knowledge and learning coincided largely with those of Liz. Class meetings were to be used for two main purposes as far as Bernard was concerned. First, they were opportunities for him to present to his students an overview of the topic to be addressed, thus providing students with some form of framework within which they could locate historical knowledge. Second, they were to be used for class discussions, often focused on questions for which the students had had some opportunity to prepare. Bernard was very clear in his view that students' acquisition of basic historical information and their initial formulation of ideas was to be achieved on the basis of their own reading out of class time. Class discussions were for the purpose of the critical examination of those ideas.

However, Bernard's students were in their first year – only four months into the course – and it was apparent that up to that point they had not shown themselves to be very effective in formulating ideas and questions on the basis of what they had read.

What would you identify as the main purposes of this session?

They'll engage in discussion based on the questions they've been given. There is a rationale behind this as in the essay I gave them last week some were just giving me the class lectures back, not taking ownership, not processing enough, not comparing with other inputs – which are all very important for history students. If they just survive by the class lectures, which the weaker ones do, it makes them not very good at using books. If you let them do it again and again, they will not get any better. . . . If I lecture them, I'll be telling them the stuff they're supposed to find out.

What will the students learn?

Some idea about the civil war. I'm not sure; they may end up confused. More inclination to use books is a major aim for the weaker ones – hopefully to force them to use books. If they develop that by the second year, they'll be more productive, they will not just be depending on lectures. It's an important skill, not just for history students but for future jobs. They're thinking in terms of reading books while I'm thinking in terms of using books.

Using books?

Extracting information from books, not just reading them. Seven or eight books, flipping through them. Reading is a luxury.

Is there any chance to go beyond the syllabus?

I mention other events – for example, how the Russian Civil War parallels situations today, but they probably don't know what is going on in today's world. History lends itself to that sort of thing. So do lots of humanities subjects.

From Bernard's account, it is quite apparent what he perceived to be the main weaknesses of his students: their use of books, their formulation of questions and ideas and their lack of general knowledge. They lacked the capacity to make critical judgements in their work and Bernard's main concern was to create the conditions in which they could learn to take risks in exercising their own imagination on the subject matter. In the class meeting which followed, he set about that task.

Bernard frequently encouraged the students to expand their answers, to elaborate and provide evidence from the documents they had studied, to offer reasoned explanation. This was, essentially, a 103 minute brainstorming session. Original thought was encouraged if it was backed up by evidence. Bernard also diverged from the set questions to discuss and explain such things as the meaning of emotive language and how to ascertain whether a fact is reliable.

(From the observer's summary notes)

However, as the following extracts suggest, Bernard did not confine himself to simply allowing the students to volunteer their insights. He pressed them vigorously, so much so that the observer was moved to describe his style as 'interrogative' rather than 'facilitative'.

BERNARD   When you say that, do you mean it is true?
CLAIRE   I presume so.
BERNARD   Why presume so?
CLAIRE   Well, it's a solid fact.
BERNARD   This is the way rumours start.
CLAIRE   Well, all the rest is prose. It's the only bit of fact.
BERNARD   You've got to be careful. It does not necessarily mean it's true.

. . .

BERNARD   Does that justify him seizing power?
TIM   Not in my opinion, no.
BERNARD   Why? How do you interpret the word, 'justification'? (Pause.) Can anyone else explain?
TIM   It's a, sort of, moral justification.
BERNARD   Now you're saying that justification is not just reasons.
TIM   Morally and ethically right.
BERNARD   But morals aren't absolute.

The session continued in this vein for much of its 103 minutes' duration although there were moments when the students turned the tables on their interrogator.

MARK   The Bolsheviks were the only people with ideas.
BERNARD   Who said that?
MARK   Well, I got it from somewhere.
BERNARD   So you found evidence although not in these sources?
MARK   Yes, I read it somewhere. I think you wrote it.

Despite Bernard's intentions, and notably his reference to the 'weaker' students, only five of the thirteen were actively involved in the 'discussion'. Most of the remaining eight did not say a word throughout. It was not, therefore, too surprising that there was variety in the students' evaluations of

126

the session. Tim, one of the active respondents in the interrogation, was quite clear about the benefits of interrogation but was less enthusiastic about the procedural directives which followed.

Could you describe how you learned?

By looking at a set of sources and discussing as a class the answers to some questions set on the sources.

Which part(s) of the session were most helpful to you?

The entire lesson was a discussion session, the most helpful being the part where I was 'on the spot' having to argue my historical opinion. I was under pressure, having to think and research very quickly, forcing me to concentrate. (The pressure was not *too* great as I had backup from others.)

Which part(s) of the session were least helpful to you?

Parts in which we discussed 'how to do questions'. I have always found this very boring so I don't concentrate and don't learn.

(Student evaluation schedule – Tim)

Leo, too, voiced approval of interrogation, but with less conviction than Tim.

Could you describe how you learned?

Through the aid of extracts from certain relevant sources and the answering of questions based on these.

Which part(s) of the session were most helpful to you?

I suppose I found the answering of my *specific* question the most helpful. It helps your logic and use of argument to answer a question both orally and in writing.

Which part(s) of the session were least helpful to you?

All of it was relevant and helpful in learning.

(Student evaluation schedule – Leo)

For Claire, another active participant, the session provided useful insights into the method or logic of argument building. Notably, it was clear in her mind that the session was not simply about acquiring historical information.

Could you describe how you learned?

By simply going through a question in great depth. Discussing and formulating opinions through logical questions.

Which part(s) of the session were most helpful to you?

The whole session because it was focused on one thing! The session was not about learning new historical information, it was about method and argument.

Which part(s) of the session were least helpful to you?

The break! The lesson was generally very good today.

(Student evaluation schedule – Claire)

Vicky participated only occasionally in the discussion but was, nonetheless, able to claim that being exposed to others' insights was in itself beneficial to the development of her own thinking and understanding. She even went so far as to claim that using her notes actually served to restrict her opportunities for learning.

Could you describe how you learned?

By listening to the other students and referring to notes made previously.

Which part(s) of the session were most helpful to you?

Listening to other students. You get to argue points, etc., or listen to other people's thoughts.

Which part(s) of the session were least helpful to you?

Referring to the notes because they were just my opinions which I had already, so I didn't learn anything.

(Student evaluation schedule – Vicky)

A quite different interpretation of the experience was offered by Alice whose preoccupation throughout appears to have been that of 'truth seeking'. While offering some recognition of the problems of reliability and bias, Alice was nevertheless dismissive of the value of others' opinions. She simply wanted the truth!

Could you describe how you learned?

The lecturer explained both [i.e. opinion and the difference between strategy and tactics] in detail. I made notes so everything I look back on I understand it.

Which part(s) of the session were most helpful to you?

When going into detail about different ways in which sources can be interpreted and how to tell if they are biased. To find out about a certain event you use sources. You have to find reliability and evidence. Now I know how to disregard sources that are biased.

Which part(s) of the session were least helpful to you?

People saying their own opinions on people and events. Because it

128

confuses me on what really happened and what is true compared to what one person thinks.

(Student evaluation schedule – Alice)

Russell had a similar viewpoint when it came to the value of group discussion and stated quite plainly his preference for dictation.

Could you describe how you learned?

Prepared notes by individual students and contribution from the lecturer to group discussion.

Which part(s) of the session were most helpful to you?

The parts done by the lecturer himself. I prefer to be dictated notes rather than the scrappy system of student contributions which are often incomplete or irrelevant.

Which part(s) of the session were least helpful to you?

The parts done by the students themselves. The students' notes were often lacking in detail and irrelevant to the subject.

(Student evaluation schedule – Russell)

Finally, another non-participant, Laura, also appeared to have reservations about the value of students' contributions, stressing instead that it was the tutor's periodic summaries which provided the most helpful stimulus to learning.

Could you describe how you learned?

Various pupils told us what they had researched the night before and Bernard clarified what they had said.

Which part(s) of the session were most helpful to you?

The explanations and clarifications given by Bernard. He makes good basic explanations when there are complications.

Which part(s) of the session were least helpful to you?

The break and the discussion about residential codes of conduct because the residential has nothing to do with Russian history.

(Student evaluation schedule – Laura)

This very varied set of responses to a common learning experience was not at all unusual in A-level or, for that matter, vocational courses. It reveals, quite strikingly, the different sets of assumptions about knowledge and learning which students bring to bear upon their learning and how these become manifest in practice, in this case in the students' participation or non-participation in discussion. It was apparent from the accounts provided by Bernard's

129

students that, as Bernard himself had intimated in his account, they were not accustomed to constructing their own understanding on the basis of given information. What was also apparent, though, was that the students showed different degrees of willingness or ability to respond to the challenge which Bernard had set for them. Alice, Russell and Laura had reacted by non-participation throughout and had occupied themselves largely by seeking to extract unambiguous truths from the discussions which happened around them. Tim, Leo and Claire, on the other hand, had entered fully into discussion and claimed to have benefited from the experience of having to exercise judgement over the historical knowledge before them. From such insights one can see the contributions which students' dispositions to knowledge and learning made to their experiences of teaching and, in turn, to the impact of that teaching upon their descriptive curricula and their learning.

The studentship of Tim, Leo, Claire and other active participants in Bernard's discussion session was evidently conformist. Some students, it transpired, had had successful previous experience of formulating and arguing their own ideas and, for them, adaptation to Bernard's expectations did not require any significant revision of previously held views of knowledge and learning. Others, whose behaviour and accounts served to confirm their conformity had had far less prior experience of this type but were nonetheless prepared to respond positively and in full to their teacher's expectations. It was what they had hoped for from their sixth form studies and represented the fulfilment of pre-course aspirations expressed at that time in terms such as 'assuming greater responsibility for my own learning' and 'contributing my own views'. Their learning careers had started to assume a new direction at this point although it was a 'turning point' that the students had planned for. The non-participating students such as Alice, Russell and Laura, however, were not able to adapt as others had. Some, given time, might well have made the kind of adaptation which Bernard sought, once they had developed sufficient confidence in their abilities to make successful contributions and had come to recognise some educational value in doing so. One such student might have been Kate who, in her account of the differences between her pre- and post-16 education suggested that she might have preferred to have had greater influence over her own learning but had not the confidence to take the risks entailed.

> School doesn't prepare you for essay writing and note taking – what you need to get points out of a lesson. Here, you're left to manage this yourself. At GCSE, they spoonfeed you – they're always on your back. Here, it's your own responsibility.

Manage this yourself?

> You haven't always got the tutor there. At GCSE, they tell you the page number and what to do.

Which do you prefer?

For the past nine years at school, I've been told what to do so I like that but that's what I've had to do. If I'd been given a freer hand, I probably would have preferred that.

What learning activities do you prefer?

Dictation, because then you can get all the relevant points.

(Student interview – Kate)

Others, and Russell in particular, were not prepared to take risks at any cost; their dispositions to knowledge and learning were set, it seemed, and that was that. The studentship of these non-participants was, for the most part, strategically compliant and they gave no outward expression to their discontent. But they were also innovative, as was Alice, in selecting from the discussion those learning opportunities which they had decided were helpful to them and disregarding the remainder. A most common innovatory response entailed the selection of Bernard's contributions and the rejection of much of what fellow students had offered simply because Bernard's accounts were seen by such students to meet their requirements for unambiguous and 'correct' knowledge.

It is not, of course, possible to make any confident predictions about the futures of Tim, Alice, Russell and their colleagues. Instead, what can be gleaned from this account is some sense of the conditions in which students' learning careers take shape and assume direction and re-direction. However, we did manage to carry out an extended interview with one of Bernard's students after he had completed his course and were able to ask him how things had unfolded for him. Matt had not, in fact, been present at the observed sessions reported above but recalled quite vividly his own experiences of similar situations.

It was a straight lecture and then write certain things on the board. And it was only every now and then he'd decide to have a seminar and he'd type out a little seminar briefing sheet for everyone and everyone had to go off and read the books and come back and have a set discussion. It was very, very disciplined – tight, sort of learning scheme.

Matt's is a retrospective account and, of course, simple comparisons cannot be made between his recollections and the accounts provided by his peers during the first few months of their course. Matt, whose story I have reported in greater detail elsewhere (Avis *et al.*, 1996: 148–152), confirmed that during his early experiences of A-level history he had not viewed the sessions with Bernard as being as 'disciplined' as he had done upon reflection. However, he had certainly been innovative in his adaptation to the learning opportunities Bernard presented, so innovative that in the second year of his course he ceased to attend the history classes except on those occa-

sions which *he* deemed necessary. While others exercised selection over
learning opportunities within class meetings, Matt did so between meetings.
He claimed in his interview that, unlike many of his peers, he entered the
course already having acquired the knowledge and skills necessary for the
critical examination of information.

> But I mean it's something which I've never really found that tricky to
> do – get what I want out of a text. . . . Of course, doing a lot of
> reading also enabled me, like I say, not to have to go to the lectures
> every week, or whatever. I could just learn about that area by reading
> books about it. So I just saw it as a way of self-motivated learning. I
> could just be my own boss with a book.

The reasons for Matt's innovative adaptation can be located in his perceptions of his teacher's and his peers' behaviour. What loomed large in Matt's
retrospective account was what he described as the 'straight lecture', something which some of his peers had perceived to be the most helpful of all
learning opportunities. Matt came to resent 'lecturing' on the grounds that
it provided information and insights which he could perfectly adequately
glean through his own reading and reflection – activities which, in fact, he
enjoyed. He also grew contemptuous of his fellow students whom he
perceived to be 'truth seekers' not prepared to exercise their own creative
thoughts on historical knowledge.

> It was quite strange. . . . I mean, they used to sit there and just write
> pages and pages of notes. And I just couldn't understand why so many
> people in my group were meticulously writing down these pages of
> notes and, you'd have folders just full of them, and you just didn't
> need to know it, really.

But he also grew resentful of what I have already referred to as Bernard's
'interrogative' style which, it transpired, was used not only to prompt
students to reflect on historical knowledge but also, more explicitly, to
communicate disapproval on a range of other issues. Matt regarded it as
hectoring and his paramount experience was one of humiliation. On the
subject of his post-16 education, he asserted,

> You, like, hear all these myths about it and about how wonderful it is
> and it's loads better than school and you get there and you think that for
> about a term, because they don't really start giving you any work, and
> after that time you realise, 'well, hang on it's exactly the same, really.
> No different!' I'm having teachers humiliating me and shouting at me
> if I'm five minutes late for lectures. I mean, there's not really an awful
> lot of difference except in certain situations when a lecturer, sort of,
> 'strikes off' or whatever and you do have a more adult relationship with
> some of your lecturers. But, then, sometimes they do always draw that,

kind of, 'I am a lecturer and you are a student' sort of one. I just began to realise that it was the same really, just in a thinly disguised form.

Matt's resentment grew as his absences began to attract further 'interrogation' from Bernard.

I just don't think he could handle what I was doing – that I was being able to . . . like I was still gaining knowledge from my own reading and still, sort of, getting good grades in my essays or whatever but not coming to every lecture, not being the model student, just spending my spare time in the library or at a computer terminal or something like that. He just didn't seem to like it that I could do it, 'cos it was something that he hadn't been able to.

Relationships between Matt and Bernard broke down and, at one point, Bernard tried to have Matt excluded from the course. Bernard's actions only exacerbated Matt's resentment, the outcome being that Matt attended in his second year only on those occasions when Bernard was to offer an overview of a new topic or to provide details of assignment requirements.

Matt's learning career, very briefly described here, is not unusual among post-16 students as they discover new self-knowledge. Many such students become alienated from their courses and, through that process, from those things which had initially compelled their interest. They may fail or drop out. But Matt's interest in history had not been damaged in this process and he was, he claimed, able to maintain his commitment to the course through private, independent study. He swore he would succeed.

But Matt's independent studies did not prompt him to regress to any simple information-seeking model of learning. He continued to exercise his critical awareness, not only in his study of history but in all three of his A-level subjects.

But, sort of, subjective reality's to do with the creation of the past and the present and I used a hell of a lot of my ideas about that and I picked up a lot more ideas on that front and put it into the extended essay in English. This was in English but there was a lot of connections in my head between what I'd picked up in communications and history and what I was doing in English with this essay and, I mean, that was one of the things where I was stretching my mind quite a lot doing that. And I felt that was the only time I really put all the skills from all my different subjects into this one thing. 'Cos it was also thinking about totalitarianism which we'd been looking at in history as well. So it drew everything that was going on in my head and put them through a literary practical criticism sense, and all together in this essay. It's one of the things I'm most pleased with, really, that I did during my college career. I think the subjects did interact with each other.

Matt had achieved some confident deeper insights into the nature of knowledge and, unlike most of the other students interviewed in the study, had been able to transcend subject knowledge boundaries. He had achieved this outside his formally prescribed courses and despite the fact that two of his A-level tutors repeatedly advised him not to incorporate knowledge from 'other subjects'.

Matt's studentship was evidently one of innovation and rebellion and yet, throughout his GCSE studies and upon entry to his A-level course, he had given every indication of being a conforming student. His new-found values and dispositions to knowledge and learning, it would appear, were attributable to his post-16 years although they were clearly not the intended outcomes of his prescribed curriculum; nor were they the fulfilment of his tutor's personal curriculum aims. They had originated in the wider context of his growing social, moral, philosophical and political awareness, in his 'becoming a person' (see discussion in Avis *et al.*, 1996), but were clearly of profound importance in shaping his described curriculum.

The reason for discussing Matt in such detail here is to illuminate some of the social conditions of what I have come to call, 'studentship', a concept which I shall elaborate in the next chapter. It is also to demonstrate that, in one case at least, rebellious and innovatory studentship was not a rejection of the value of knowledge or of learning. Matt was driven by a realisation that knowledge is more than information, that knowledge categories are in part arbitrarily determined and are restrictive, that learning can be rewarding providing it allows for both a personal construction of knowledge and the exercise of personal judgement over how to learn, and by a personal conviction that teacherly authority rests not just upon subject knowledge or hierarchically ascribed status but upon shared values and a mutually satisfactory person–person relationship. Ironically, it is these very observations which have been widely advanced as the necessary conditions for the autonomous lifelong learner and flexible knowledge worker upon which the economic and social stability of the twenty-first century depends.

SUMMARY

From the A-level history groups reported here, it is again apparent that a diverse range of practices operates under a single heading. Indeed, the variety of students' and teachers' views of knowledge, learning and teaching reported here is comparable with that found to exist in the vocational and chemistry courses described in the previous two chapters. Arguably, the variation in values, expectations and practices existing *under* each of those course headings is greater than that which exists *between* them. Indeed, the results of analysis of quantitative data obtained from student questionnaires supports this claim: greater variation was found to exist within than between course types in respect of students' reports of predominant course learning activities.

Comparative analysis of the qualitative data served to support a number of the claims reported already in connection with the chemistry and vocational courses and I will note some of these very briefly here.

First, there was considerable variety among students in their expectations of course knowledge and learning. Some were evidently inclined to search only for objectively verifiable knowledge while others looked more closely to their own resources for the generation and critical inspection of course knowledge. Their dispositions to learning were equally varied: some valuing only receptive activities and others interactive activities. It was quite noticeable, though, that over the duration of their courses, some students' dispositions to knowledge and learning had undergone significant transformation while others' had not. Some, it seemed, had been more readily influenced by the expectations brought to bear upon them within their A-level courses than had their colleagues, while the changes which had affected others appeared to be attributable more to their general personal growth and development and their lives outside their formal education. Matt, for instance, was one of a number of students who had experienced massive transformations in their dispositions to knowledge and learning but not as a result of the planned outcomes of his prescribed curriculum.

Second, the curriculum values claimed by the three history teachers reported here overlapped with one another to a greater degree than those of the teachers in either of the groups reported in earlier chapters. However, they revealed themselves quite differently in practice. While Liz's described and idealised curricula appeared congruent, Maria's and Bernard's were clearly not. Indeed, the emergent descriptive curricula of these three groups varied considerably while the factors which could explain the variation are numerous and include: teachers' dispositions to course knowledge and learning; students' dispositions to the same; the institutional and wider contexts in which the courses were located; the extent to which tutors and students were prepared to suspend their own convictions in the interest of their greater good (and a very great number of factors may be held to contribute to this); teacher–student relationships; and many more.

Third, these cases, alongside those reported in earlier chapters, reveal something of the complexities of teaching, studentship and curriculum making. Despite the fact that many of the examples considered here were examples of successful teaching and learning, none could be described simply as the same. They were each unique. The same observation might be made about the less successful examples. Above all, it is apparent that the working relationships described here were *achieved* by teachers and students on the basis of what each brought to bear upon the situation; they were not simply *prescribed*. In short, the power of prescription has been found to be lacking, particularly in its effects upon students' learning and their descriptive curricula. The significance of teacher and student agency has been highlighted.

Finally, the observations made here, especially in respect of the significance of student agency in learning, have important implications for educational planning into the twenty-first century. National economic and social futures have been frequently reported as resting upon the capacity of young people to exercise their judgement autonomously and confidently, to construct their own solutions to as yet unanticipated problems, and to be able to work flexibly and collaboratively. The last three chapters have offered a degree of insight into the problem of adapting to those future requirements. They have also provided some indications, however, that many young people are already remarkably skilled in some of these capacities and that what they need is a curriculum that will allow them to exercise and develop those strengths. The prospect of such a curriculum is the subject of the final three chapters of this book.

POSTSCRIPT

It is probably not surprising, given the insights recorded here, that Matt achieved a grade 'A' in the final examinations for each of his three A-level subjects. It may not come as a surprise, either, that he elected to tour the world for a year rather than to proceed directly to higher education. That year rolled into two, after which he returned home. Last week, having decided not to seek entry to Oxbridge, he was making a final decision between two university courses in media studies. This week, he is pursuing government funding for a media enterprise he proposes to set up with two friends.

7

STUDENTSHIP AND LEARNING CAREERS

ON THE SUBJECT OF STUDENTSHIP

The qualitative data accumulated through the Leverhulme Study reveal, quite strikingly, the important part played by teachers in curriculum making. Teachers are not merely points in some conduit linking centralised *pre*scriptions to learners' desks. They are not technicians, faithfully acting out the detail of prescribed blueprints. Rather, they 'act upon' prescriptions in order to create learning opportunities. They exercise judgement and discretion in the light of *their* interpretations of the broad aims of prescriptions, in accordance with what *they* perceive to be the needs of the students in their charge and within the confines of what *they* understand to be significant constraints. How teachers act, as has been amply demonstrated in the last three chapters, is very much affected by the views of knowledge and learning which they bring to their work.

Just as teachers exercise agency in their creation of learning opportunities, so students act upon those learning opportunities in the creation of their *de*scriptive curricula and their learning. It is this expression of human agency, 'acting upon', which I have termed 'studentship'. As revealed in earlier chapters, there are many different ways in which studentship is exercised. Within all of the groups observed and interviewed, there was evidence of diversity of studentship: students accepted, selected from, made modifications to, rejected or supplanted those learning opportunities which their teachers made available to them. But their selectivity was not confined to learning tasks; it was equally visible in the ways in which they adapted to course knowledge and to expectations in respect of both student–teacher relationships and student–student relationships. Within all of the groups considered here, students were variously observed filtering knowledge, modifying learning activities and withdrawing from, or investing of themselves in, activities according to the values embedded in their expectations, aspirations and dispositions to knowledge and learning.

Other writers have endorsed the claim that learning is pre-eminently to do with student agency and have been moved so far as to argue that it is

137

fallacious to view it as an outcome of teaching or curriculum prescription at all. 'Learning is an upshot of studenting, not an effect that follows from teaching as a cause' (Fenstermacher, 1986: 39). However, it is not my concern here to debate the relative impact of teaching, curriculum prescription and studenting, or as I prefer, studentship, upon learning. Structure–agency dualisms, in any event, have been widely condemned as inadequate representations of the forces bearing upon human action and behaviour, despite their frequent usage within popular discourse. Many competing alternative conceptualisations of the relationship between structure and agency have been articulated (Bandura, 1977; Giddens, 1984; Archer, 1988; Jones, 1988; Lave and Wenger, 1991; Haugaard, 1992), all of which are acutely sensitive to the complexities of the matter and some of which will be visited in the following chapter. The 'traditional' dualism is a time-honoured distraction from the pursuit of more critical and relevant questions, the likes of which I intend to concern myself with here. These are questions about the *origins and nature* of agency (in the form of studentship) and of structural opportunities (in the form of teaching and curriculum prescriptions) and, crucially, about the *ways* in which these impact upon students' experiences of learning.

The young people who participated in the Leverhulme Study displayed many different forms of studentship which, it was soon apparent, were neither randomly determined or entirely predictable. The research revealed rationality behind actions and a patterning among the ways in which individual learners 'acted upon' learning opportunities as they perceived them. This patterning was explicable by reference to students' dispositions to knowledge and learning – dispositions which, for the most part, remained stable but which also changed perceptibly or imperceptibly from time to time and from one situation to the next. Changes in dispositions, and hence studentship, were profoundly influenced by both in-course and out-of-course experiences. In-course experiences of learning frequently prompted students to reappraise themselves as learners (and exceptionally as persons) and to revise the values they ascribed to particular forms of knowledge or types of learning activity. There are many cases of students who came to revise their views of knowledge and learning in a manner consistent with the expectations of their tutors and peers; they had become socialised by routine into new schematic perceptions and their studentship had transformed accordingly. But equally apparent were students who had revised their views in a manner which placed them in conflict with the dominant expectations of their tutors and groups. For them, identity and routine had become contradictory with a consequent transformation in studentship. As I have reported elsewhere,

> Overall, it was a significant proportion of students who claimed that
> their own values, beliefs and expectations on matters concerning what

to learn, how to learn and why to learn contradicted those which they met in their post-16 courses. Students' responses to such situations took the form of *strategic compliance* (highly visible in many students), *retreatism* (absenteeism or non-completion), *rebellion* (in the form of petty disruption, albeit in a very few cases) or *innovation* (where students devised some novel means of enabling them to achieve what they wanted from their courses). Added to the *conformism* of those students whose values and beliefs were confirmed by their course experiences or who had become socialised into accepting and sharing course expectations, this categorisation of the ways in which students 'acted upon' their courses – that is, their studentship – is not dissimilar to Merton's (1968) typology of modes of individual adaptation (conformity, innovation, ritualism, retreatism and rebellion).

(Avis et al., 1996: 141–142)

From interviews with students, many different factors appeared to have a bearing upon studentship. Pre-course aspirations and in-course experiences were frequently mentioned by students in their various accounts of confirmatory and contradictory transitions into new routines. But such insights into existing dispositions and in-course socialisation held only limited explanatory power: other, out-of-course, experiences were important. Matt was not alone in pointing to other socialising influences in his account of his studentship. He had, as he put it, 'become a different person' during the time he completed his A-level studies and it was plain that his 'new person' was not simply the product of his *pre*scribed curriculum. For Matt and many others the most powerful influences lay outside their post-16 courses. The personal growth and development of these students was rooted largely in a world outside school and college, a world which afforded new friendships, new social activities, new knowledge and new questions. It fostered new opportunities for self-appraisal, new criteria for such appraisals and new stimuli to political, philosophical, moral, social, economic and sexual awareness. Indeed, the 'other world' proved to provide many rich and challenging experiences from which students truly learned and which gave shape to, and was shaped by, their emergent personal identities. The processes by which that other world impacted upon students' dispositions to knowledge and learning and, in turn, upon studentship, warrant more than fleeting consideration here.

DISPOSITIONS, HABITUS AND IDENTITIES

Bourdieu (1977a) uses the concept, 'habitus', to describe 'that system of dispositions' (1977a: 487) which is framed within social and cultural experience but which also enables the individual to give meaning to those experiences. He describes habitus as, 'the site of the internalization of exter-

139

nality and the externalization of internality' (Bourdieu and Passeron, 1990: 205). For Bourdieu, dispositions extend beyond mere attitudes; the concept of disposition is taken to mean, ' "the result of an organising action"; . . . a "way of being" or an "habitual state"; and "tendency", "propensity" or "inclination" ' (Bourdieu, 1977b, cited in Jenkins, 1992: 76).

> Habitus includes transportable dispositions such as way of thinking, values, and patterns of interpretation. One's habitus operates at two levels: it determines what and how one perceives, and also what expressions and actions one generates and in what manner. . . . Habitus is not an individual phenomenon but is mainly 'a family, group and especially class phenomenon, a logic derived from a common set of material conditions of existence' (Garnham and Williams, 1980).
>
> (Okano, 1993: 27)

Habitus arises from a dialectic between subjective and objective, in which dispositions both shape and are shaped by experience of external social and cultural conditions. It is,

> acquired by implicit or explicit learning [and] functions as a system of generative schemes; [it] generates strategies which can be objectively consistent with the objective interests of their authors without having been expressly designed to that end. . . . To put it briefly, the *habitus* is a product of conditionings which tends to reproduce the objective logic of those conditionings while transforming it. It's a kind of transforming machine that leads us to 'reproduce' the social conditions of our own production, but in a relatively unpredictable way, in such a way that one cannot move simply or mechanically from knowledge of the conditions of production to knowledge of the products.
>
> (Bourdieu, 1993: 76 and 87)

All of the learning and other social experiences described in this book, whether they originated from within or without institutionalised education and whether they were consciously or unconsciously experienced, contributed to habitus and to the shaping of students' predispositions and dispositions to learning. Those dispositions, in turn, set limits to the meanings which students attributed to their new experiences. But dispositions to learning and knowledge cannot be separated from other dispositions which comprise habitus; dispositions to political, philosophical and moral considerations were found to be inextricably bound up with dispositions to learning, as illustrated in Matt's case.

For Bourdieu, the experiences which contribute to habitus are heavily circumscribed by class-derived cultural values and his work has been criticised both for the ambiguity of its account and for its overly deterministic view of human growth and development (Brown, 1987; Jenkins, 1992). However, these criticisms are to be balanced against Bourdieu's own claims that habitus mediates between structures and practice, where the notion of mediation can be taken to indicate a reflexive relationship between the two. Other critics (Hodkinson, 1995; Okano, 1995) have emphasised such an interpretation of Bourdieu's work, accounting for changing habitus on the basis of dialectical relationships between structure and practice, culture and personal identity.

At this point, I should like to confirm those aspects of Bourdieu's work which I consider to be most relevant and helpful to the present study. The concept of habitus, as I use it here, may not accord entirely with Bourdieu's account but it has proved adequate for the description and analysis of young people's learning over time. Habitus allows for the dialectical interplay of the objective and subjective while providing some opportunity to account for both continuities and transformations in dispositions to studentship and to knowledge and learning. As such, it has a 'goodness of fit' with students' experiences of learning as revealed in this study. The repeated claim, throughout this book, that prescriptive action (in this case, in the form of prescribed curricula) has only limited impact upon human behaviour or action (in this case, learning) is also, it seems, provided for in Bourdieu's thesis:

> [Habitus] ensures the active presence of past experiences, which, deposited in each organism in the form of schemes of perception, thought and action, tend to guarantee the 'correctness' of practices and their constancy over time, more reliably than all formal rules and explicit norms.
>
> (Bourdieu, quoted in Harker, 1992: 16)

But this is no simple assertion of the power of agency over structure since the 'deposits' which Bourdieu speaks of are, themselves, structurally prescribed:

> the *habitus* makes possible the free production of all the thoughts, perceptions and actions inherent in the particular conditions of its production – and only those.
>
> (Bourdieu, quoted in Harker, 1992: 16)

Bourdieu's method has been described as an attempt,

> to steer a course between (on the one hand) the subjectivism of phenomenological accounts in which social actions and subjective meanings have primacy, and (on the other hand) structuralist accounts which look for environmental determinants or social patterns of human behaviour in order to give objective expression to causes or regularities.
>
> (James, 1995: 457)

But the extent to which Bourdieu is seen to have maintained such a course has been the source of much critical comment. As I have already mentioned, he has been widely criticised for having placed too great a stress upon external objective conditions in his account of habitus, providing an overly deterministic view. Other critics, however, have sought to stress that there is no crude determinism to be associated with habitus; while it sets boundaries to actions, its effect is that of orienting not determining (Harker and May, 1993: 174).

There is already an expanding library of critique of Bourdieu's work (see, for instance, Swartz, 1977; Giroux, 1982, 1983; Elster, 1983; Harker, Mahar and Wilkes, 1990; Robbins, 1991; Jenkins, 1992; Calhoun, LiPuma and Postone, 1993) and I have neither the need nor the facility to contribute to its expansion here. My reflections on habitus and other concepts here are purely pragmatic: are they adequate for the purposes of describing and analysing the experiences reported by young people in this study?

I have already noted a number of respects in which habitus is adequate for the purpose. The concepts of disposition, studentship, perception, action and interaction are, in my judgement, similarly adequate. However, Bourdieu's habitus, despite its analytical power and relevance here, seeks to locate learning – and all social action – within social and institutional structures. While due emphasis is placed by Bourdieu upon subjective experience, it is a view of subjectivity as prescribed ultimately by objective probability. Objective conditions are the cornerstones of his theory. Thus, while there may be 'goodness of fit' between Bourdieu's habitus and the experiences of the young people who participated in this study, there is not 'exactness of fit'. Or, at least, the study does not provide the facility for testing for 'exactness'. It would, therefore, be erroneous to import the full weight of Bourdieu's thesis into this work and more appropriate, in my judgement, to proceed strictly within the scope afforded by the data. Thus, I shall discount what I regard as Bourdieu's fundamental emphasis upon structure but retain a notion of habitus which rests upon a dialectical interdependence of subjective experience and objective structure. This is, in fact, far more in keeping with the traditions of phenomenology and social action theory.

The work of Phil Hodkinson from which I have drawn here utilises elements of schema theory and situated cognition theory to provide particularly helpful insights into the development of habitus (Hodkinson, 1995; Hodkinson and Sparkes, 1995). As Hodkinson puts it,

> a repertoire of schemata contributes to the dispositions that make up habitus. As new experiences are gained, schemata are modified and developed and as they change so does what is recognised in the surrounding world . . . the life history of the individual shapes and is shaped by his/her common sense experience.
>
> (Hodkinson, 1995: 92)

Thus, learning, in the form of changed dispositions, arises out of a dialectical interplay between schemata and action and between both of these and the cultural and social contexts within which they are located. This gives rise to new social and cultural experiences and to changes in 'sense' – in dispositions and habitus. This much is also captured by Eisner:

> whatever it is we think we know is a function of *transaction* between the qualities of the world we cannot know in their pure, non-mediated form, and the frames of reference, personal skills, and individual histories we bring to them. . . . It is in the transaction between objective conditions and personal frames of reference that we *make* sense. The sense we make is what constitutes experience.
>
> (Eisner, 1993: 53)

More commonly, changes in dispositions are gradual and indiscernible although, on occasions, they can be swift and dramatic.

> though difficult to change fundamentally (Chinn and Brewer, 1993), the schemata which are part of habitus develop and modify incrementally as new information is absorbed and new experiences or situations encountered. Haugaard (1992) suggests that when schemata are challenged by accumulated or powerful anomalous experiences they may transform and transfers of knowledge between practical and discursive consciousness are likely. Thus, a person's habitus can occasionally change radically.
>
> (Hodkinson, 1995: 93)

Hodkinson and Sparkes (1993, 1995) introduce the concept, *horizons for action* – not dissimilar to Eisner's 'frames of reference', it seems – in order to illuminate the conditions under which habitus and dispositions might or might not change and under which actions may or may not be taken. An horizon for action distinguishes that which lies within existing habitus from that which does not, the perceptible from the imperceptible. But horizons are also restricted by external opportunity structures. It is the combination of habitus and external opportunity structures which delineates the scope for action since it is perceptions of their appropriacy and availability, respectively, which affect opportunities for decisions. Thus, to re-work Hodkinson's own discussion (1995: 93–94), the fact that a teacher might go to excessive lengths to make interactive learning opportunities[1] available is irrelevant if the students concerned cannot perceive them as appropriate or do not perceive it appropriate to explore the possibilities they might hold. A number of students in the Leverhulme Study fell into this category, sometimes because their existing habitus sustained for them some hardened, semi-immutable disposition to knowledge or learning, and often because of their inability to perceive interactive learning opportunities as likely to produce the kinds of knowledge which they considered they would need in order to meet the requirements of examinations or employment. The cases of Alice, Russell and Laura, reported in Chapter 6, illustrate this point. Engagement with interactive learning activities did not 'fit with their existing schematic views of themselves or their perceptions of appropriate opportunities' (Hodkinson, 1995: 94). On the other hand, many students did make gradual adjustments to new expectations. Some did so because, on the basis of prior experiences, they perceived interactive learning opportunities as likely to produce the kinds of knowledge or other experience which they adjudged would be of benefit to them. Others did so because, again on the basis of their prior experiences, they were disposed to suspend such concerns as they might have held and to explore the opportunities before them in the belief that to take such a risk *might* ultimately be for their greater educational benefit. The experiences of these students serve to underline the point that horizons for action are to be seen as *both* enabling and restricting. Moving to the case of Matt, again, it is possible to see how both his evolving habitus and the external opportunity structures *as he perceived them* provided the impetus for his particular studentship.

The point that it is students' *perceptions* of opportunity structures which contribute to horizons for action as well as the objective presence of those structures is illustrated in the case of Henry Stapleton's A-level chemistry group considered in Chapter 5. While Henry considered himself to be the 'brain stirrer' – a catalyst to make his students think for themselves – the students experienced the learning opportunities he created for them in an entirely different light. To them, Henry was 'completely off his rocker'. Whether the students' horizons for action were attributable to their habitus, to their inability to perceive the opportunities presented to them as appropriate, or to the inadequacies of their teacher is totally immaterial. The outcome was that, working within existing habitus and the opportunity structures they *perceived* as being available to them, they embarked upon a remedial education of their own design: a search for 'correct' information from external authoritative sources and grounded in the very principles which Henry claimed to be trying to shift them away from. Their studentship had taken shape *in spite of* the opportunity structures which their teacher and course planners had sought to construct for them and in accordance with opportunity structures *as they perceived them* on the basis of their existing habitus. But this phenomenon is far more widespread than the single case of Henry Stapleton's chemistry group. As the earlier chapters have shown, in all groups, students perceived opportunity structures differently from one another. Indeed, throughout this entire study, evidence of *pre*scribed structures determining student action has been somewhat thin, despite the fact that assumptions of some such causal relationship underpin virtually all contemporary educational planning.

Horizons for action is a helpful conceptual device for accounting for the development of studentship in post-16 education. As reported earlier, students made a variety of adaptive responses as they encountered new routines. They 'acted upon' the opportunities as they perceived them in accordance with existing habitus, either confirming existing dispositions to learning and knowledge or embarking upon gradual or, occasionally, radical changes in dispositions and, consequently, learning careers. Their various conforming, critical or creative responses to the learning opportunities made available to them – their studentship – arose from within the boundaries of, and were facilitated by, their horizons for action and are to be understood in terms of the dialectical interplay between systems of dispositions within existing habitus and perceptions of the opportunity structures available. The development of new habitus, new dispositions to learning and knowledge, new perceptions of opportunities and new actions (studentship) was symbiotic.

For students whose habitus became transformed and who acquired new dispositions, there followed a gradual or occasionally dramatic change in studentship. Some, albeit a few, abandoned their studies, unable to reconcile perceived conflicts between course expectations and their new-found habitus. Most were moved to strategic compliance, retreatism, innovation and even rebellion. Some appeared able to manage conflicting demands by maintaining what, on the face of it, seemed to be two distinct identities: one as 'student' and one as 'person'. One such case was Natalie who, by the mid-point of her A-level physics course, had decided that she did not want to continue to study physics beyond A-level. During her mid-teens, Natalie had become progressively more preoccupied with ecological and moral problems such as those concerning pollution, global warming, civil wars, third world famine and animal rights. These interests of Natalie's had not been promoted by her A-level physics course but could be traced to events which took place in her GCSE English classes and to insights afforded by peers and the media. In fact, in her experience, her A-level physics course firmly excluded opportunities for any examination of the problems in which she had become deeply interested: the moral dimension had been 'separated out' of her science. Natalie's identity as 'person' was starkly revealed in her interview as having a significant and powerful moral component. Her identity as 'student', as scientist, in contrast, had no such component. Her view of knowledge, as 'person', was one which seemed to stress the essential unity of all knowledge, while her view as 'student', was strongly affected by a logical fragmentation of knowledge into subjects. Her dispositions to learning, as 'person', were to be understood very much in terms of her personal satisfactions and her intrinsic needs to command her own understanding of the world in the terms in which it was important to her; her dispositions as 'student', on the other hand, were largely instrumental, having no discernible connection with Natalie as 'person'. Both of Natalie's identities can be accounted for in terms of shifting horizons for action: they arose out of her evolving habitus and were circumscribed by her perceptions of the new structural opportunities available to her. In Natalie's case, it is not

145

possible to say whether her management of conflicting expectations through the maintenance of two distinct identities should be described as an act of conformity, strategic compliance or even retreatism, since we did not get to know her well enough at the time of the interview to be able to make such a judgement. It is even possible that the situation we witnessed was an early phase in the transformation of her studentship into innovation or rebellion. Indeed, stories such as Natalie's concerning the maintenance of two identities were not uncommon among students' retrospective accounts of their evolving dispositions to knowledge and learning and of transformations in their studentship. However, deeper insight into change processes can only really be afforded by longitudinal research in which the evolution of habitus, dispositions and studentship can be monitored more closely and more fully.[2]

A considerable number of the young people who participated in the Leverhulme Study reported that their studentship was somehow altered as the result of changes in their habitus. Although I might, perhaps, be more cautious in attributing causality here, it was certainly the case that many made reference to their 'extra-curricular' development when seeking to account for changes in studentship. However, it would be quite wrong to assume that the students themselves had the means of distinguishing clearly between the various factors contributing to their own development, even supposing that they were ever conscious of all the influences to which they had been subjected. An alternative (but complementary) proposition is that habitus and studentship were, for most students, mutually reinforcing. While some, as I have already mentioned, appeared able to maintain separate identities as 'student' and 'person' for a period without apparent difficulty, most displayed either a consistency between personal identity and studentship or were engaged in some kind of struggle to achieve such a consistency. Of those young people striving for consistency, many disclosed some degree of uncertainty about themselves both as learners and as persons, their identities being subjected to the sometimes conflictual values and expectations of their post-16 studies and their 'extra-curricular' worlds. The instability of identity revealed by students in this latter group is a strong reminder that, no matter how fully or carefully the post-16 curriculum might be prescribed and articulated in terms of content and process, the development of identities and, hence, studentship is left very much to chance. Despite their profound influence upon learning, personal identities and studentship have been largely ignored in processes of technical rational prescription of mainstream post-16 education. Where there has been recognition of their importance at all, it has been through the provision of counselling, tutoring and study skills support services based on a 'casualty' or 'deficit' model. But then, technical rationalism is hardly suited to providing an effective response to needs which emanate as much from situations beyond its purview as from those within, or to problems whose inherent complexity has to be recognised before they can be understood.

DISPOSITIONS TO KNOWLEDGE AND LEARNING

The qualitative data from the Leverhulme research reveal a strong relationship between students' views of knowledge and their preferences for particular learning activities. Students who were most prone to describing course knowledge in terms of its fact-like or objective qualities – as information – were also most likely to state strong preferences for receptive learning activities and to reveal themselves to be among the less critical and more dependent learners. These students were likely to discount the relevance of a general knowledge to their subject studies and the value of non-utilitarian knowledge in general. They were also more inclined to speak of knowledge as commodified and tightly compartmentalised within subject and syllabus boundaries. Others, who stressed the importance of conceptual, declarative or logical knowledge and, particularly, the subjective and problematic qualities of knowledge, were more apt to acclaim the merits of interactive learning activities. A number of these students, albeit only a few, were seemingly prepared to transcend knowledge boundaries and to utilise their (externally grounded) general knowledge in their critical appraisal of course knowledge.

Although it is true that some clearly subscribed to one of these sets of views while rejecting the alternative, others claimed not only that both were valid but that they were positively disposed to both. Often, it seemed, these included the more successful students. Some of the A-level history students considered in the last chapter are a case in point. They distinguished between historical information, to be acquired through private reading and note taking and historical theorising, to be developed through private thought and tested or refined through whole-group questioning and discussion; and they acclaimed the importance of both. It was, of course, noted that some of these students nonetheless appeared to participate more fully in some types of activity than in others. I should also note here that there were other students who tended to stress the fact-like qualities of knowledge but who also stated a preference for interactive learning activities. However, it was often found that these young people's preferences owed more to the fact that interactive learning activities were perceived to offer release from the monotony of receptive learning than to their value as learning opportunities. But how is it that students who experienced a more or less similar secondary curriculum should emerge with such varied views and preferences in respect of knowledge and learning?

Almost certainly, the single most important factor was prior experiences of success in learning, particularly in secondary education. Students frequently acclaimed learning strategies which had served them well in the past in the sense that they had proven effective in helping them secure desired grades, examination successes or other personal rewards. On the basis of prior successes and failures, by whatever criteria were consistent with their habitus, their dispositions to learning and studentship had become shaped. However, students' appraisals of learning activities also varied in the value attached to particular characteristics of the learning experience. Whether learning activities entailed group work, competition or public presentations of work, or whether they yielded intrinsic or extrinsic rewards, for instance, counted prominently in some students' evaluations but not in others. While there was some evident variation between feeder schools in students' dispositions to learning, the greater variation was found to exist between individual students drawn from a single feeder school. Although it would be unwise to claim this as conclusive evidence, it is at least consistent with the earlier discussion of the emergence of students' dispositions to learning. The structural opportunities provided by schools had had some impact upon horizons for action, despite their mediation by pupils' perceptions, while pupils' wider habitus appeared to have had the greater impact. Some students clearly rejected the learning activities which predominated in their pre-16 education and actively pursued alternative opportunities once at college or in the sixth form. For the majority, however, it was their schooldays' experiences which formed the mould in which their post-16 dispositions to knowledge and learning were cast.

In these opening sections, I have offered an overview of the social conditions of studentship, of dispositions to knowledge and learning and of habitus. Such insights, in so far as they illuminate particular cases of student learning, help to confirm that learning is at least as much a social as a psychological phenomenon. However, there are serious limitations attached to any theoretical claims about learning which do not incorporate an account of the dynamics of change. Learning is, after all, change. Moreover, despite the fact that the Leverhulme research was not a longitudinal study, there were many occasions when both students and teachers recounted change or hypothesised change in their attempts to give meaning to the present. Their pasts and anticipated futures were *ingrained in* their presents. Thus, it is important for concepts of studentship, disposition and identity to be relocated within the various contexts of their evolution and unfoldment: the learning careers of young people.

LEARNING CAREERS

The most common use of the term, 'career', is one which emphasises its objective properties: its constitution in terms of statuses and offices and, often, some continual, trajectory-style, upward movement through externally defined occupational structures. This is, arguably, a phenomenon of our time and place where occupation, as the principal determinant of income and status, is the most unambiguous indicator of a person's means of procuring life chances. It connotes a '"fixed and inevitable process" . . . which depicts a career as having an ideal-typical path of upward progression' (Armstrong, 1987: 9).

But such a concept of career is not appropriate to the theoretical model being sought here. The Leverhulme data indicated very clearly that reference only to positions within institutional structures – to course and subject group membership, year of programme, entry qualifications and such like – is not an adequate way of capturing the essential qualities of the learners concerned. At least equal emphasis has to be placed upon some subjective definition of career:

> a career is the moving perspective in which the person sees his life as a whole and interprets the meaning of his various attributes, actions, and the things which happen to him. This perspective is not absolutely fixed either to points of view, direction, or destination.
>
> (Hughes, 1937: 409–410)

Career, therefore, can be, and in the context of this discussion, has to be, experienced as an interpretive schema, linked not purely to a single domain of human activity but to *life* and to whatever impinges significantly upon that life in the experience of the interpreter. Moreover, it has to be conceived in some way other than as an occupational career for there are other points at which one's life and the external social world touch more tellingly, as Hughes (ibid.) noted and as many of the students who contributed to the Leverhulme Study reported.

The concept, *learning career*, has the potential to meet the various needs highlighted here. It allows for the incorporation of both objectively and subjectively defined experience; it has the capacity for describing, in both objective and subjective senses, continuity and transformation in learning by relating the present to both past and future; as subjectively experienced, it is about seeing 'life as a whole' and, thus, it is not bound to include or exclude experiences from one sphere of human activity more than those from any other; and, certainly, it is not limited to the insights afforded by any single discipline perspective. In order to illuminate its qualities further, I shall examine learning career against some of the data from the Leverhulme Study.

Students' dispositions to knowledge and learning and their studentship are susceptible to change from context to context and from time to time. Learning careers describe those changes. However, although dispositions may fluctuate from moment to moment, they are often relatively stable in the short term. In the longer term, however, they invariably change and many of the young people who participated in this study were able to provide insights into the different conditions under which their horizons for action had shifted and under which their dispositions to knowledge and learning had undergone change during their secondary school years. Among these were students who had come to perceive a new relevance of their studies to their personal or occupational aspirations (often due to changes in the latter), to value intrinsic rewards attached to certain learning activities or to discover a moral basis for some body of knowledge or learning activity. In some cases, teacher intervention in the form of praise or constructive help was advanced as the catalyst for students' reappraisals of themselves as learners. While some reappraisals and consequent changes in dispositions to knowledge and learning had led to a stronger commitment of students to their studies, it was also true that, for others, reappraisals had given rise to a weakening of commitment, even alienation. The horizons for action of students' reappraisals, as I have noted, were constrained on the one hand by the structural opportunities available to them, and on the other by their emerging habitus.

Important in determining horizons for action, it appeared, were students' personal values and identities which, themselves, owed at least as much to the opportunities afforded by family, culture and peer group as they did to the structural opportunities of formal educational prescriptions. The importance of family and culture in explaining the limited effects of externally imposed prescriptions has already been noted by Moore and by Bourdieu and Passeron:

> Their effects at any point in time are conditional upon the state of the entire system of relationships within which they are located (and through which they acquire their specific value) and mediated by both the dispositions acquired within the 'habitus' of the home and expectations held under a prevailing system of 'objective probabilities' within key social systems such as the labour market.
>
> (Moore, 1988b: 117)

> everything in the conduct of the families and the children (particularly their conduct and performance at school) will vary, because behaviour tends to be governed by what it is 'reasonable' to expect.
>
> (Bourdieu and Passeron, 1990: 226, cited in Moore, op. cit.)

The concept of learning career refers to the *development* of a student's dispositions to knowledge and learning over time. But that development is not to be understood simply as arising from the determined impact of enduring psychological traits upon dispositions. Rather, dispositions change as the result of the partly unpredictable influences of a variety of social and other factors, themselves mediated through horizons for action. Thus, learning career does not carry with it the assumption that given external influences have similar effects upon different individuals; it cannot, for the reasons already presented here concerning the dialectical relationship between structure and habitus and concerning the significance of individuals' perceptions of structural opportunities in the development of their habitus. Indeed, it is the *particular* characteristics of each learning career and not only the conditions under which it has developed which hold the key to understanding the behaviour, or I should say action, of the learner concerned.

Dispositions to knowledge and learning, and the learning careers to which they contribute, 'rarely remain unchanged by experience . . . [but] are revised in keeping with experience' (Hughes, op. cit.: 410). They do not cease to change simply because a young person reaches the age of 16 or 18 or some state of maturity. In so far as dispositions are attributable to habitus, they are liable to continual change as the social, moral, economic and other conditions of habitus themselves change. Changes in habitus continue throughout life. Even without systematic research, there is ample evidence of quite dramatic transformations in dispositions to knowledge and learning occurring well beyond adolescence. Religious conversions provide some of the most vivid illustrations. The new generation of information technology teachers 'born' in the 1980s is also an example of a large number of people who, from a wide variety of different backgrounds and often through very different routes, became newly disposed to knowledge and, potentially, learning. The further education sector itself offers, perhaps, the clearest illustration of all, containing as it does a large proportion of people who have moved into teaching from other career routes for reasons that have more to do with transformations in their own relationships with knowledge and learning than with logical progressions through predetermined career routes, trajectories or pathways.

But here I am primarily concerned with late adolescence, that most volatile stage in human growth and development. Adolescence is not simply a stage in the natural process of psychological or biological maturation; it is a profoundly social phenomenon. It is a social product – a means of regulating and controlling transition from childhood to adulthood (Clarke and Willis, 1984). There is ample documentation from researches and critiques in a variety of traditions to support the claim that, during their secondary and post-secondary years, young people encounter the most dramatic changes in both freedom and restrictions upon opportunities for social, moral and physical behaviour (see, for example, Erikson, 1968). It is the period in which their exposure to new, strong and sometimes conflicting expectations is of a scale and intensity greater than at any other period in their lives. For many young people, it is a period of turmoil as they turn to confront problems of their moral, social, cultural, political and sexual identities, in their striving for identities as persons. The case of Matt, considered in Chapter 6, comes clearly to mind.

> It has been described as an unstable and unpredictable age, when physical changes, including the development of sexual maturity, are accompanied by heart-searching and the trying out of new experiences in the adult world. In all these activities a central driving force can be discerned: the striving for self-realisation . . . a central feature of human progression from child to adult . . . accomplished in every sphere of life activity – personal relationships, creative efforts, leisure and so on.
>
> (D'Aeth, 1973: 7)

It is also the period in which strong cultural expectations combine with the structural conditions of British education to exert pressure upon the young to exercise choice – over subjects, courses and careers – and to confront the prospect of their economic independence of both family and state. But this combination of expectations and opportunities – of pressures – does not exert its effect upon young people in any easily predictable fashion. Rather, much of it is mediated through existing habitus. The personal careers of young people have become more diverse and 'individualised' (Beck, 1992; Evans and Heinz, 1994; Roberts *et al.*, 1994; Roberts, 1995) as they are moved to 'try things out while keeping their options open'. Thus, such transformations in dispositions as do take place under these conditions are to be understood as deriving from young people's *perceptions of* the opportunities and expectations to which they are exposed – perceptions which are continually framed and re-framed within the limits of progressively realised selves.

But accounts of the uncertainties of adolescence, and the significance of the freedoms and restrictions afforded by cultural expectations and structural conditions are not sufficient to capture the full complexity of 'becoming a person' in a postmodern age. 'The sources of certainty on which life feeds are changed' claims Beck (1992: 50) in the development of his influential 'individualisation thesis' and 'risk paradigm'. It is a period in which there is 'widespread scepticism about providential reason, coupled with the recognition that science and technology are double-edged, creating new parameters of risk and danger as well as offering beneficial possibilities for humankind' (Giddens, 1991: 27–28). It is a period of 'all change' in which once stable cultural and symbolic systems of meaning have become transformed and multiplied. The demise of the nation state as an economic unit, the globalisation of economies and work, rapid transformations in the nature, distribution and availability of work, the de-normalisation of the maritally bound family and, perhaps paradoxically, widespread bureaucratic rationalisation – the *McDonaldization of Society* (Ritzer, 1993) – are just some of the changes which threaten whole, stable and enduring personal identities, or selves. The individual is confronted with a multiplicity of sources of identification, sometimes contradictory and about which there is seldom a widely shared knowledge or opinion. As available courses of action have multiplied, so have the attendant risks. 'Within us are contradictory identities, pulling in different directions, so that our identifications are continuously being shifted about' (Hall, 1992: 277). If postmodern claims about the destabilisation of existing selves have any ring of truth – and I happen to believe that they do, despite some scepticism about certain views of the origins of the postmodern condition – their implications for the emergent selves or personal identities of late adolescents are profound indeed.

Thus, in the present study, it is hardly surprising that in explaining uncertainties or ambiguities in their learning careers or in laying claim to changes in their dispositions to knowledge and learning, young people sometimes made reference to significant changes in their wider habitus, including transformations in their predispositions and in their most fundamental dispositions. This was evident in cases where changes in personal

152

values accompanied greater political, moral or sexual awareness, where changes in motivation occurred following the identification of new personal needs, or where attitudinal and behavioural changes followed the experience (successful or unsuccessful) of exercising judgement and control over matters of new-found interest or importance. If these types of transformation of habitus, arising out of the interaction of existing habitus with newly perceived structural opportunities, can prompt changes in personal values, motivation, locus of control and, in effect, personal identity, it is to be anticipated that these, in turn, will prompt new horizons for action, new experiences and insights and further transformations of habitus.

The situation described here is, therefore, one of ever-changing disposition, habitus and personal identity – each finding a new equilibrium as newly perceived structural opportunities disturb the old. This contrasts vividly with those over-psychologised views of human growth and development which seek to explain dispositions to learning by reference to relatively constant personality or other human traits which are deemed to influence or even determine learning. It also contrasts with those accounts which describe processes of learning solely in terms of some highly generalised sequencing of psychological states. Such views are reflected in popular discourse but are also heavily implicit in concepts of 'learning styles' (Honey and Mumford, 1992) and in undifferentiating approaches to individual differences such as Kolb's (1984) 'Learning Cycle'. Dispositions to learning are infinitely more complex than those conceptualisations allow.

Learning careers describe transformations in habitus, dispositions and studentship, over time. They cannot be planned in any technical or rational sense; they happen or 'unfold'. Their futures are unpredictable to the extent that there is much that is unpredictable about the conditions under which unfoldment or happenstance take place. But they are not wholly unpredictable since, from our widely grounded and long-standing knowledge of the capacity of those conditions to reproduce themselves through successive generations of young people, we can still assuredly predict the perpetuation of inequalities by class, gender and race (Layder et al., 1991). Learning careers may be both idiosyncratic and ideal-typical.

Learning careers are biographical. They have pasts which are repeatedly constructed, deconstructed and reconstructed in response to new-found purposes (Heinz, 1987); 'people do not just grow older: they change and their relationships change as well' (Jones and Wallace, 1992: 14). They have futures, or at least anticipated futures, which are framed and reframed in the light of continually changing perceptions of opportunities. Their presents are configurations of those pasts and futures, and cannot be separated from them (Baert, 1992).

Learning careers thus incorporate notions of structure, of agency, and of action, providing some basis for a unified theory of learning. In as much as the concept of learning career is grounded in the dialectical and sometimes highly energised interplay of structure and agency in the processes of young people's growth and development, it stresses a dynamic component to the theorising of learning. It is some such dynamic component which is noticeably absent from much of the contemporary thinking affecting policy, practice and planning. Assumptions that human attributes are inherently stable, enduring, and even static, have had a powerful effect upon modern-day thought, as the literatures on intelligence, personality, motivation and self-theory amply testify. Moreover, along with parallel assumptions about inert, commodified knowledge, they are heavily implicit in a good deal of the rhetoric which gained sway in Britain in the 1980s and 1990s. Technicist concepts such as 'subject application' (DfE, 1992) and 'transferable skills' (see Hyland's indictment: 1994a: 111), for example, are products of an intellectual reductivism which has promoted the understanding of learning about as much as painting by numbers has advanced the interests of aesthetics. To be sure, social theorising of any description has, of necessity, to reduce reality to some simplified form in order that understanding might be communicated. The problem that I am describing here is one of reification where academics and policy makers alike have been swept away in the belief that the simplification is the reality.

The concept of learning career places studentship, learning and personal development in a dynamic, mutually constitutive, relationship. Inter-related as it is with a theory of habitus, it also links, dynamically, the formation of personal identity and dispositions to the transformation of social, moral, economic and other conditions. Such a theoretical construction releases the study of learning from the stifling constraints of static and reductive conceptualisations such as those referred to above. It thus has the potential to yield not simply the knowledge *that* young people 'act upon' learning opportunities in the ways that they do through their studentship but to generate an understanding of *why* they do. This is made possible because of the eclectic grounding of the concept of learning career and also because of its capacity, when located in an appropriate theoretical framework, to account for change. A theory of learning, incorporating a concept of learning career such as has been described here, is, thus, crucially important to the successful description and explanation of young people and their learning.

Before proceeding in the next chapter to further discussion of a theoretical framework for the description, analysis and development of post-16 education, I should like to offer some diagrammatic representation of the concept of learning career described thus far. The problem with diagrammatic representations, of course, is that they inevitably result in some over-simplification of the phenomena in question, and this example is no exception. However, the purpose here, in Figure 7.1, is to provide a map of the concepts embedded in learning career and of the various relationships between them, given that the discussion up to this point has tended to focus at any one time only upon small groupings of the key concepts.

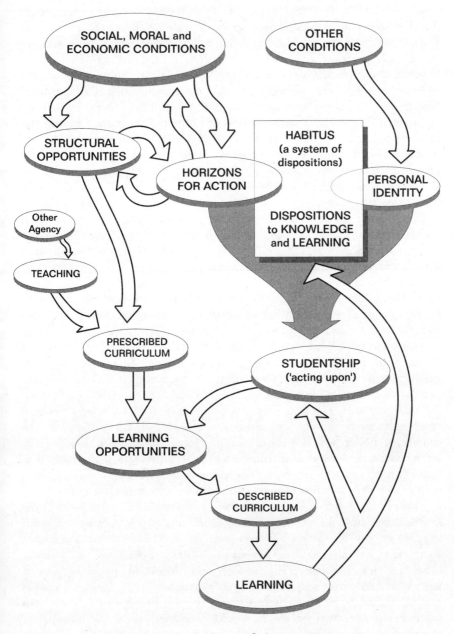

Figure 7.1 The landscape of a learning career

At first sight, it might appear that Figure 7.1 does not adequately describe the all-important development of learning careers over time and that it merely maps out the categories and concepts which constitute, or which have some other relationship with, learning career. However, the kinds of change which occur in the development of learning careers are not to be understood mechanistically; they are not the outcomes of some simple determinism. The development of a learning career is best seen as organically constituted. It is to be understood in terms of perpetual transformations in, on the one hand, the constituent conceptual categories and properties and, on the other, the relationships which exist between them. The categories, properties and their relationships are, of course, interdependent and mutually transformative and the development of learning careers rests ultimately upon those transformations.

But to hang the development of learning careers solely upon a notion of mutual transformation is to fail to provide any account of the impetus for change or development – the 'dynamic' component referred to above. It is in this connection that the arrows used to denote relationships between the categories and concepts identified in Figure 7.1 are important. In many cases, the relationships denoted by the arrows are reciprocal as, for example, 'structural opportunities' having a limiting effect upon 'horizons for action', and 'horizons for action' effectively limiting perceptions of 'structural opportunities'. It is such a reciprocity of relationships which provides for the vital interplay of structure and agency that is the impetus for change. It is through such relationships that external structures impinge upon and orient habitus and personal identities while, simultaneously, the self acts reflexively upon those external structures. Elsewhere in the figure, reciprocity is achieved through a more elaborate 'chaining': dispositions to knowledge and learning set the conditions under which studentship develops; studentship delimits the described curriculum and, in turn, what is actually learned and how it is learned; finally in this sequence, learning impacts, strongly or weakly, upon both studentship and dispositions. Thus, learning careers are transformed.

This chapter has focused on a number of issues which, on the basis of the Leverhulme Study, have been shown to be worthy of closer inspection if learning in post-16 education is to be comprehended in anything like its full complexity. The discussion has served to confirm the need and the opportunities for new theorising in a number of important respects. This is particularly so with regard to the agency-structure dialectic in its various manifestations. Some initial steps towards that further theorising have been taken here, particularly with the initial developments of the concepts of studentship and learning career, and one of the purposes of the following chapter is to deepen and widen some of those discussions. A further purpose of Chapter 8 is to re-address questions of future needs and opportunities and to contemplate the implications that these hold for curriculum development for the twenty-first century.

8

TOWARDS A RECONSTRUCTION OF THE POST-16 CURRICULUM

There are two central strands in the development of the conclusion to this book. The first concerns progressive economic globalisation and the problem of economic, social and political destabilisation confronting Britain, Europe and the Western world. It is to do with the types of demand that the twenty-first century will impose upon post-16 education. The second is to do with learning careers and the need to reconceptualise knowledge, learning and teaching in post-16 education in terms which are grounded more securely in students' experiences than in policy makers' assumptions about students' experiences of learning. These two strands of argument provide the basis for the examination, in the final chapter, of the knowledge, aims and organising principles of a curriculum for the future.

GLOBALISATION AND A CURRICULUM FOR THE FUTURE

The phenomenon of economic globalisation – 'simply the intensification of global interconnectedness' (McGrew, 1992: 63) – and its impact upon the British economy have already been briefly described in Chapter 2. Regardless of the views one might hold on the merits of competing economic and labour market analyses, there can be no escaping the need to break out of the vicious circles (Ball, 1991) surrounding the low-skill, low-productivity equilibrium of the present (Finegold and Soskice, 1988). There can be no denying, either, the imperative to plan properly for a high-skill, high-productivity alternative, although the difficulties of achieving such an end should not be underestimated. The implications which globalisation holds for educational change are the subject of a growing literature (Thurow, 1992; Reich, 1993; Ilon, 1994). The future for Britain depends ultimately upon its capacity for innovation and for responding to an expanded market for customised products. It is only through these kinds of economic endeavour that future growth can be achieved and sustained.

The establishment of a productive economy on the basis of customisation and innovation as opposed to the repetitive activities of Fordism will place heavy demands upon the education system. While I reject any notion of a simple causal relationship between education and the economy, it is becoming apparent that the economy of the future will be particularly demanding of the creative capabilities of its labour force and that the education system can do much to foster these. It is, perhaps, ironic that at the very time that Britain might have begun to grasp this nettle, the development of its secondary and post-secondary curriculum and assessment procedures should come to stress a technicist reduction of the learning act, a decontextualisation, fragmentation and commodification of knowledge, 'outcomes' over aims, and utilitarian values over any others, so significantly diminishing opportunities for the promotion of creativity. I shall return to the problem of creativity in the curriculum in the discussion of a curriculum for the future in Chapter 9.

But product customisation and innovation, at least if the post-Fordist analysis is to be believed, will also entail significant changes to units of production and to working practices. Post-Fordists claim that there are clear signs that such changes are already taking place – that smaller units of production with leaner, flatter hierarchies of multi-skilled personnel are becoming the norm. While it is hard to deny that significant 'down-sizing' has taken place across the productive economy, evidence of more egalitarian labour relations is far less easy to discern.

> Britain has adopted the *neo*-Fordist option in which the rights and opportunities of citizens and workers have been increasingly diminished . . . [as] terms such as flexibility, diversity and choice have . . . become euphemisms for inequality, control and deprofessionalization.
>
> (Avis *et al.*, 1996: 179 and 8)

Of course, if Britain is presently lurching towards neo-Fordism, and I believe it is, some massive political and cultural change will be necessary in order to set things on the post-Fordist track – and this will certainly have major implications for education. But whether it is post- or neo-Fordism which most adequately describes the present is actually immaterial to this discussion. The point is that future prosperity and stability rest heavily upon our capacity to achieve the cooperative, high-trust, democratic, working relationships envisaged under post-Fordism and also to foster 'flexible' or 'multi-skilled' knowledge workers. It is these requirements that are likely to make the heaviest of all demands upon the education system. In so far as the working practices of the future will be especially demanding of human agency, of team work, of self-reliance, and of the capacity for the generation of new substantive knowledge and such like, and less reliant upon the 'application' of externally verified knowledge and the uncritical enactment of externally structured work roles, so the education system of the future must enhance provision for the liberation and harnessing of human agency and be rid of its excessive dependency upon externally structured knowledge and authority. Once more I should point up the irony of recent curriculum developments in British secondary and post-16 education, which, in respect of their treatment of knowledge, planning and assessment, have become dominated very much more by the concerns of neo-Fordism than by those of post-Fordism. In as much as neo-Marxist theories about the reproduction of social order through the content and organisation of schooling (Althusser, 1972; Bowles and Gintis, 1976; Apple, 1979) have validity at all, this latter observation is acutely disturbing.

While changes to the nature of work and to working practices of the types alluded to so far, assuming they are achievable, may go some way towards securing future economic growth and stability, they are by no means the complete recipe for success. Economic development cannot be planned without proper regard to the social, political and moral conditions with which it is inextricably linked. There is no simple causal relationship between education and economic performance and there is an abundance of historical and contemporary evidence to confirm the importance of social and political stability in the equation. Of particular importance is the need to protect against the social ills of unemployment.

The prospect that structural under-employment will persist well into the foreseeable future is perhaps the most disquieting feature of our present predicament. The inequalities to issue from unemployment, alone, are causes for concern. However, prognoses such as that by Hutton (1996) of a 30/30/40 society are matters of particular concern.

Society is dividing up before our eyes, opening up new social fissures in the working population. The first 30 per cent are the *disadvantaged*. These include the more than 4 million men who are out of work, . . . unemployed women and women married to economically inactive men. . . . The second 30 per cent are made up of the *marginalised* and *insecure*. . . . People in this category work at jobs that are insecure, poorly protected and carry few benefits. This category . . . includes the growing army of part-timers and casual workers. There are now more than 5 million people working part-time, of whom over 80 per cent are women. The last category is that of the *privileged* – the just over 40 per cent whose market power has increased since 1979. These are the full-time employees and the self-employed who have held their jobs for over two years . . . and the part-timers who have held their jobs for more than five years.

(Hutton, 1996: 106 and 108)

There is now widespread agreement with the type of analysis that Hutton has offered and mounting concern about its implications (see, for instance, CPAG, 1996). Social polarisation, as the result of a de-regulated labour market, is the back-cloth against which poverty, stress and insecurity are illuminated all too clearly. But these conditions are not confined to the disadvantaged, the marginalised and the insecure; their effect is pervasive, 'affecting everything from the vitality of the housing market to the growth of social security spending – and ultimately the growth prospects of the entire economy' (Hutton, 1996: 109). Thus, even the privileged have little cause for contentment since, ultimately, it is the employment, social stability and cohesion of their fellow citizens as well as their own individual market positions and capital which make for their security.

The broad economic, political and moral implications of these analyses are abundantly clear. A divided and potentially volatile society is not a suitable basis for economic advancement and stability. A political establishment whose primary investment is in its own re-election is not the responsible body politic that will commit itself to the long-term planning and investment required for the project described here. Nor is that 'Thatcher/market-liberal emphasis on "possessive individualism"' (Hickox, 1995: 154), promoted in Britain throughout the 1980s and 1990s, in which any notion of shared interest or common good is subordinated to personal and private interests, at all suited to sustaining the essentially collaborative working relations of post-Fordism. Communitarianism, once lauded by Tony Blair's Labour Party as the platform for their assault on poverty and social polarisation, is also unequal to the task. In so far as communitarianism rests upon a moral responsibility of individuals to look after others, it offers no promise of social healing. The affluent are more likely to be preoccupied with looking after their own than forming close ties with the poor. Even Amitai Etzioni, the guru of communitarianism, recognised the possibility of rebuilt communities becoming insular and indifferent to others. He would probably not disagree with the following worst case scenario for Britain:

> The rhetoric of community has a powerful resonance in a society which has witnessed the destruction wrought by rampant individualism. It could be replaced by a rampant 'communitism' that would leave the poor as invisible as ever.
>
> (Thomas, 1996)

Education has an important part to play in all of these matters and, although it will entail looking well beyond the scope of the particular curriculum developments that have taken place in recent years, it is not too difficult to see what this part is and how it might be played. However they are to be formulated, the secondary and post-16 curricula for the twenty-first century will entail an economic education, a political education and a moral education of a form that will give proper meaning to the term, 'education for citizenship'.

> The conditions of Habermas's 'communicative rationality', whereby, in unfettered contexts, people can explore the integrity of their accounts in order to reach shared understandings, are demanding ones and will

160

require institutional settings that promote reason in public discourse. . . . These are the conditions of our own times. If the transformations are to be coped with a new polity is required that enables more active public participation and discourse to generate the legitimate foundation for any new moral and political order. The need can generate the institutional prerequisites for a broader and more active educated public.

(Ranson, 1994: 104–105)

But the achievement of such a situation will be no straightforward matter since the political agendas of both the New Right and New Labour are firmly set against any curriculum development which cannot be expressed in terms of short-term utilitarian ends. Their sights are limited to an education for making a living; they have little vision of an education for making a life (Postman, 1996).

real and lasting educational reform cannot be subordinated to the causal determinants of economy, or traditions of hierarchy and exclusion. Genuine alternatives must embrace an active view of *citizenship* which links partnership and empowerment in personal education and economic relations, beyond market, qualification and employer-led considerations . . . [they] must embrace an *educationally constructed* view of citizenship on the lines advocated by Clark (1994) which interlinks partnership and empowerment in personal, education and economic relations.

(Avis *et al.*, 1996: 98 and 100)

The problems of economic globalisation and social polarisation as I have briefly described them here give rise to important questions about nation state economics, identity and culture. These are matters which Britain, of all nations, can ill afford to ignore. As control over expenditure has shifted out of the hands of national exchequers and into those of multi-national or transnational industries, a process greatly assisted by the privatisation project of the New Right, so the facility for the nation state to exert control over its 'own' affairs has been much reduced.

But the impact of globalisation is not confined to transformations of national economies; globalisation has forced political and cultural adaptation, too. Despite the fact that there are numerous examples that such adaptations have taken place relatively swiftly and smoothly, pockets of resistance are highly visible. The defence of nationalism, for example, has found strong and cynical expression in recent upsurges in neo-Fascism throughout the West while the defence of religious identities is maintained as forcefully as ever by militarised fundamentalist groups across the world. Although of less sinister proportions, the British government's intransigence on the Maastricht Treaty – notably the Social Chapter and the European

Exchange Rate Mechanism (ERM) – must also be seen as an attempt to defend national sovereignty and identity in the face of more widely grounded pressures to surrender elements of both.

Clearly, these observations raise crucial questions for the education of the young in this postmodern society. In so far as an education system is responsible for transmitting the essentials of a culture from generation to generation, the question 'what culture?' looms large. Is it, for instance, to be the Anglo-centric culture envisaged by the Hillgate Group: 'a solid foundation in British and European history and . . . no concessions to the philosophy of the global curriculum advocated by the multi-culturalists' (Hillgate Group, cited in Whitty, 1989: 333)? Clearly, if Britain is to make an adequate response to the demands of globalisation, it must reject small-minded outpourings such as these. Its education system must strive to promote multi-cultural and multi-national understanding and to assist in creating the conditions upon which cross-national economic and social projects can flourish. Although an increased commitment to the learning of foreign languages would represent a significant step forward in Britain's case, this alone would be inadequate without a similar commitment to an education for European and world understanding.

I have made a number of claims here about the importance of promoting creativity, flexible and collaborative working relationships, human agency, self-reliance, citizenship (in the form of an economic, political and moral education) and multi-cultural and multi-national understanding in a curriculum for the twenty-first century. However, these claims are unlikely to attract any meaningful support in the 1990s from either the New Right or New Labour since they are not expressed in the strict technicist and utilitarian terms in which those political groups have come to describe, and conceive of, education. But it is specifically because they are not reduced to technical and crude utilitarian proportions that the claims are important.

There are many reasons to suspect that Pacific Rim countries will dominate the global economy of the early twenty-first century. However, despite the fact that a ruthless adherence to utilitarian technicism in educational planning has contributed greatly to their substantial economic growth and development, advancing nations of the Pacific Rim are already showing the foresight to think and plan in accordance with the needs I have described here. The following extract from a publication by the Korean Ministry of Education offers a set of aims and values that the West in general, and Britain in particular, will ignore at their peril. It is a sobering thought that this particular statement originates from a country which, only thirty-five years earlier, ranked among the poorest and least stable in the world.

To prepare for the upcoming 21st century, Korean education has established humanization, refinement, informativeness, human welfare and open-mindedness as its ultimate goals. Various efforts are made to raise

a self-reliant individual equipped with a distinct sense of independence, a creative individual with a sense of originality, and an ethical
individual with sound morality and democratic citizenship.

(Republic of Korea Ministry of Education, 1995: 4)

LEARNING, LEARNING CAREERS AND A CURRICULUM FOR THE FUTURE

I have already argued for a concept of learning career in the study of
learning. Here, I simply want to signal the importance of such a theoretical
construction for curriculum planning.

The observations that dispositions to knowledge and learning change over
time and that such changes are more volatile and less predictable among
adolescents than among others are by no means profound. In fact they are
strikingly obvious to anybody who has contemplated the problems of
learning or adolescence more than momentarily. But what should be equally
obvious are the friction and 'energy losses' which arise from the 'force-fitting'
of those same young people into curricula straitjackets designed on the
implicit assumption that learners' dispositions are essentially stable and
enduring or that they will change in ways that can be prescribed. There are
few curriculum designs, it appears, which have made any real attempt to
harness the creative energies of unfolding learning careers to the promotion of
learning. It must be said that the design of BTEC courses took some important steps in this direction, as did certain TVEI and even some A-level
projects, in as much as they promoted individual and group experimentation,
project work and other interactive learning activities, although, as this study
has revealed, the extent to which those prescriptions were translated into any
described curriculum depended greatly upon the teacher and student agency
introduced to the situation. BTEC and a precious few other developments
aside, the norm in post-16 curriculum development has been to reject,
prompt rejection by, or coerce compliance from those young people whose
changing dispositions or unfolding learning careers happened to place them
in conflict with the requirements of the prescribed curriculum. The labels
'failure' and 'drop-out' have been used all too readily as the values of technical
rational structures have been wrongly asserted over those of human agency.

A curriculum for the twenty-first century must hold a primary responsibility for the transmission of a corpus of knowledge and skill from one
generation to the next. I shall return, in Chapter 9, to the problem of determining what should constitute that corpus. At the same time, though, the
curriculum must make provision for harnessing the creative energies of
dynamic learning careers. It must not suppress but must support the realisation of the full potential of human agency in learning if future generations
are to be adequately equipped to meet the requirements of post-Fordist
economic and work relations. Of course, any proposition such as this,

concerning the release of forces of human agency, is seriously at risk of being associated with the promotion of individualism – and that is not what I have in mind. This, too, I shall return to later.

The curriculum I am alluding to in this discussion demands careful conceptualisation in relation to the all-important learning careers and studentship described earlier. It should be patently clear already that the reconceptualisation of knowledge, learning and teaching required for such a project will entail significant shifts of viewpoint from those implicitly or explicitly maintained in the post-16 curriculum of today. The present emphasis upon fragmented, decontextualised, cerebral and reified knowledge must be abandoned and greater importance attached to the essential unity and situatedness of all knowledge. Technicist and reductivist treatments of knowledge as a commodity for exchange and uncritical internalisation must also be rejected and fuller recognition given to the individual, social and cultural structuredness of knowledge. On the matter of learning, theorising must move well beyond the restrictive scope of those psychologies which,

> [interpret] learning and context as two separate entities, treating the former as if it could be discussed in terms of universal applicability and the latter as a changing pattern of process and structure which makes an 'impact' on the former and 'within' which the former is located.
>
> (Quicke, 1996: 103)

There must also be a shift away from conceptualisations which attach primary importance to cognitive processes, motivation or other intrapersonal categories towards alternatives which stress the interpersonal and social conditions of learning and, above all, the mutually constitutive nature of learning and being. Shifts in the conceptualisation of knowledge and learning such as I am describing here will, in turn, raise critical questions about the practice of teaching. These will include questions about whether teaching has any necessary connection with learning and, if so, what connection. Needless to say, any reconceptualisation of teaching which follows from this may well offer a strong challenge to long-standing and dominant assumptions about what teaching is.

Many of the conceptual distinctions made here in respect of knowledge, learning and teaching have been scrutinised elsewhere, notably in more radical rethinking of the problems of knowledge and learning. The significance of the social conditions of learning, for instance, is recognised in the work of Vygotsky (1978) and this, in turn, has influenced the thinking of a great many others.

> animals are incapable of learning in the human sense of the term; human learning presupposes a specific social nature and a process by which children grow into the intellectual life of those around them.
>
> (Vygotsky, 1978: 88)

But it is in Vygotsky's discussion of the 'zone of proximal development' that he reveals the essentially social character of learning:

> We propose that an essential feature of learning is that it creates the zone of proximal development; that is, learning awakens a variety of internal developmental processes that are able to operate only when the child is interacting with people in his environment and in co-operation with his peers.
>
> (ibid.: 90)

Bandura's social learning theory (1977) has also received recognition for its critique of those theories which seek to explain behaviour with reference to the 'joint influence' of personal and environmental factors. He argues that it is crucially important to conceive not of joint influences but of the 'interdependence of personal and environmental influences' (Bandura, 1977: 195). He claims that social learning theory is an attempt

> to provide a unified theoretical framework for analyzing human thought and behavior. . . . [It] approaches the explanation of human behavior in terms of a continuous reciprocal interaction between cognitive, behavioral and environmental determinants. Within the process of reciprocal determinism lies the opportunity for people to influence their destiny as well as the limits of self-direction. This conception of human functioning then neither casts people into the role of powerless objects controlled by environmental forces nor free agents who can become whatever they choose. Both people and their environments are reciprocal determinants of each other.
>
> (ibid.: vi and vii)

Although it is hardly radical, there are key aspects of Bandura's work which resonate with the present discussion of learning. Social learning theory attaches importance to the power of human agency and, notably, in Bandura's later works (1982, 1989), has been much concerned with the problem of self-efficacy. It also conceives of the personal and the environmental as not only interdependent but as reciprocally determining, thus transcending the dualism of agency versus structure. However, although Bandura's interests do extend well beyond the purely cognitive, social learning theory is person-centred and ahistorical. It is essentially concerned with psychological processes and, thus, its usefulness and relevance to the present discussion of learning is effectively limited to the few observations noted here.

More recently, the work of Brown et al. (1989), among others, has drawn attention to the difficulties of establishing an all-encompassing conceptualisation of learning. They claim that knowledge is intricately related to the context in which it is learned: learning is, therefore, situation specific and performance is context dependent. They are highly critical of the separation of knowing and doing such as occurs under the arrangements of formal schooling and argue for the

> centrality of activity in learning. . . . The activity in which knowledge is developed and deployed . . . is not separable from or ancillary to learning and cognition. Nor is it neutral. Rather, it is an integral *part of* what is learned.
>
> (Brown *et al.*, 1989: 39 and 32, emphasis added)

Brown *et al.* stress that learning entails the social construction of knowledge on a basis of collaborative social interaction. They employ the notion of cognitive apprenticeship in their account of the methods by which learning can be achieved.

> In essence, cognitive apprenticeship attempts to promote learning within the nexus of activity, tool, and culture. . . . Within a culture, ideas are exchanged and modified and belief systems developed and appropriated through conversation and narratives, so these must be promoted, not inhibited. Though they are often anathema to traditional schooling, they are an essential component of social interaction and, thus, of learning.
>
> (ibid.: 40)

There is clearly much in the insights offered by Brown *et al.* which has direct relevance to the present account of the post-16 curriculum and learning careers of young people. Situated cognition theory is the most radical and eclectic of the various attempts to theorise learning which I have considered thus far. It locates learning securely within its social, cultural and historical contexts and conceptualises knowledge, learning and teaching in a manner suited to the description and analysis of the kinds of problem identified on the basis of the Leverhulme Study. I shall return to these points shortly.

Claxton (1996a and b) is one of the few Britons striving to re-theorise learning. He is highly critical of the partiality and simplicity of academic psychology, claiming that 'no even half-way adequate psychology of real-life learning exists' (1996b: 6). In setting out his case for an integrated learning theory, Claxton argues that

> learning has to be seen as reflecting a tacit, or at least intuitive, decision-making process that includes social, emotional and material, as well as cognitive, considerations, the resultant of which is a *stance* towards the learning opportunity that determines whether, and if so when, how and with what intent, learning will proceed. . . . [The] significant risks, rewards and so on, which weigh in the balance of a person's learning decisions, are themselves underpinned by a host of views-of-the-world that are the residues of past experiences and teach-

ings ... and which are brought to bear on current events in order to attribute significance and meaning to them.

(Claxton, 1996a: 46; 1996b: 3 and 4)

Claxton makes particular use of 'implicit theories' – not dissimilar to Argyris and Schön's (1974, 1978) 'theories-in-use' – and claims that individuals' implicit theories of self, knowledge, learning and ability lead them to make judgements which have important implications for their own learning. He also points to collectively held 'implicit theories' which are effectively disabling of whole communities of learners. One example, particularly relevant to this discussion, concerns that post-Cartesian 'psychomythology' of mind which asserts the virtues of the explicit, the articulable and of consciousness in learning, over those of the implicit, the non-articulable and the non-conscious.

> Our contemporary education ... being based on a view of mind in which, if the unconscious has any role, it is as an emotional disrupter of learning rather than as a cognitive resource, has come to rely predominantly, if not exclusively, on learning modes in which one can 'show one's working', and in which the assessment of learning is based on the ability to describe and explain what one knows, rather than to reveal it spontaneously under appropriate real-life conditions.
>
> (Claxton, 1996a: 49)

Clearly, Claxton's integrated learning theory relates strongly to a number of the themes of the present discussion, notably those concerning a 'stance towards learning opportunities' (referred to here as dispositions), learners' attributions of meanings to events, the importance of human agency and, of course, the notion of implicit theories. His account of the decision making process could synthesise well with Beck's (1992) 'risk paradigm'. But integrated learning theory is still essentially person-centred. It is located firmly within the psychological tradition of social constructivism and its central concern remains the prediction of human performance on the basis of an understanding of those cognitive processes underpinning learning as an individual act. However, despite this cautionary note, Claxton's work offers much to the present analysis by way of its constructive and challenging insights.

The work of Nixon et al. (1996) is also noteworthy in the context of this discussion. In their presentation of an 'analytical model of learning', Nixon and his colleagues briefly examine relationships between learning institutions, culture, and secondary school pupils' learning. But they also make strong claims in respect of the mutual constitution of learning and being and about the central place of human agency in the learning process.

> the deeper significance of learning lies, through its forming of our powers and capacities, in our unfolding agency. ... Learning is becoming. It is an unfolding through which we learn not only what

167

makes us unique – what individuates us – but how we can learn to make that distinctive agency work in the world.

(Nixon et al., 1996: 49)

The work of Nixon et al. clearly has much in common with the arguments advanced here. This should not prove too much of a surprise since, despite focusing upon learners from different age groups, both projects are attempting to address the same root problem: how to promote learning relevant to the future in a context where opportunities for curriculum reform and development are hamstrung on the one hand by New Right ideology and, on the other, by popular technicism. But the claims made by Nixon and his colleagues also resonate strongly with one of the key themes to have emerged from both the Leverhulme Study and the other literature reviewed here – that of the socially situated nature of knowledge and learning.

> Reasoning and testing ideas . . . reveals the indispensable mutuality or sociability of learning. It is not just that any competence is learnt with and through others, but that the subjectivities which define what we become as persons, and therefore our agency, are social creations.

(Nixon et al., 1996: 51)

But perhaps the most radical re-theorising of learning of all, to date, is that offered by Lave and Wenger (1991) in their work on situated learning and legitimate peripheral participation. They define learning as the product of social participation in contra-distinction to the acquisition of knowledge; learning processes are, therefore, the processes of social participation, not the personal cognitive processes upon which much conventional learning theory has been hinged. The concept of situated activity is central to Lave and Wenger's general theoretical perspective which, they maintain, provides,

> the basis of claims about the relational character of knowledge and learning, about the negotiated character of meaning, and about the concerned (engaged, dilemma-driven) nature of learning activity for the people involved. That perspective mean[s] that there is no activity that is not situated. It implies emphasis on comprehensive understanding involving the whole person rather than 'receiving' a body of factual knowledge about the world; on activity in and with the world; and on the view that agent, activity, and the world mutually constitute each other.

(Lave and Wenger, 1991: 33)

They advance a social practice theory of learning in which learning is integral to social practice in an historical and generative sense.

> learning is not merely situated in practice – as if it were some independently reifiable process that just happened to be located somewhere;

168

learning is an integral part of generative social practice in the lived-in world.

(ibid.: 35)

Lave and Wenger's theory of learning is in keeping with the Marxist historical tradition of theorising about social practice and it is as much concerned with the problem of reproduction of the social order as it is with those of situated knowledge and learning. Indeed, the problems are inter-related; they are mutually constitutive and it is the concept of legitimate peripheral participation which provides a framework for their examination.

> Conceiving of learning in terms of participation focuses attention on ways in which it is an evolving, continuously renewed set of relations; this is, of course, consistent with a relational view, of persons, their actions, and the world, typical of a theory of social practice .... Insistence on the historical nature of motivation, desire, and the very relations by which social and culturally mediated experience is available to persons-in-practice is one key to the goals to be met in developing a theory of practice. Theorizing in terms of practice, or praxis, also requires a broad view of human agency, emphasizing the integration in practice of agent, world, and activity.
>
> (ibid.: 49–50)

'One way to think of learning', according to Lave and Wenger, 'is as the historical production, transformation, and change of persons' (1991: 51). Learning, therefore, implies the construction of identities.

> Viewing learning as legitimate peripheral participation means that learning is not merely a condition for membership, but is itself an evolving form of membership. We conceive of identities as long-term, living relations between persons and their place and participation in communities of practice. Thus identity, knowing, and social membership entail one another.
>
> (ibid.: 53)

Clearly, Lave and Wenger's work has much to contribute to the present analysis of learning careers. It offers insight into the potential of human agency in learning while transcending any crude distinction between agency and structure; its treatment of situated knowledge and learning resonates very strongly with earlier reports of the dispositions of the students and teachers who participated in the Leverhulme Study; and the notions of learning as a social act and of legitimate peripheral participation in communities of practice would appear to be highly relevant to the further description and analysis of learning needs of the post-Fordist era such as I have briefly mentioned already. Most compelling of all, Lave and Wenger have employed an analytical focus sufficiently broad to provide for a realistic

169

harnessing and integration of 'agent and world, activity, meaning, cognition, learning and knowing' (ibid.: 50).

Finally in this overview of some of the more radical contributions to a re-theorising of knowledge and learning, I should like to note the work of Gibbons *et al.* (1994) on the subject of knowledge production. Gibbons and his colleagues contrast 'traditional' (mode 1) knowledge production with 'mode 2' which they claim has become increasingly evident of late. Mode 1 production is set securely within a disciplinary framework and is characterised by a predominance of codified knowledge, by largely academic interests, and by the primarily cognitive contexts in which it occurs. The organisation of production is hierarchical with clear divisions of labour into increasingly diversified, specialised and narrow fields. The emergence of a new mode of knowledge production (mode 2), supplementing rather than supplanting mode 1, is seen as resulting from 'the existing dysfunctionalities and breakdowns of disciplinary forms of problem-solving' (Gibbons *et al.*, 1994: 29) and from coincident increases in both the supply of potential knowledge producers and in demands for new knowledge. Mode 2 knowledge production is defined as that which is

> carried out in the *context of application* and marked by its: *transdisciplinarity*; *heterogeneity*; organisational heterarchy and transience; social accountability; and *reflexivity*; and quality control which emphasises context- and use-dependence.
>
> (ibid.: 167, original emphasis)

> In mode 2 creativity is mainly manifest as a group phenomenon, with the individual's contribution seemingly subsumed as part of the process. . . . Mode 2 knowledge is accumulated through the repeated configuration of human resources in flexible, essentially transient forms of organisation. The loop from the context of application through transdisciplinarity, heterogeneity, organisational diversity is closed by new adaptive and contextual forms of quality control. The result is a more socially accountable and reflexive mode of science.
>
> (ibid.: 9)

Mode 2 knowledge production is distinguished by its *transdisciplinarity* and by the production of transdisciplinary knowledge within an '*application context*'. This, it seems, is exactly what Esland had in mind more than a generation beforehand when he asserted:

> the content of knowledge may become subservient to the development of a cognitive technology which is capable of projecting multiple inferential structures containing both enactive and theoretical knowledge. There is no reason to suppose that these will remain within the 'boundaries' of what are now heuristically labelled as 'subjects'. New

170

configurations of knowledge are likely to emerge from the combinations of questions whi-h arise in the learning situations.

(Esland, 1971: 96)

But transdisciplinarity is not to be confused with inter- or multi-disciplinarity. It 'corresponds to a movement beyond disciplinary structures' (Gibbons *et al.*, 1994: 27), generating its own theoretical structures, methods and procedures. 'Working in an application context creates pressures to draw upon a diverse array of knowledge resources and to *configure* them according to the problem in hand' (ibid.: 27, emphasis added). Transdisciplinary knowledge production consists in

> a continuous linking and relinking, in specific clusterings and configurations of knowledge which is brought together on a temporary basis in specific contexts of application. Thus, it is strongly oriented towards and driven by problem-solving. Its theoretical-methodological core, while cross-cutting through well-established disciplinary cores, is often locally driven and locally constituted, thus, any such core is highly sensitive to further local mutations depending on the context of application.
>
> (ibid.: 29)

Mode 2 knowledge production depends more explicitly upon tacit knowledge and competence than does its mode 1 counterpart. Its organisation is sufficiently flexible to accommodate contradictory, even conflicting, interpretive communities – arguably the requisite conditions for creativity – while 'preference [is] given to collaborative rather than individual performance and excellence judged by the ability of individuals to make a sustained contribution in open, flexible types of organisation in which they may only work temporarily' (ibid.: 30).

Plainly, the claims of Gibbons and his colleagues on the subject of knowledge production have much in common with those of Brown *et al.*, 1989; Lave and Wenger, 1991; Claxton, 1996a and b; Nixon *et al.*, 1996, and others considered here. Notions of situated knowledge and learning are carried implicitly in mode 2 contexts of application, while Gibbons' claims in respect of transdisciplinarity and the erosion of demarcations between the theoretical and the practical and even between knowledge and culture (Gibbons *et al.*, 1994: 84) closely parallel others' objections to the separation of knowing and doing (Brown *et al.*, 1989) or learning and being. The importance attached to tacit knowledge is prominent too in Claxton's work and also in claims made by Giddens (1984) in respect of reflexivity and practical consciousness, while the view that the generation of knowledge is a collaborative social act is also one of the mainstays of the work of Brown *et al.*, 1989; Lave and Wenger, 1991 and Nixon *et al.*, 1996. I should add, finally, that the claims which Gibbons and his

171

colleagues make in respect of the requisite basic knowledge and skills for learning bear more than a passing correspondence with those advanced by Reich (1993): *'abstraction, system thinking, experimentation,* and *collaboration'* (1993: 229).

There are many points which have been raised in this discussion of the problems of conceptualising knowledge and learning that mirror arguments and observations made earlier in respect of both learning careers and the post-16 curriculum. First among these are the ways in which different writers have seen fit to articulate relationships between structure and agency as 'interdependent', 'reciprocally determining' or 'mutually constitutive'. Such accounts not only provide the means for transcending the structure–agency dualism but serve to underscore claims made in Chapter 7 in respect of the mutually transformative categories and properties of the constituent concepts of learning careers and of the relationships existing between them. They also allow for what I described in the last chapter as, 'the vital interplay of structure and agency that is the impetus for change' in learning careers.

A second area of broad consensus concerns the claims which different theorists have attached to the significance of human agency – either individual or group-collaborative agency – in processes of learning and particularly in the generation of new knowledge. But these claims are not simply that learning is agency-driven; rather, they stress the importance of the social conditions with which agency is mutually constituted. They argue for recognition of the situatedness of knowledge, learning and performance; of the socially constructed nature of knowledge; and of the reciprocal relationships which exist between personal and collective implicit theories of self, knowledge, learning and ability on the one hand and learning processes on the other. This same emphasis is at the very core of the concept of learning career and is quite visible in the earlier discussions of habitus, of the relationships between structural opportunities and horizons for action and between studentship and learning opportunities. But demands for greater recognition of, and for a harnessing of, the energies and creative capacities of individual and group-collaborative agency derive also from changing economic, political and social conditions and will find full expression in any plausible curriculum for the future.

Third, there is a common sense in which recent attempts to re-theorise learning have described relationships between personal identity and learning: they are treated as mutually constitutive. Such assumptions of interdependence also lie at the core of the concept of learning career. In fact, under learning career, the immediate network of interdependent concepts extends also to studentship, dispositions, values and beliefs. But while identity and learning might, indeed, be regarded as mutually constitutive, that is not to suggest that their interdependency is tight and that changes in one immediately effect changes in the other. The Leverhulme Study provided cases of quite a number of students such as Natalie, mentioned in Chapter 7, who appeared to be trying to manage conflicting demands by maintaining two distinct identities. Identities of self as 'person' and as learner, or 'student', were 'out of phase'; there was a 'gap' – one had simply not caught up with, or accommodated to changes in, the other. This 'gap' is essential in understanding the dynamics of learning careers; while it does not account for the impetus for change, it does explain the adaptive transformations which follow. Moreover, the notion of a 'gap', of a loose constitutive dependency between personal identity and learning, highlights the limiting features of that technical rationalism so prevalent in contemporary curriculum development which presumes, for example, that effective personal and social skills learning is achieved simply through effective instruction in 'personal transferable skills'. Oh, that the matter were nearly that simple!

TOWARDS A CURRICULUM FOR THE FUTURE: RECONCEPTUALISING THE BASICS

Throughout this book, there have been numerous reports and claims about the inadequacy of prevailing conceptualisations of knowledge and learning in post-16 education. These reports, in many cases, have been grounded in empirical data of the Leverhulme Study. Elsewhere, claims have been deduced from an examination of future needs and opportunities. Throughout, technically rational prescriptions of knowledge and learning opportunities have been found to be singularly lacking. Such observations have been broadly echoed by those researchers and writers reported in the last section and by others both in Britain and elsewhere. There is now an urgent need for the reconceptualisation of knowledge and learning lest more of yesterday's 'answers' are allowed to stifle the questions for tomorrow. It is towards such a reconceptualisation that the remainder of this chapter is directed.

In this last section, I set out what I believe to be the key founding principles of a theory of learning for the future. These are based upon empirical evidence from the Leverhulme Study, a reasoned critique of relevant literature on the subject of learning and an analysis of future economic and social needs.

Any theory of learning must be informed by some clear conceptualisation of knowledge, of learners, of the context(s) in which learning takes place, of the relationships between learning and context, and of human behaviour and action. It should also make explicit its presuppositions – in as much as that is ever possible – in order that the reader can have the fullest opportunity for critical engagement with the work concerned. In order to help meet these requirements, I have chosen to lay out my claims under seven propositions, each accompanied by a brief discussion of its underpinning rationale.

1 *Knowledge is socially situated and socially constructed*

The evidence of the Leverhulme Study has provided some illustration of the crucial bearing which the social conditions of learning have upon the content as well as the processes of learning. The situatedness of knowledge is central to any adequate understanding of learning and learning careers. Such claims are echoed in a large number of other reports of research into learning and knowledge production potential. The Leverhulme Study, again in common with other researches, also highlights the lack of any proper recognition of the gravity of these claims in contemporary curriculum prescriptions. With few exceptions, British curriculum development in the 1980s and 1990s has had scant regard for the situated nature of knowledge, emphasising instead the 'objectivity', value-freeness, universality and reifiability of a decontextu-alised, absolute, subject-bound knowledge: 'curricular fundamentalism' (S. J. Ball, 1993). But analyses of post-millennia needs and opportunities, whether couched in terms of post-Fordism, flexible knowledge workers, high-skill/high-trust work relations or democratic citizenship, all point to the need to exploit the potential of human agency in the generation of new knowledge in response to as yet unforeseen problems. The imperative for curriculum reform is obvious and urgent. But even more pressing is the need to reconceptualise knowledge in British post-16 education in ways that will enable reform to be *thought about*. Those metaphors and discourses which shape coherent systems of thought (House, 1986) around a view of knowl-edge as a context-free (even teacher- and learner-proof), transferable commodity must be rejected as impediments to the advancement of learning in the twenty-first century. In their place must be put alternatives which provide the facility to conceive of knowledge as situated and as heavily reliant upon teachers and learners for its construction and reconstruction. In this regard, observations such as those disclosed by Gibbons *et al.* (1994) in respect of mode 2 knowledge production are timely and telling.

2 *Learning is socially situated; it is a social act*

It is not only the context of learning which is socially situated but both the learners themselves and the processes of their learning. As demonstrated by the Leverhulme data, young people's dispositions to learning are inextricably bound up in the social conditions that are their wider habitus: the condi-tions under which they develop as 'whole persons'. Values, beliefs and dispositions develop within the context of that wider habitus, serving to circumscribe both 'horizons for action' and perceptions of available struc-tural opportunities. But such claims in respect of the social and cultural situation of learners do not signal some crude determinism. While habitus sets boundaries to actions, its effect is that of orienting, not determining (Harker and May, 1993). Habitus and personal development are mutually constitutive.

But processes of learning are situated in an additional sense. Learning opportunities are not simply the points at which dispositions become manifest in action with formulaic predictability; rather, they are the sites on which dispositions, personal identities and learning are mutually transformed in the manner described in the earlier discussion of learning careers. The conditions under which these transformations take place are, in crucial respects, social. As Claxton (1996a and b) has claimed, learning can be seen as occurring on the basis of tacit or intuitive decision making informed by implicit theories of self, knowledge, learning and ability. To be sure, these are enduring theories whose foundations are essentially social. They form part of the biographical context of decision making and are reciprocally linked to learning. But decision making in learning has other contexts, notably social contexts *of the moment* which 'overlap' with biographical contexts and which are also reciprocally linked to learning. 'Immediate contexts of the moment' are objective in the sense that they consist often of teachers and other learners; but they are also, importantly, subjective – they consist of *meanings* which learners attribute to those other witnesses. These are social meanings which are highly susceptible to change from moment to moment and from situation to situation but which, despite this, have significant implications for learners' dispositions to learning opportunities and for their decision making in learning. Changed meanings promote, permit and restrict adaptations in dispositions and decisions while changed dispositions and decisions promote, permit and restrict new meanings.

Meanings, dispositions and decisions may be partly explained biographically but they are also profoundly affected by 'matters of the moment'. Dispositions to learn and to learning are affected in no small measure by learners' perceptions of what others bring to the learning situation. Thus, meanings, dispositions and decisions turn significantly upon matters such as a teacher's demeanour on a given occasion or their tone or vocabulary in some communication. They may turn upon such things as the layout of the room or the structuring of a learning task or plans for its assessment. Equally, they may be affected by the ways in which fellow learners present themselves as, say, collaborative and collegial or as competitive – and there are a good many reasons why such presentations of self might change even over the shortest time scale.

While I do not wish to labour the point here, I should also note that beyond the 'immediate contexts of the moment' are less immediate contexts. These consist of parents, friends and others who, while not present in the immediate context, are every bit as significant in framing and shaping learners' meanings, dispositions and decisions as those who are. Less immediate contexts also consist of those others not yet experienced, 'anticipated others', such as future employers, partners and the like. And they may also consist of projections of selves: 'the person I want to become' or 'the person I imagine I am becoming'. These subjectively constituted selves and others impact as much upon learners' constructions of meaning, their dispositions and decisions as do those which have a more visible objective presence.

The Leverhulme Study has yielded evidence to support claims made here in respect of socially situated learning. Other researches have done likewise although some have contested or sought to qualify such claims, pointing out, for example, that context dependency is affected by the kind of knowledge learned (Anderson *et al.*, 1996). However, most curriculum development in British post-16 education through the 1980s and 1990s has been based upon objectives-led, outcomes-dominated models of learning, assessment and, to tie in with the New Right political agenda, accountability. These models do not admit the complexities of learning as described here. They regard learning as nothing more than an act of transference of some knowledge commodity from expert to novice; effective learning is that which is 'uncontaminated' by social interference. Not only is this particular distortion of reality hopelessly naive, obscuring as it does the essentially social nature of learning, but it effectively denies any opportunity to think about learning in a manner suited to meeting the challenges of the twenty-first century, as described earlier. There must be a radical reconceptualisation of learning as a social act if opportunities for the achievement of high-trust work relations, flexible knowledge workers, independent learners, a learning society or democratic citizenship are to be fulfilled. This must be coupled with a deeper appreciation of the mutual constitution of learning and being.

3 *Learning is a personal act; it is an expression of human agency*

I am certainly not at this juncture seeking to assert the importance of agency over structure or culture, of voluntarism over determinism or subjectivism over objectivism. Rather, my concern is to reiterate a key theme of this chapter, namely to stress the mutually constitutive nature of agency and structure and, for that matter, of the entities of other such dualities. I want to 'balance' my earlier emphasis upon the social conditions and the social character of learning by re-telling aspects of my story of learning from the perspective of the individual or actor.

Anthony Giddens, in his 'Introduction' to *The Constitution of Society*, claims that most schools of contemporary social theory have rejected that orthodoxy which views human behaviour as resulting from forces of which actors are not aware and over which they can exert no control, and have adopted, instead, a view which emphasises the 'active, reflexive character of human conduct'.

> Human agents or actors . . . have, as an inherent aspect of what they do, the capacity to understand what they do while they do it. The reflexive capacities of the human actor are characteristically involved in a continuous manner with the flow of day-to-day conduct in the contexts of social activity. But reflexivity operates on a partly discur-

sive level. What agents know about what they do, and why they do it . . . is largely carried in practical consciousness. Practical consciousness consists of all the things which actors know tacitly about how to 'go on' in the contexts of social life without being able to give them direct discursive expression.

(Giddens, 1984: xxii–xxiii)

Giddens' account of agency resonates strongly with the earlier discussion of the 'immediate (and less immediate) contexts of the moment' in which actors attribute meaning to their experiences. The notion of practical consciousness, as described by Giddens, also, it seems, has much in common with the implicit theories of self, knowledge, learning and ability which inform dispositions, and the intuitive decision making in learning referred to earlier. In so far as human agency embraces all of these notions, it harnesses some of the key concepts in the theoretical framework sketched out here, and does so within a wider understanding of reciprocally linked structure and agency.

Observations such as these are supported in other researches and they have been well borne out by the findings of the Leverhulme Study. The concept of studentship, for instance, is wholly grounded in cases of students 'acting upon' learning opportunities in accordance with a practical consciousness. Studentship is a product of decision making in learning; it is the most visible expression of human agency in learning. Moreover, discussion in the last chapter about the implications which postmodernity holds for the stability of personal identities serves only to underscore claims that opportunities for self-realisation, self-actualisation and such like must be treated as central to the problem of planning for learning. Dispositions, learning and personal identity are inescapably linked. Unfortunately, much recent curriculum development in post-16 education has placed problems of human agency at the periphery of its concerns or disregarded them altogether.

But there is one further reason why human agency must figure prominently in a reconceptualisation of learning. It is not adequate to regard effective learning as that which is unaffected by matters of agency, as though it is something which happens in laboratory-style conditions, independent of human interference. Rather, it is the 'active reflexive character of human conduct' which is the essence of the learning process, not its passive, dependent character. This brings me back, yet again, to future needs and opportunities. In so far as these demand creativity, innovation and collaboration within smaller, flatter hierarchies, with learners/workers continually moving into and out of semi-marginalised or peripheral positions in the economic matrix, emphasis upon independence, reflexivity and human agency in plans for learning for the future is crucially important. In so far as that future will demand the greater political awareness and participation of all, it is essential.

177

Having argued that curriculum development must be harnessed more closely to the potential of human agency, there is a danger that this might be interpreted as the promotion of individualism, as I have remarked already. However, to presume this would be to lose sight of the central importance which an education for democratic and participative citizenship has in any curriculum for learning for the future. Of course, an education for citizenship in the form of a critical, political, economic and moral education will not, in itself, offset the sway of individualism. However, it will bring moral questions back to the fore in everyday deliberations upon education, work and social life, thus contributing to a strengthening of the moral fabric of those local, national and international communities which individualism has done so much to destroy. It is through their controlled but direct exposure to the moral dilemmas of our time that the creative and moral energies of human agency can be harnessed to the common good.

4 Learners' dispositions to learning are visible in their studentship

The concept of disposition is central to understanding the act of learning. As the findings of the Leverhulme Study have demonstrated, fluctuations in dispositions to learning may be affected by a wide variety of considerations. These include meanings which learners attribute to the instrumental value of the knowledge or skill concerned, to the intrinsic rewards of the learning activity entailed, to the audience in front of whom, or in collaboration with whom, the learning is to be carried out, and more. Fluctuations in meanings often do not amount to any permanent or long-term changes in dispositions to learning. What was experienced as an object of anxiety or confusion yesterday may well have become a source of confidence or illumination by today, while today's rudeness, aggression or hurtful criticism may be regarded by tomorrow as good humour, exuberance or honest, helpful critique. Of course, it is not easy to distinguish those fluctuations which have only short-term impact upon dispositions and learning from those which contribute to more profound and lasting change. That is the nature of a learning career: frequent fluctuations and adaptations in context-specific meanings, perceptions and dispositions on a relatively short-term basis take place within the grander scheme of the adaptation of the whole. But whether they are short term or more lasting, changes in dispositions are reciprocally linked to changes in learners' 'horizons for action' and in their perceptions of structural opportunities. There is no simple causality here; dispositions, 'horizons' and perceptions are continually adapting towards some equilibrium of mutual consistency – an equilibrium which, if ever reached, would not necessarily represent a higher or healthier state of mental life.

Changes in meanings, perceptions, 'horizons' and dispositions are also linked to changes in studentship, as has been demonstrated on a number of occasions in reports of the findings of the Leverhulme Study. Examples of studentship to have issued from what appeared to be short-term fluctuations in meanings and dispositions included Pauline's nursery nursing students in Chapter 4, whose energies switched from the contribution of ideas to group discussion to the conscientious recording of 'correct' teacher-dispensed knowledge, apparently because of their teacher's failure to give value to their contributions to discussion. Another case was those students of Henry Stapleton who took to group work in their attempts to demystify A-level chemistry. Of course, I cannot claim with certainty that these adaptations did not somehow contribute to more substantial or lasting change in studentship. It is not possible to establish that, even though there were indications from Pauline's students that their withdrawal from group discussion did not carry forward into subsequent class meetings, and from Henry's students that voluntary group work did not extend into their other studies.

But there were, quite evidently, students whose changes in perceptions, 'horizons' and dispositions were accompanied by more profound changes in their studentship. Matt, referred to in Chapter 6, was an obvious case, as were some of his conformist peers in Bernard Lewis's A-level history group. Cliff, from Keith Delve's engineering group, was another student who, over time, had come to acquire a new disposition to knowledge and learning which, in so far as one can ever be certain about these things, appeared to have resulted in some lasting change in his studentship and, possibly, his learning career.

But it is not only *changes* in dispositions which impact upon studentship. There were many cases of students observed and interviewed in the Leverhulme Study whose dispositions to knowledge and learning remained largely unaltered even in the face of the most challenging conditions. Alice, Russell and Laura in Bernard's history group, for instance, steadfastly refused to partake of the learning opportunities their tutor contrived for them. Their existing dispositions to knowledge and learning were set firmly against any idea of the value of group discussion in the generation or consolidation of course knowledge and proved all-important in the determination, or in their case the confirmation, of their studentship. The same was probably true of Steve in Keith's engineering group and of Sarah from Richard's chemistry group. Indeed, it was not uncommon for tutors to express concern about those students who proved resistant to, or had difficulty in accommodating to, some new appreciation of knowledge and learning.

At the beginning of this chapter, I made brief reference to five modes of individual adaptation or studentship: *conformism, strategic compliance, retreatism, rebellion* and *innovation*. Of course, we should not presume that the categories of the typology represent 'types' of people in any absolute sense – the student who is strategically compliant in certain circumstances may well turn out to be the rebel in others; moreover, students conforming under different conditions may have little in common with each other, at least as far as their dispositions to knowledge and learning are concerned. But the

179

typology does assist the description of individual cases and, in the case of the Leverhulme Study, the illumination of the diversity of students' experiences. Some cases are marked by visible changes in studentship, often attributable to identifiable in-course or out-of-course experiences; others are more clearly marked by a stable and strong sense of studentship which has proved resilient to pressures to change. In most cases, though, studentship is attributable to *both* continually changing *and* relatively stable and enduring perceptions, 'horizons' and dispositions. Studentship can be predictable or erratic, depending upon the relative bearing that new-found and long-standing perceptions, 'horizons' and dispositions have at any one moment upon an individual learning career. It is the outcome of a complex decision making process where decisions are shaped, on the one hand, by enduring personal or tacit theories, values, beliefs and dispositions, and on the other by recently, even temporarily, acquired perceptions, 'horizons' and dispositions.

5   *Through their studentship, learners construct their descriptive curricula, thus delimiting what is actually learned and how it is learned*

This proposition needs little elaboration here. It is fairly self-evident. The processes of studentship are those processes whereby learners 'act upon' learning opportunities made available to them. The findings of the Leverhulme Study have illustrated not only varieties of studentship but, also, how studentship is linked to both the creation and confirmation of personal knowledge and learning careers. Studentship, knowledge and learning careers are mutually constitutive.

6   *Learning and being are mutually constitutive, continually transforming within the context of learning careers*

The Leverhulme Study has provided numerous insights into relationships between, on the one hand, learning within the prescribed context of a formal post-16 education and, on the other, the more general personal growth and development of young people. One thing that is strikingly clear is that the 'outside' world impinges strongly upon young people's learning and *vice versa*. Any separation of 'learning', even learning for expressly utilitarian reasons, from issues of other personal growth and development is an artificial separation. Learning is the process of 'becoming a person'. It is integral to social practice in an historical and generative sense (Lave and Wenger, 1991). It is, therefore, regrettable that so much of the curriculum development to have taken place since the 1980s has had conspicuously little regard for the development of the 'whole person', preferring instead to base its prescriptions upon a commodified, 'objective' and often decontextualised knowledge instead of one grounded in a fuller recognition of the essential unity of all knowledge and of the subjective origins of much practical knowledge.

Some of the complexities of relationships between learning and being or 'becoming a person' have already been described here. While there is a mutual dependence, the relationships are plainly not those of a crude determinism. The most adequate account that I can offer here is that they are mutually transformative, subject to the dynamics of a learning career which has *both* continually changing *and* relatively stable and enduring elements.

7 *'Becoming a person' and the transformation of a learning career are inextricably linked. Both are to be understood as constituents of a partly unpredictable but powerful dialectic between agency and structure. They are not simply the outcomes of prescriptive intervention*

The first and second parts of this proposition have already been argued and illustrated here. The third part points to the limitations of prescriptions in the achievement of change. Structural prescriptions do not effect change in themselves; they have to be interpreted and understood before they will ever bring about change in practice. The problem of interpretations and understandings has already been addressed here in the earlier discussions of meanings, perceptions, 'horizons' and dispositions. The extent to which these impinge upon practice has also been examined in the discussions of decision making and studentship. But what has been most apparent from the Leverhulme data is that the prescribed curriculum has only very limited explanatory power over studentship, learning and learning careers. How absurd, then, that contemporary curriculum planners and policy makers should ignore the importance of human agency in the curriculum–learning equation and persist in the belief that the categories and concepts which they have appropriated for the purposes of communicating their vision of a curriculum are unproblematic, relevant and 'real in their consequences' (Thomas and Thomas, 1928). How inappropriate that the metaphors chosen to communicate information about knowledge and learning have been metaphors of linearity, stability, predictability, exactitude and technical rationality (consider, for example, 'objectives', 'routes', 'trajectories', 'pathways', 'bridges', 'performance indicators' and 'outcomes') when the world they purport to represent is at least as much a world of happenstance, irregularity and uncertainty.

9

TOWARDS A CURRICULUM FOR THE FUTURE

This final chapter pinpoints key areas in which changes must be made in order to facilitate a reconstruction of post-16 education. There are a number of major structural issues, including funding, which I shall note briefly in the first instance. Next, I shall turn to a number of ideological and cultural problems which will need to be addressed if change is to be achieved. I shall also discuss the principal aims, values and organising principles of a curriculum for the future, highlighting as appropriate key summary points.

CLEARING THE DECKS

The massification of further and higher education during the 1990s has compounded problems of a progressively weakening nation state economy. There is no escaping the fact that the exchequer purse is virtually empty and that, in the absence of dramatic economic or political change, there will be little or no money in the twenty-first century to fund the maintenance of the present scale of post-16 education, let alone an enhancement of it. The situation is not helped by the fact that British industry and commerce, unlike those of many other countries, have no strong history of investment in education and training.

In these circumstances, one of two broad strategies could be adopted. The first would entail bolstering public funding of education through taxation. But neither the Conservatives nor the Labour Party have shown the slightest inclination to adopt this approach – only the Liberal Democrats have advocated any move of this type. Such has been the effect of the New Right's promotion of economic de-regulation and individualism throughout the 1980s and 1990s that both major political parties consider increased taxation to be too great a political risk to take. How different to the situation of only one generation earlier where, in a period of greater economic buoyancy, neither of these political groups would have seen fit to question seriously the dependency of education upon the public purse. The political and cultural change that has taken place under the New Right project has been enormous and its legacy is a political hedonism which embraces New Labour every bit as much as it does the Conservatives.

The alternative strategy is to seek funding from private sources. While it is distinctly possible that more could be extracted from commercial sources by compulsory levy, thus bringing Britain more into line with, say, Germany, the impact of such a move upon Britain's economic 'competitiveness' cannot be ignored. In any event, the political will to bring it about is, for the present, non-existent.

This leaves the learner or, in the language of New Right marketism, the customer or consumer. Arrangements for students to borrow funds to cover their further or higher education fees and subsistence and to repay them over an extended period by graduate taxation or some other means are not uncommon in industrialised nations and some such plans may well figure in future British policy. This is a principle which already underpins the higher education student loan system. However, there is no doubt that such measures can prove extremely divisive. An alternative style of proposal which has been linked to provision of opportunities for lifelong learning is for Individual Learning Accounts (Labour Party, 1996) which would be built up through some combination of government, employer and learner contributions, and it seems likely that the future funding of British post-16 education will be met, at least in part, by some such arrangement. However, while Individual Learning Accounts might reduce the iniquities of a student loans system they would, in the absence of appropriate safeguards, carry with them all the considerable drawbacks of consumer-led education.

But however the problem is addressed there should be no mistaking its importance: British investment in education and training at the present time is extremely low and some substantial upturn in that investment must be made before the effects of any revised post-16 curriculum can be fully realised.

> After two years of inquiry and detailed assessment of the present position of education and training in the UK, we are wholly satisfied that, if our vision is to be realised, additional spending from both public and private sources is essential.
>
> (National Commission on Education, 1993: 388)

A second practical problem arises from the proliferation of quangos in the 1980s and 1990s. While lack of democratic accountability must always be a major source of concern regarding such bodies, those which were established under the regime of the New Right are distinguished also by their minimal provision for professional representation. Bodies such as the Further and Higher Education Funding Councils, Training and Enterprise Councils, the Office for Standards in Education and the Qualifications and National Curriculum Authority and its predecessors have all been constituted in this way. But post-compulsory education and training are central to the maintenance of the social fabric and to the stability and future growth of the economy and, for this reason, it is too great a risk to leave their management and control to doctrinaire quangos. The management of education must be democratically and professionally accountable.

A third major practical obstruction to the future development of post-16 and, for that matter, any other education is the technical rational structuring of public education consolidated during the 1980s and 1990s. The development of such structures has been essentially for the purposes of accountability and control and has been part of a larger project of the deprofessionalisation of educators. But an equally serious concern, here, is that the structures to which I am referring are obstructing the very advances which, I have argued in earlier chapters, are essential if key problems concerning social and economic stability are to be confronted.

National Vocational Qualifications, for instance, impose a highly reductivist conception of knowledge upon learning and assessment. They fragment knowledge and, in so far as assessments for NVQs focus upon discrete elements, they serve to heighten the significance of fragments over wholes. This does not assist the integration of knowledge but serves only to reinforce its discreteness and boundedness. Moreover, NVQs focus very tightly upon the most readily observable and measurable: the behavioural 'outcomes' of learning. Lost altogether are those other less tangible but nonetheless crucially important qualities that are to do with originality, creativity, confidence, self-reliance, political and moral awareness, ethical conduct, collaborative learning and work, and such like. While these latter qualities may prove to be no great loss in a curriculum for Fordism or neo-Fordism, although that would be an extremely narrow view to adopt, their exclusion from the education and training of a large proportion of the post-16 age group will seriously undermine Britain's chances of exploiting such opportunities as may exist under any post-Fordist project of the twenty-first century. Of course, it is not only NVQs which constrain learning in the way I have described. GNVQ assessment practices have a similar effect (Bloomer and Hodkinson, 1996) while the technical reductivism which treats knowledge as a commodity is also apparent in the assessment practices which operate under the schools' National Curriculum.

A very different example of technical rational structuring which impinges adversely upon young people and their learning careers concerns the basic structure of the post-16 curriculum and also the guidance and advice services which have grown up around it. I have already remarked in Chapter 2 that notions of 'academic' and 'vocational' tracks, of pathways, bridges, trajectories and such like do not correspond with the natural 'unfoldment' of young people's learning careers. As I noted at the end of Chapter 8, it is ironic that the metaphors of predictability and stability are used to represent a world which is essentially irregular and uncertain – at least when experienced from the point of view of students. If Britain is to develop its provision of post-compulsory education and training in such ways as will enable the intellectual, practical and other energies of young people to be tapped to the full, a far more responsive and flexible system than that operating at present will be necessary. To achieve such responsivity and flexibility will not only entail the dismantling of structures such as I have described here but, equally importantly, a shift away from the technical rational thought systems which have given rise to them.

IDEOLOGICAL AND CULTURAL CHANGE

There are many forms of ideological and cultural change which might be considered to be in the interests of promoting economic and social wellbeing in the twenty-first century. A number of these have been touched upon already in the course of this book. However, there are just two aspects of the problem of change that I wish to highlight in this instance.

The first concerns what I have described elsewhere (Avis *et al.*, 1996: 164–166) as a 'culture of answerism'. It refers to the conditions under which the decision making of successive UK governments in recent years has come to be driven more by the pursuit of short-term political kudos than by any penetrating or critical appraisal of the problems in question. Policy making has come to be propelled by the felt need of politicians to produce not informed, reasoned and carefully articulated responses to problems but 'answers' that, purely and simply, are acceptable to an electorate. The fact that a lay public might apply criteria grounded in reconstructions of their own school days when assessing the merits of a contemporary policy proposal is not considered a cause for concern. There can be little wonder, then, that so many recent 'solutions' to the problems of today have the distinct flavour of yesterday's answers. The refusal to reform A-levels, the failure to address the problem of the academic–vocational divide by anything more imaginative than subject or occupationally focused, modular-based cores and options, and the persistence of tri-partitism in the form of 'academic', 'vocational' and 'occupational' pathways are clear illustrations of the incapability of governments to plan *ahead*. The sad truth is that informed, long-term, forward planning offers no short-term political gain. Turning out answers which appeal to people's recollections of some mythical golden age, it seems, does!

But the political practices I have described here have not evolved at this time simply in response to some heightening of self-interest among politicians. They are the product of 'ideological filtering' (Keep, 1991) and are linked strongly to the free market, consumerist philosophy of the New Right – a philosophy also evident in the policies of New Labour. Major changes in this state of affairs must be brought about if Britain is to take proper control of its own destiny. The emerging culture in which the capacity to produce 'answers' counts for everything and the capacity to address questions counts for nothing must be contested. Commitments to free market practices will have to be reversed and governments made to accept their responsibilities for the common good. Abdication of those responsibilities to the free market is not a responsible act of government – any government. It is only the electorate which can make governments face up to their full responsibilities but electoral pressure is likely to emerge only after a systematic dismantling of the free market thought systems which operate at present. This does not sound promising. Probably, the only plausible way of breaking into the present circle of mutually reinforcing public individualism and governmental marketism is through educationally assisted ideological and cultural change. I shall return to this point in the discussion of the curriculum for the future which follows.

The second issue that I wish to highlight here in connection with the problem of ideological and cultural change concerns change *processes*. Again, this entails a critique of the technical rationalism which has come to dominate contemporary thinking and planning and of the structuralist analyses in which it is embedded.

A very large proportion of the energy and finance which has been devoted to educational development and change throughout the 1980s and 1990s, in particular, has been channelled into changes in the objective structures of educational provision. The National Curriculum has come to absorb (or nullify) almost entirely the creative capacities of teachers in primary and secondary education. Bodies like the Schools Council have closed while others such as the Qualifications and National Curriculum Authority, dedicated to the production of all-encompassing and all-binding structures, have been established. FE sector institutions have become incorporated (1993) while national funding councils have been set up in order to regulate their affairs. All of these examples, and more, have been based squarely upon the assumption that change is effected simply through the external structuring of educational experience. They have been based upon a technical rationalism which does not merely discount the idea of a mutually constitutive structure and agency; it disregards agency altogether. Even the dogma and rhetoric which have accompanied recent attempts to change educational practice have been a dogma and rhetoric of structured externality with due emphasis upon concepts such as 'standards', management, formula funding and heavily prescribed course content. Seldom has there been any overt recognition of the importance of the subjective component of educational experience, of agency.

It is, however, as the Leverhulme Study has demonstrated, subjective experience and action which is all-important in the process. Teachers and students do not merely receive and 'act out' externally imposed prescriptions of their tasks, they 'act upon' those prescriptions in the construction of their own practices. They are *actors*, acting in accordance with their own understandings and constructions and it is precisely for this reason that programmes for change, if they are to have effect, must be directed to those understandings and constructions.

> But to provide individuals with new concepts is not simply to offer them a new way of thinking. It is also to offer them the possibility of becoming more self-conscious about the basic pattern of thought in terms of which they usually make their own actions intelligible. . . . Practices are changed by changing the ways in which they are understood.
>
> (Carr and Kemmis, 1986: 91)

To be sure, there are structural alterations which might be made and which could assist the achievement of the kinds of change alluded to here – I am thinking, for example, of such things as a reduction in 'content' and 'outcomes' dominated curricula and the more explicit and widespread participation of teachers in curriculum planning. However, these must be accompanied by a substantial shift away from the technical rational thought systems which have promoted dependency upon external structuring: 'coherent curriculum experiences result not from deterministic models of rationality, but from a naturalistic approach that focuses on the deliberative solution of practical problems' (Holt, 1996: 241). Again, educationally assisted ideological and cultural change is called for.

AIMS, VALUES AND ORGANISING PRINCIPLES FOR A CURRICULUM FOR THE FUTURE

In this penultimate section I have set out what, on the basis of the Leverhulme Study and the examination of that wider set of concerns reported in Chapters 7 and 8, I believe are the major issues to be addressed in the reform of British post-16 education for the twenty-first century. The discussions here are brief – more detailed considerations having been incorporated into earlier chapters – and each discussion point concludes with a clear and unambiguous proposition.

In the first instance, under the heading of 'New Orientations', I have identified a number of matters which require changes in the ways in which they are thought about. Second, I have focused on the 'Practicalities of Providing for Learning'.

New orientations

Curriculum in practice

There has, during the 1980s and 1990s been a progressive narrowing of the concept of curriculum. In policy, planning and, to some extent, practitioner circles it has come to mean little more than a prescription of 'content' coupled with a series of checks for its successful implementation. 'Objectives', 'outcomes' and 'quality assurance' now cover all, while 'delivery' is the metaphor to describe the process. But this book has raised two major criticisms of this view of curriculum: first, it seriously restricts opportunities to think about and plan for educational development in the way that many analyses of the opportunities and needs of the twenty-first century suggest is necessary; second, as the Leverhulme Study has demonstrated, it bears little relation to what actually happens in practice.

We have seen in earlier chapters how teachers and students 'act upon' curriculum prescriptions in the creation of their various *de*scriptive curricula and how curriculum making is, in the final analysis, a heuristic process heavily dependent upon the participation of those who it is intended will be affected by it. Curriculum 'invites critical testing rather than acceptance' (Stenhouse, 1975: 142). Thus, the practitioner's first task is that of

> interpreting the 'curriculum' as text. . . . [But] an interpretive view of textual analysis would deny the authority of the document to impose its own meaning. Such a view implies that the practitioner has not only the right, but also the obligation, to make his/her own meaning of the text. . . . If practitioners take seriously their obligations to regard the interpretation of curriculum texts as a practical action, that is, as one which engages their judgment, they will also take seriously the status of the students as learning subjects, not objects in the curriculum event. . . . Moreover, learning will involve, not the production of certain artefacts . . . but the making of meaning.
>
> (Grundy, 1987: 69)

Such claims and observations about knowledge, learning and curriculum accord strongly with those that have been presented in my earlier discussions of the social conditions of learning, situated knowledge and learning, and of future needs for a collaborative, creative, independent and critical citizenry and work force.

While the points raised so far have numerous implications for a curriculum for the twenty-first century, it is apparent, above all, that curriculum development can no longer proceed on the assumption that prescriptions count for all and that teachers and students are little more than technicians and consumers in the process; rather, curricula must be planned in full recognition of the essential contributions which teachers and students make to their final constructions. They must be planned *around* those contributions.

Knowledge and skills

I have already made detailed observations and claims concerning future educational, economic and social needs and opportunities. In short, these will require citizens and workers able to work both independently and collaboratively in the construction of innovative and creative responses to novel problems, often on the basis of a confident and articulate synthesis of knowledge and skills of different forms and drawn from many different sources. The Leverhulme Study has also offered a number of illustrations of the capabilities of post-16 students for thinking, learning and working in this way, sometimes in spite of the curricula prescribed or the learning opportunities selected for them.

There is much to suggest that the present post-16 curriculum is limited in its capacity to meet the full requirements of a curriculum for the twenty-first century such as I have identified. I have already demonstrated in Chapter 3 and elsewhere the high premium that A-levels attach to the re-circulation of second-hand knowledge and to an uncritical mastery of rules and conventions. While the BTEC National courses described earlier offered some promise of transdisciplinary, problem-centred and person-centred course knowledge, the fulfilment of that promise was patchy, resting as it did both upon the idiosyncrasies of vocational areas and how teachers and students 'acted upon' the syllabuses and learning opportunities presented to them. But BTEC Nationals have been largely replaced by Advanced GNVQ courses which, it appears, in some crucial respects, have dampened the hopes which BTECs, for a time, inspired (Bloomer and Hodkinson, 1996). The GNVQ structure is strictly unitised and does not make for the easy integration of knowledge across unit boundaries; practices are more standardised than under BTEC while the whole is subjected to an assessment regime which is partly driven by the NCVQ behaviourist-inspired notion of competence and largely directed to ensuring uniformity of outcome. Dare I mention NVQs at this juncture?

> Instead of a holistic framework, CBET [competence-based education and training] atomizes and fragments learning into measurable chunks; rather than valuing process and experience, NVQs are concerned only with performance outcomes; and, most importantly, instead of encouraging critical reflection on alternative perspectives, the NCVQ model offers a monocultural view based on the satisfaction of narrow performance criteria and directed towards fixed and predetermined ends.
>
> (Hyland, 1994a: 54)

The NCVQ model of knowledge and competence is entirely compatible with other technicist and reductivist notions such as 'transferable skills'. These concepts serve not merely to over-simplify and trivialise problems of knowledge but to distort them; they are the tools by which the whole debate about knowledge and learning is rendered manipulable by those who persist only in the technical interest (Habermas, 1972). 'Transferability' is a highly contestable concept when applied to skills (Oates, 1996); it implies an unproblematic 'sideways shift' of knowledge from one context to the next as distinct from any process of knowledge deconstruction and reconstruction with regard to the particular opportunities afforded within the new context. It takes little or no account of knowledge context – the situated nature of knowledge – which, in both the Leverhulme Study and elsewhere, has been deemed fundamentally important in accounting for learning.

There is much of the existing post-16 curriculum and the thought systems which sustain it which must be dismantled before plans for education and training for the twenty-first century can be properly laid. On the particular subject of knowledge and skills, increased emphasis must be placed upon the essential unity and situatedness of all knowledge, traditional demarcations between 'the theoretical' and 'the practical' must be challenged and the mutually constitutive nature of theory and practice be drawn into the central focus of educational inquiry. Notions of knowledge and skills as fragmented, commodified entities must be swiftly dispatched and replaced by others which accord status to the personal and social construction of knowledge and skill and to implicit, non-articulable, reflexive or tacit knowledge and 'practical consciousness'.

Learning and knowledge production

The Leverhulme Study has illustrated the significance of the social conditions of learning – of situated learning as described by Lave and Wenger (1991) – in the generation of knowledge. At least it has been shown that the concept of 'situated learning' more adequately reflects students' personal experiences of learning than do those sanitised, culture-free notions of learning with their footholds in behaviourism. And yet, it is that latter view of learning, with its emphasis upon the supremacy of abstracted theoretical knowledge over practical knowledge which predominates still both in the public imagination and in politically driven educational policy making and planning. The implicit assumption of those curriculum developments which have sought to reduce opportunities for learners to experiment in the process of learning or to base their learning in *real* problem-solving activities or project work (and there have been many such reductions, often for the reason that assessments can be made more reliable and comparable in the interests of accountability) is that learning takes place in a vacuum rather than in a complex social milieu.

> The learning milieu represents a network or nexus of cultural, social, institutional, and psychological variables. These interact in complicated ways to produce, in each class or course, a unique pattern of circumstances, pressures, customs, opinions, and work styles which suffuse the teaching and learning which occur there.
>
> (Parlett and Hamilton, 1987: 62)

Indeed, it is the re-configuring of the learning milieu which takes place from moment to moment and place to place which provides an important platform for creativity, whether conceived as an individual or group phenomenon. It is also not difficult to see the relevance for the flexible, responsive and flatter work (and social) heterarchies of the future, of a learning environment in which learners assume responsibility for the *configuration* of knowledge resources, rather than for elements of somebody else's configuration.

There must be a shift from reductivist conceptualisations of learning which attach primary importance to cognitive processes and other intrapersonal categories, towards alternatives which emphasise the *inter*personal and social conditions of knowledge production and, above all, the mutually constitutive nature of learning and being.

The person learner

Both the findings of the Leverhulme Study and the rich variety of new literature on knowledge and learning referred to in Chapter 8 endorse the claim that learning is crucially dependent upon learner agency and is not, simply, an 'outcome' of prescription. Prescriptions alone do not effect change. Moreover, those research findings and literatures also offer insights into ways in which the heavily prescriptive curricula of contemporary post-16 education may dampen the creative energies which human agency brings to bear. They also argue that the positive incorporation of human agency in curriculum development and practice is necessary for the achievement of a greater creativity, innovation, independence, collaboration and critical reflexivity in learning – those same qualities which analyses of future economic and social needs suggest are most urgently required.

It has also been shown here, and amply demonstrated elsewhere, that learners, like learning, do not exist in a vacuum. Learners are actively and often profitably engaged in learning outside their formally prescribed learning settings and curricula and those experiences can and often do impact upon studentship and learning careers, positively or negatively. The simple fact is that being a person and being a learner are essentially the same thing; they are both 'being'. Much of Chapter 7 was devoted to describing the interdependency of learning, dispositions, habitus, personal identity and perceptions within the context of learning careers and it is recognition of these claims which needs to be carried forward into new thinking about the post-16 curriculum.

The detailed implications of these claims will have to be examined at some later stage. However, before questions of detail can be addressed at all, it will be necessary to effect significant changes in the ways in which these matters are understood and acted upon.

There must be a rejection of those conceptions of learning which, explicitly or implicitly, attach greatest importance to the prescription of content and 'outcomes' and least importance to learner agency in the process of learning. Greater recognition must now be given to the interdependency of learning and context and to the mutually constitutive nature of learning and being and of structure and agency. To support these essential changes in perspective, a dynamic theory of learning in post-16 education which gives full regard to the significance of studentship and, most importantly, learning careers, is crucial.

About 'teaching'

It is timely to consider the implications which the foregoing claims about learners, learning and curriculum hold for long-standing and dominant conceptions of teaching. In my view, there are four broad requirements which are very strongly implied. The first implication is that teachers must assume a new authority, or renew their authority, in the construction of curricula. By and large, they have rarely succumbed to pressures to become passive recipients of externally imposed prescriptions but have 'acted upon' such prescriptions, often on the basis of their tacit, moral or professional understanding. As David Yeomans put it at the 1996 conference of the British Educational Research Association, 'Despite all the planning and prescription, TVEI still had to be invented by teachers'. That understanding, invention and 'acting upon' must now be properly recognised as a legitimate and essential part of curriculum making.

Second, the teaching act must be defined in terms consistent with the kinds of learning activity described above. This will entail a rejection of teaching as grounded essentially in a mastery of specialist subject knowledge. New definitions of teacher expertise and professionalism will focus much more tightly upon the knowledge, understanding and skills that are required to assist learners in finding and utilising their own new knowledge across subject boundaries and across the theoretical–practical divide. Teaching must be much more to do with creating the conditions under which knowledge can be generated than with 'delivering' the knowledge itself. I should, of course, note here that there have been significant attempts to define teaching in this way in recent years (e.g. the philosophy of BTEC, some TVEI ventures and even certain proposals to revise A-level). However, I should also note that such developments had become seriously curtailed by the 1990s.

Third, a radical redefinition of teacher–learner relationships must be achieved. This will need to reflect the collaborative nature of the 'new learning', the *making* of curricula and knowledge generation. It may even reflect, as some (Young, 1993; Brown and Scase, 1994) have suggested it should, the flatter heterarchical working relationships of a post-Fordist economy.

The fourth and final requirement is that educational policy makers and planners be reminded that education is not concerned simply with what goes on in classrooms – although that should clearly have an important bearing upon education. Education is located within the much broader economic, political, social and moral contexts referred to above, and must be recognised as such. Bodies such as the Teacher Training Agency, the Office for Standards in Education and others seeking criteria by which to describe teaching must abandon the classroom-focused technicism that is their current preoccupation and pursue, instead, a professional model of teaching such as is implied by the first three requirements described here.

Future conceptions of the authority of teachers must not rest upon their status as knowledge holders (or, for that matter, as crowd controllers) whose whole task is understood in terms of their observable classroom behaviour. They must rest instead upon teachers' knowledge, skills and understanding in the support of learners in knowledge generation in collaborative, heterarchical relationships in and beyond the classroom.

Assessment

Following directly from the above claims are important questions about the ways in which we regard the nature and purposes of assessment. Until now, the dominant purposes of assessment in post-16 education have been for the selection and allocation of students and for accountability, with increasing emphasis, of late, upon the latter. This has served to limit the types of assessment practices which have been developed and deployed. The emphasis upon so-called 'objective' testing, the pursuit of reliability and the search for comparability has increased considerably, as the practices accompanying the changes from BTEC National to GNVQ Advanced courses and the moratoria on the use of assessed course work in A-levels amply illustrate. The upshot is that assessment practices are distinctly 'product' or 'outcome' focused, not 'process' focused.

Current assessment practices lay great stress upon the virtues of memorisation, the presentation of abstracted second-hand knowledge and the rehearsal and application of given procedures; they do not provide for genuine experimentation and the type of risk taking activity requisite for new knowledge generation. Moreover, in so far as they focus upon individual mastery of universal knowledge – and some courses, it must be said, do exclusively this – the situatedness of knowledge and learning and the values of collaborative knowledge production are effectively denied.

Assessment arrangements are crucially important in shaping teachers' and learners' dispositions to knowledge and learning. The Leverhulme Study has afforded some insights into this, although the observation is by no means new. On the subject of primary education: 'the curriculum is too often cramped and distorted by over-emphasis on examination subjects and on

193

ways and means of defeating the examiners. The blame for this rests not with the teachers but with the system' (Board of Education, 1943b: 6).

Similarly, on secondary education:

the examination dictates the curriculum and cannot do otherwise; it confines experiment, limits free choice of subject, hampers treatment of subjects, encourages wrong values in the class-room. Pupils assess education in terms of success in the examination; they minimise the importance of the non-examinable and assign a utilitarian value to what they study. They absorb what it will pay them to absorb, and reproduce it as second-hand knowledge which is of value only for the moment. Teachers, recognising the importance of the parchment to the individual child, are constrained to direct their teaching to an examination which can test only a narrow field of the pupil's interest and capacities, and so necessarily neglect the qualities which they value most highly; they are forced to attend to what can be examined and to spoon-feed their weakest pupils. Originality is replaced by uniformity.

(Board of Education, 1943a: 31)

Of course, claims that examinations stifle opportunities for creativity and knowledge generation should not be taken to suggest that all assessments have this effect. Where the purposes of assessment are formative – integral, rather than an appendage, to learning – assessments can enhance opportunities for learning, particularly if they are revealing of the intrinsic qualities of the learner and their learning. Various records of achievement, profiles and diagnostic tests have been designed expressly for this purpose – to enable learners and their teachers to gain deeper insights into the progress and achievements concerned, in order that they can take more informed action. Indeed, it is this principle which underpins much of the crucially important, yet frequently discounted, informal assessment which is carried out by both learners and teachers within and throughout the routines of learning. However, assessments designed for such 'educational' purposes, if I might call them that, must be clearly distinguished from those whose function is external, essentially political. The benefits of the former will never be realised where they are confused with the latter.

The purposes of assessment must be clearly distinguished and, although it will be extremely difficult to achieve, assessments for purposes of selection, allocation and accountability must not be allowed to determine the nature of assessment for learning. Rather, assessments designed expressly for the purposes of assisting learning should provide the means by which any other purposes of assessment are fulfilled. Specifically, and most important of all, the scope of educational assessment must be widened to include far greater attention to 'process' (as distinct from 'outcome') and to other less readily measurable qualities of learning and attainment.

Practicalities of providing for learning

In the following section, I have set out what I consider to be the foundation principles of a curriculum for the twenty-first century.

The multiple purposes of post-16 education

The various purposes attributed to post-16 education over recent years have already received some consideration in Chapter 2. The Leverhulme Study has afforded further insight into these, at least in as much as they are visible in the various expectations, dispositions and behaviours which students exhibit in the course of their learning. There can be no doubt that there is still a strong and persistent tension between those declared purposes which stress the utilitarian benefits of education or training, and those which assert the greater importance of a 'general', often called 'academic', or even 'liberal' education. The academic–vocational divide is a partial reflection of this historically, culturally and institutionally reproduced phenomenon – a phenomenon which Dearing's (SCAA, 1996) report, with its advocacy of three tracks, would serve to reinforce if incorporated into policy.

Of course, the more I persist with this discussion, the more I risk reinforcing one of the all too frequently occurring weaknesses in contemporary thinking: the creation of dualisms. The simple fact, as analyses of future economic and social needs have shown repeatedly, is that *both* of the major purposes I have described should be applied to *all* post-16 education (and, for that matter, all pre-16 education). We need to look beyond dualisms to dualities of purpose to discover ways in which hitherto contradictory purposes might be reconciled into single and coherent statements of purpose.

There has, as yet, been only one serious attempt[1] to confront the practical implications of this question in any wholesale form:

> While most current policy proposals take as given the separation of academic from other studies, we take the abolition of this separation as the starting point for reform. The interests of a fairer society and the demands of a modern economy both point to the need for a more unified and inclusive system of education and training. . . . No amount of tinkering – for instance with 'core skills' embedded in separate vocational and academic qualifications – will overcome the problems posed by the division itself.
>
> (Finegold *et al.*, 1990: 4–5)

Finegold and his colleagues moved on, of course, to propose 'A British Baccalauréat', the like of which must be entertained seriously if the necessary transformation in British post-16 education is ever to be achieved.

Post-16 education of the future must foster independence of judgement, collaborative knowledge generation, creativity, innovation and adaptability on the basis of an integration of knowledge and experience drawn from across all boundaries. While new specialisms are to be encouraged, these should be located securely within the provision of a strong and robust general education. The variety of interests within education and training must, of course, be properly entertained. No single interest can be allowed to dominate and, most certainly, that narrow utilitarian view expressed from time to time on behalf of employers and through the consumerist policies of the New Right must be guarded against with extreme caution.

The selection of knowledge and skills

There are two sets of criteria by which course content might be selected and evaluated. The first concerns the relevance of knowledge and skills to the needs and interests of the individual learner; the second concerns their relevance to the economy and society of the future. But both sets of criteria are hugely problematic. The extent to which any provision meets the first set depends upon who defines 'needs' and 'interests'. In any event, it will vary considerably from one learner to the next. The extent to which it meets the second set of criteria turns on definitions of relevance, and also upon the future economy and society envisaged.

Notwithstanding these observations, I should like to make four proposals which, taken together, should enable the criteria broadly described above to be met. The proposals are for four compulsory components of all post-16 curricula. The first is not in the least novel and concerns 'basic' knowledge and skills. It would seek to ensure a minimal level of competence among all young people in communication (via the media of host language, foreign language, mathematics and new technologies) and in the generation, retrieval and utilisation of knowledge.

The second is more complex and would consist of (a) a general education, and (b) opportunities for some specialisation, both achieved through (c) the proper integration of knowledge from different sources and, particularly, theoretical and practical knowledge. The general education I have in mind in (a) extends well beyond those envisaged by the National Commission on Education (1993) or by Dearing (SCAA, 1996); it is not simply the study of a string of compulsory 'subjects' spanning the 'breadth' of available knowledge. Rather, it would take the form of a liberal education to promote a wide range of 'ways of experiencing' everyday as well as less commonplace phenomena. 'Some specialisation' would not entail the abandonment of *any* field or type of study; nor would it be achieved only through progressive focusing on subject knowledge. Specialisms would be just as likely to focus upon given 'problems' or processes, necessitating the harnessing of knowledge and skills from a variety of different fields and sources. However they are achieved, the general education and new specialisation that I refer to here

196

must contribute to the continued development of personal understanding or 'knowing'.

> To have knowledge requires understanding and understanding often requires in turn a grasp of the interconnections that relate one part of the picture to another. . . . This is, of course, a difficult matter to be clear about. But at least it means this – that the exposure to particular facts or to particular statements or to a selection from the data can so easily distort an understanding of what then is made public, for it removes that which is to be known from the context in which it must be understood or from the process to which it is logically related as product.
>
> (Pring, 1987: 286)

The third element that I have in mind links directly with the first and second: it concerns both the development of basic skills and the enhancement of a general education. The Leverhulme Study has amply demonstrated the power of human agency in the learning process. It has provided evidence of the resourcefulness and creativity which considerable numbers of young people displayed in their studentship. At the same time, it has shown examples of learners unable to maximise their opportunities for learning, often because of a basic lack of knowledge and understanding about how to confront the problems they faced. The study has also shown that many young people, though by no means all, became newly disposed to knowledge and learning as they were socialised into the new routines of their post-16 courses. It also cast light on a number of students who seemed equally positively disposed to a variety of forms of knowledge and opportunities for learning and who, it appeared, proved the most effective learners of all.

These observations are all indicative of a considerable potential for the further development of young people's command over their own learning capabilities. They point, specifically, to a curriculum for the future in which the problems of knowledge and learning will be made explicit focuses of study, in which learners will participate in the critical examination of their own learning dispositions and capabilities, and in which all will be encouraged towards the perfection of the most extensive repertoire of learning skills.

My fourth compulsory element concerns education for responsible citizenship. In my discussions of the interdependency of economic and social stability in Chapter 8, I have argued for an economic, political and moral education that will give proper meaning to the term, 'education for citizenship'. Underpinning this call are my deeply held personal convictions that a lively, informed, participating and critical citizenry, living and working within a secure democratic framework, is the most viable recipe for economic and social stability and regeneration, and that the present formula for social participation, which rests solely upon the licensing of individualism within a free market, is part of the recipe for the social polarisation which Hutton describes in *The State We're In* (1996).

> curricula which do not face the need to open up knowledge to the pupils are often the staple of an education designed for the underprivileged and reinforcing their exclusion from the education and knowledge most valued and most valuable.
>
> (Stenhouse, 1975: 19–20)

Education for citizenship must, therefore, promote the critical engagement of all learners with the social, economic, political and moral worlds they inhabit, and foster their autonomy within, and control over, those worlds – as persons and as learners.

While I have described my four compulsory elements separately, this should not be taken to suggest that they would best be addressed separately in the course of curriculum development and implementation. There are compelling reasons why the four elements should be integrated as fully as possible and, providing the changes in thinking and practice described earlier are effected, there would be relatively few practical obstructions. However, it will be important to establish suitable aims and principles for the integration of these elements in a post-16 curriculum and to resist the distractions of the technicist pursuit of content mapping.

The knowledge and skills made available to students through the post-16 curriculum must, for each individual student, offer the promise of *both* intrinsic and extrinsic reward. A consequence of this is that there can be no uniformity of curriculum content, only uniformity of aims, principles and curriculum structure. Each student will contribute to *making* their own post-16 curriculum, thus providing for the accommodation of individual studentship and learning careers. It is the knowledge, skills and attitudes acquired through this process which are the necessary foundations for 'lifelong learning' and a 'learning society'.

The post-16 curriculum must include education and training in basic skills, a general education, some specialisation and an education for citizenship for *all* students. Perhaps of paramount importance, it must require that students are able to study the problems of knowledge and learning and to examine and perfect their own capabilities as learners. These elements must be fully integrated and organised in such ways as to promote the critical engagement of all learners with the world they inhabit. The curriculum aims must have in mind *both* the present personal interests of individuals *and* their prospective social and economic interests, in so far as it is possible to identify these in advance, and they must do so for *every single learner*. The curriculum must also equip learners for lifelong learning. This will entail a radical restructuring of post-16 educational provision and will not be achieved by tinkering with existing routes, pathways and trajectories.

The organisation of knowledge

The concept, 'flexible specialisation' was introduced by Piore and Sabel in the context of economic production to refer to, 'a strategy of permanent innovation: accommodation to ceaseless change, rather than an effort to control it' (1984: 17). They argue that the legacy of stark divisions of labour promoted under mass productive economies seriously restricts opportunities for adaptation to new economic opportunities and requirements. Specifically, the models which dominate Britain's present industrial, commercial and service practices rest not only upon the fragmentation of specialist subject or occupational knowledge, but upon the separation of design, production and evaluation processes and, often, of mental and manual labour. Piore and Sabel stress the need for labour to possess a broader base of more integrated knowledge as the means of ensuring the responsivity and adaptability required of industries of the future.

Michael Young (1993) has weighed the concept of 'flexible specialisation' against contemporary educational policy and curriculum. On the one hand, he observes a strong correspondence between the 'divisive specialisation' of the mass productive economy, the 'academic–vocational divide' and the strong classification (Bernstein, 1971) of subjects of the curriculum. On the other, he argues for a post-16 curriculum better suited to supporting young people in their preparations for meeting the challenges of new economic opportunities and requirements.

The case which Young argues for his 'Curriculum for the 21st Century' is directly relevant to the problem of knowledge organisation being addressed here. It is also well supported by some of the claims stemming from the Leverhulme research and is consistent with points made in Chapter 8 in the discussions of 'a curriculum for the future'. We should do well at this juncture to dwell a little longer on Young's treatment of the curriculum problem.

He claims that those new forces of production based around flexible specialisation will require a congruent curriculum. Principally, this will entail an end to demarcations rooted in the 'academic–vocational divide' or in subject specialisms. However, this is not to imply a curriculum without order, structure or even internal boundaries. In Young's proposal, coherence would be achieved through,

> new and innovative kinds of connectiveness between knowledge areas and different forms of specialised study interwoven with a generic core of knowledge, skills and processes . . . change is not away from specialisation, but towards new forms that can (at least in principle) free specialisation from its association with selection and insulation. *The separation of specialisation from its association with divisions and the insulation of subject areas is the key basis for distinguishing between a divided curriculum or 'curriculum of the past' and a 'curriculum for the future'.*
>
> (Young, 1993: 213 and 214, original emphasis)

Young argues that the reasons for the dominance of 'divisive specialisation' in the curriculum lie not in the inherent nature of knowledge or in the inevitable behaviour of practitioners. Rather, they lie in the historical insulation of communities of practitioners. Thus, it is amenable to change.

Young employs the term, 'connective specialisation' when describing his curriculum vision. It stresses the interdependency of specialisms, however these specialisms are conceived (cognitively, practically, technically, affectively or in other ways) and of all participants sharing

> an overall sense of the relationship between their specialisation and the whole curriculum. . . . At the individual level it refers to the need for an understanding of the social, cultural, political and economic implications of any knowledge or skill in its context, and how, through such a concept of education, an individual can learn both specific skills and knowledge and the capacity to take initiatives, whatever their specific occupation or position.
>
> (ibid.: 218)

This view of the organisation of knowledge lies at the heart of the IPPR proposal for a British Baccalauréat (Finegold et al., 1990) – a project in which Young played a key part. Given the observations arising from the Leverhulme Study and also from the various appraisals of future economic and social needs such as I have identified here, it must be apparent that the British Baccalauréat was the most far-sighted and comprehensive proposal for post-16 education of its time.

But Young's analyses also resonate strongly with claims originating from quite different concerns, a number of which I have reviewed in Chapter 8. In so far as the notion of 'collective specialisation' implies the situatedness of knowledge and learning while attaching importance to the social, cultural, political and economic contexts of knowledge and learning, it harmonises strongly with the claims of Brown et al. (1989), Lave and Wenger (1991) and even Vygotsky (1978) discussed earlier. But 'collective specialisation' also attaches great importance to the removal of subject or disciplinary demarcations and, as such, implies a *transdisciplinarity*. Given this, and the stress placed upon the context of knowledge and learning, Young's claims would also appear to have a great deal in common with those made by Gibbons et al. (1994) in connection with mode 2 knowledge production.

Notions such as 'collective specialisation', mode 2 knowledge production and situated knowledge and learning are crucially important to our capacity to think about and respond to the challenges of the future. But they alone will not provide the blue-print for the organisation of knowledge. There are other principles which need to be incorporated into the new scheme, not least those which will provide guidance for the achievement of 'collective specialisation' and 'transdisciplinarity'. Most importantly, we must grasp the nettle of student choice. The policies and culture of free marketism and voluntarism have created considerable pressures for students to be granted the right to exercise choice over the content and organisation of their studies. At best, this has resulted in direct student participation in the creation of curricula suited both to their personal needs and interests and to the wider social and economic needs sketched out earlier, possibly resulting in students' deeper understanding of themselves as learners and persons. At worse, the exercise of free choice has given rise to unwise 'choices' or an incoherent 'lego curriculum' where each component is selected only for reasons of its intrinsic (or extrinsic) appeal at a given point in time and without any necessary regard for the wider implications of the educational development of the young person concerned or for the context in which that development takes place. Dearing's (SCAA, 1996) report, it must be said, does not entertain such problems. Indeed, one of the key weaknesses of that report is its own voluntarism (Spours and Young, 1996). It is profoundly important to recognise the drawbacks of raw free marketism and to set in place those procedures that will ensure both the internal coherence of a course of study and its adequacy as a preparation for the economic and social futures described here. This will entail the imposition by educators of educationally grounded judgements, in the face of competing interests, and implies, of course, a weakening of current political, managerial and 'consumer' control over education and training, and the strengthening of professional control. While we would be unwise to underestimate the strength of oppositional forces, we should not lose sight of the central importance of achieving such a shift in power over post-16 education.

Further issues which must be addressed arise from the implications of knowledge production and dissemination under transdisciplinarity. What form will an organisational heterarchy take if, indeed, that is how production and dissemination are to be organised? The principles and procedures of operation will need to be clearly laid out not least because a shift from hierarchical to heterarchical organisation is likely to prove the most radical of all the proposals considered here.

However, before concluding this section on the subject of the organisation of knowledge, I should at least acknowledge one major factor which has served to obstruct the revision of British secondary and post-secondary curricula for generations. As Bernstein (1971) put it:

> The major control on the structuring of knowledge at the secondary level is the structuring of knowledge at the tertiary level, specifically the university. Only if there is a major change in the structuring of knowledge at this level can there be effective . . . change at lower levels.
>
> (ibid.: 69)

The success of the post-16 curriculum for the future will depend upon the capacity of policy makers and planners to break through such historically and culturally sustained barriers. It will mean confronting political pressures for comparability and for crude technical accountability. It will also rest heavily upon the quality of thought invested in the selection and organisation of knowledge, its production and dissemination.

Future policy making and planning must promote the integration of knowledge across those boundaries which currently dominate and fragment the post-16 curriculum: the 'academic–vocational divide' and subject and occupationally defined specialisms. The new curriculum must be planned around new notions of specialisation which reflect not only the inter-relatedness and interdependency of knowledge but the situated nature of both knowledge and learning. It must ensure that the educational experience of *all* learners includes not merely a 'breadth' of subject-defined knowledge but, crucially, that of producing, testing and utilising knowledge in a variety of practical contexts. It must also ensure the opportunity to examine all knowledge both from various disciplinary and occupational standpoints and from within a variety of social, cultural, political, economic and moral contexts. The primary aims of such curricula for all learners must be twofold: the acquisition of the fullest understanding of oneself as a learner and the development of one's command over the generation, utilisation and critical evaluation of knowledge. However, planners and educators must realise that this will not be assisted by free market practices where students have complete freedom of choice. A curriculum for learner empowerment will, of necessity, impose restrictions upon student choice.

Progression

There are two main problems concerning progression into, through and out of post-16 education. The first is to do with how decisions are made if, indeed, it is reasonable to conceive of progression as being, in part, the outcome of learners' decisions. The second concerns prevailing assumptions about routes of progression.

As I have remarked already in the previous section, freedom to choose is no guarantor of empowerment. Freedom of choice, as Hodkinson (1996) has pointed out, does not ameliorate inequality but can exacerbate it. 'If anything . . . choices within markets benefit the haves more than the have nots partly because they have more resources, including cultural capital, with which to make and take choices' (ibid.: 9).

> What is called for is a commitment to the concept of *universal provision*, based on entitlement and equity rather than on elusive notions of choice and diversity. Once established, the principle of a unified system of post-compulsory education and training need not necessarily preclude new thinking about access, credits and markets – *but neither should it be replaced by them*.
>
> (Avis *et al.*, 1996: 101, original emphasis)

The terms, 'decision' and 'choice' are widely used to describe how young people progress to one course or job rather than another when, in fact, choices are often heavily circumscribed not only by the opportunities over which choice might be exercised but by the choice maker's capacity to exercise choice making knowledge and skills.

> We found that in England, careers advice at school and beyond was plentiful, especially for those on vocational routes, but most of it was of an information-centred kind with little attempt to build up the young person's own autonomy as a seeker and user of advice on which to base decisions.
>
> (Bynner and Evans, 1994: 237)

Such choices as are made are frequently poorly informed: few of the young people in the Leverhulme Study, when describing their progression into post-16 education, for example, demonstrated deep knowledge of themselves as learners and only exceptionally did they possess clear, informed insights into the knowledge and learning entailed in the courses they had 'chosen'. This brings me to the second problem.

Progression is frequently portrayed as a step onto some route, trajectory or pathway. As I have remarked here, the metaphors used to described this process are invariably 'linear', the portrayal mirroring the technical rational assumptions which underpin it. These assumptions are essentially two-fold: (1) that young people can and do make well informed decisions about their progression, and (2) that once 'correctly' chosen, the progression route will remain perfectly matched to the person who chose it. However, young people do not and, arguably, cannot make informed 'once-and-for-all' decisions about their futures, not least because they have no direct experience of those futures in their totality to base their decisions upon. Moreover, the utility and good sense of choice making of this type is also extremely doubtful given the speed and scale of change in the nature of employment. But most importantly, as I have repeatedly argued here, young people's learning careers are anything but stable, particularly between the ages of 16 and 19. Learning careers can be exceedingly volatile and it is a nonsense for the entire educational system to be structured in such a way that frustrates many young people in their natural growth and development. The technical rationalism of the present system is counter-productive: it is one of the main reasons for non-completion and under-achievement.

Progression must be conceived in new ways. First, the post-16 curriculum, if planned along the lines described earlier, will contribute to a more common educational experience for all, though not, of course, by means of a uniformity of curriculum content. At the very least, this will ensure that, in their choice making, young people will not become cut off, effectively for ever, from whole areas of educational experience. The risks attached to choice at 16 must be reduced. Where choices are made, they must be reversible with minimum penalisation, in order to provide 'space' for the unfoldment of learning careers and the expression of human agency in learning. Finally, the post-16 curriculum of the future must equip young people with sufficient 'breadth' of experience that any directions they might subsequently assume in their higher education or employment can, themselves, be changed easily as needs arise, without heavy costs.

Curriculum organisation

By way of a conclusion to this section on the practicalities of providing for learning, I should like simply to reiterate the key aims of a curriculum for the future and to confirm some of the main organisational features of that curriculum.

The main over-arching aim of a curriculum for post-16 education and training must be the liberation of human agency in learning. We must move well away from the dependency relationships fostered by contemporary curricula. The purposive utilisation of agency and the promotion of self-reliance, independence of thought, collaborative working attitudes and practices, social, political and moral awareness and greater knowledge of self as a learner and as a person are what must be achieved. The means of achieving these ends demand changes in our practices, based upon changes in the ways in which we see and theorise knowledge, learning and teaching. Specifically, they will entail regard for the inter-relatedness of knowledge and for the promise of notions of collective specialisation and transdisciplinarity; for the situated nature of knowledge and learning and for the social conditions of learning; for the use of assessment for the purpose of aiding learning and not for political domination; for heterarchy in learning practices and, crucially, for teachers and learners as agents in the construction of their descriptive curricula.

However it is finally achieved, the post-16 curriculum for the future must provide the 'space' for teachers to exercise professional judgement and for learners to contribute to the process of curriculum making. It must provide 'space', also, for young people to be able to become the persons they do not yet know they will become: it must be developed and continually re-negotiated around learning careers, not in spite of them.

ENDNOTE

The key purpose of the Leverhulme Study was to gain access to students' and teachers' experiences of learning and teaching. That research has drawn two firm conclusions. First, it has shown that claims made in respect of the power of curriculum prescriptions are often overstated; it has confirmed the profound significance of student and teacher agency in the process of curriculum making. Second, in so far as it has been able to offer some insight into students' and teachers' lives outside the context of their formal learning and teaching, it has added weight to the claim that 'students as learners' can only be properly understood within the context of 'students as persons'. Thus, the concepts of studentship and learning career are the key to communicating these essential claims.

Given the claims presented in this book, and given also the demands that life and work in the twenty-first century are likely to place upon future generations, one might be prompted to question the suitability of the present post-16 system and its various curricula for future purposes. The problem is not that we don't already know and acknowledge the importance of student and teacher agency in curriculum making, it is that we don't realise the full implications of such observations. The discourse which most commonly accompanies the curriculum debate is one which embraces the view that prescription counts for all: change the prescription and you will change the practice. As long as such views are allowed to persist and hold sway, opportunities for the full exploitation of human agency in learning will be lost. As Roland Barthes put it, 'the birth of the reader must be at the cost of the death of the Author' (Barthes, 1977: 148).

NOTES

CHAPTER 3
KNOWLEDGE AND THE PRESCRIPTION OF LEARNING OPPORTUNITIES

While it is true that every construction of curriculum is different, it is important to distinguish between two broadly different types: *prescriptive* and *descriptive*. The former is most commonly adopted by teachers and planners to convey the intentions of some curriculum design or other. It is in this sense that it is used in formal statements of intent – as an attempt to prescribe what the student experience *will be*. But by far the richer usage is the descriptive, based as it is upon experiences of what *actually* happens. It is the descriptive curriculum that is the student's construction and which is accessible primarily through students although there are, of course, others, including teachers, parents, peers, higher education tutors and employers who have other experiences of the descriptive curriculum through their direct knowledge of students. In practice, the prescriptive and descriptive constructions of curriculum are not discrete entities: it is hard to imagine how any curriculum can be prescribed in the absence of some knowledge of its likely effects, although there are numerous examples where 'effects' have made seemingly little impact upon prescription; similarly, it would be unusual for descriptive constructions to bear no resemblance to the prescriptive, although, exceptionally, this might happen.

CHAPTER 4
KNOWLEDGE AND LEARNING IN PRACTICE: VOCATIONAL COURSES

1 The distinction between 'receptive' and 'interactive' learning activities has been reported elsewhere (Bloomer and Morgan, 1993). Receptive learning activities include those where the learner is presumed to be essentially passive in the uncritical acceptance and retention of knowledge or information. Note taking from dictation or demonstration are examples of common receptive learning activities. Interactive learning activities entail the interaction of the learner with some knowledge source in the form of their critical engagement with that source. Examples may include debate or experimentation, providing the activity entails the learner contributing to decisions about the course, shape and form of such

activity and not merely following procedures set out by others. Interactive activities imply the learner's production of knowledge.

CHAPTER 5
KNOWLEDGE AND LEARNING IN PRACTICE: A-LEVEL CHEMISTRY COURSES

1 See Chapter 4, note 1, above.

CHAPTER 6
KNOWLEDGE AND LEARNING IN PRACTICE: A-LEVEL HISTORY COURSES

1 See Chapter 4, note 1, above.

CHAPTER 7
STUDENTSHIP AND LEARNING CAREERS

1 See Chapter 4, note 1, above.
2 Such a longitudinal study sponsored by FEDA, *The Experience of the Learner in FE: A Longitudinal Study (RP912)*, is currently being carried out by Phil Hodkinson and myself.

CHAPTER 9
TOWARDS A CURRICULUM FOR THE FUTURE

1 At the time of writing, the final report of the *Learning for the Future* project (Richardson *et al.*), which might well constitute a second serious attempt, is still awaited.

BIBLIOGRAPHY

Abrams, F. (1994) 'Two-thirds of Students Fail to Complete GNVQs', *The Independent*, No. 2449, 25 August.

Althusser, L. (1971) *Lenin and Philosophy and Other Essays*, London: New Left Books.

—— (1972) 'Ideology and the Ideological State Apparatus', in B. R. Cosin (ed.) *Education: Structure and Society*, Harmondsworth: Penguin, 242–280.

Anderson, J. R., Reder, L. M. and Simon, H. A. (1996) 'Situated Learning and Education', *Educational Researcher*, 25, 4: 5–11.

Apple, M. (1979) *Ideology and the Curriculum*, London: Routledge and Kegan Paul.

Archer, M. S. (1988) *Culture and Agency: The Place of Culture in Social Theory*, Cambridge: Cambridge University Press.

Argyris, C. and Schön, D. A. (1974) *Theory in Practice: Increasing Personal Effectiveness*, San Francisco: Jossey-Bass.

—— (1978) *Organisational Learning*, Reading, Mass.: Addison-Wesley.

Armstrong, P. F. (1987) *Qualitative Strategies in Social and Educational Research: the Life History Method in Theory and Practice*, Newland Papers, 14, University of Hull.

Ashton, D. N., Maguire, M. J. and Garland, G. (1983) *Youth in the Labour Market*, Research Paper No. 34, Department of Employment, London: HMSO, cited in Moore (1988a) 'Education, Employment and Recruitment', London: Hodder and Stoughton, 266–271.

Association for Colleges, The Girls' Schools Association, The Headmasters' Conference, The Secondary Heads' Association, The Sixth Form Colleges' Association and The Society of Headmasters and Headmistresses in Independent Schools (1994) 'Post-Compulsory Education and Training', A Joint Statement, October.

Atkinson, J. S. and Meager, N. (1990) 'Changing Working Patterns: How Companies Achieve Flexibility to Meet New Needs', in G. Esland (ed.) *Education, Training and Employment*, vol. 1, Wokingham: Addison-Wesley/Open University, 70–85.

Audit Commission (1991) *Two Bs or Not... ? Schools' and Colleges' A-level Performance* (Working Paper), London: Audit Commission.

—— and OFSTED (1993) *Unfinished Business: Full-time Educational Courses for 16–19 Year Olds*, London: HMSO.

Avis, J. (1993) 'Post-Fordism, Curriculum Modernisers and Radical Practice: the Case of Vocational Education and Training in England', *The Vocational Aspect of Education*, 45, 1: 3–14.

——, Bloomer, M., Esland, G., Gleeson, D. and Hodkinson, P. (1996) *Knowledge and Nationhood: Education and the Transformation of Work*, London: Cassell.

Ayer, J. (1994) *The Great Jobs Crisis: Mobilising the UK's Education and Training Resources*, Cambridge: Tory Reform Group.

Bacon, F. (1876) *Advancement of Learning*, W. A. Wright (ed.) (second edn), Oxford: Clarendon Press, The Second Book, VII, 6.

Baert, P. (1992) *Time, Self and Social Being*, Aldershot: Avebury.

Ball, C. (1991) *Learning Pays*, London: Royal Society of Arts.

—— (1993) *Towards a Learning Society*, London: Royal Society of Arts.

Ball, S. J. (1981) *Beachside Comprehensive: A Case Study of Secondary Schooling*, Cambridge: Cambridge University Press.

—— (1982) 'Competition and Conflict in the Teaching of English: A Socio-Historical Analysis', *Journal of Curriculum Studies*, 14, 1: 1–28.

—— (1993) 'Education, Majorism and "the Curriculum of the Dead"', *Curriculum Studies*, 1, 2: 195–214.

Bandura, A. (1977) *Social Learning Theory*, Englewood Cliffs: Prentice-Hall.

—— (1982) 'Self-efficacy Mechanism in Human Agency', *American Psychologist*, 37: 122–147.

—— (1989) 'Regulation of Cognitive Processes through Perceiver Self-efficacy', *Developmental Psychology*, 25: 729–735.

Banks, M., Bates, I., Breakwell, G., Bynner, J., Elmer, N., Jamieson, L. and Roberts, K. (1992) *Careers and Identities: Adolescent Attitudes to Employment, Training and Education, their Home Life, Leisure and Politics*, Milton Keynes: Open University Press.

Barnes, D. and Shemilt, D. (1974) 'Transmission and Interpretation', *Educational Review*, 26, 3: 213–228.

Barthes, R. (1977) *Image – Music – Text*, London: Fontana.

Bates, I. and Riseborough, G. (eds) (1993) *Youth and Inequality*, Milton Keynes: Open University Press.

——, Clarke, J., Cohen, P., Finn, D., Moore, R. and Willis, P. (1984) *Schooling for the Dole?*, London: Macmillan.

Beck, U. (1992) *Risk Society: Towards a New Modernity*, London: Sage.

Behrens, M. and Brown, A. (1994) 'Finding Jobs: Institutional Support and Individual Strategies', in K. Evans and W. R. Heinz (eds) *Becoming Adults in England and Germany*, London: Anglo-German Foundation, 174–207.

Bennett, R., Glennerster, H. and Nevison, D. (1992) *Learning Should Pay*, London: London School of Economics/BP Educational Services.

Bernstein, B. (1971) 'On the Classification and Framing of Educational Knowledge', in M. F. D. Young (ed.) *Knowledge and Control: New Directions for the Sociology of Education*, London: Collier-Macmillan, 47–69.

Bloomer, M. (ed.) (1991) *Transition from School to College* (A school-based evaluation report), University of Exeter.

—— (ed.) (1992) *Students' Experiences of Transition from School to College* (A school-based evaluation report), University of Exeter.

—— (1994) *NVQing Teacher Education (FE): The Struggle Within a Profession*, Paper presented at the Conference of the Universities Council for the Education of Teachers, Coventry, November.

—— and Hodkinson, P. (1996) *The Experience of the Learner in FE: A Longitudinal Study (RP912)*, First Research Report to the Further Education Development Agency, August.

—— and Morgan, D. (1993) 'It is Planned, Therefore It Happens – Or Does It?', *Journal of Further and Higher Education*, 17, 1: 22–37.

Board of Education (1943a) *Curriculum and Examinations in Secondary Schools* (The Norwood Report), London: HMSO.

Board of Education (1943b) *Educational Reconstruction* (White Paper), Cmnd 6458, London: HMSO.

Bobbitt, F. (1918) *The Curriculum*, New York: Houghton and Mifflin.

Bourdieu, P. (1977a) 'Cultural Reproduction and Social Reproduction', in J. Karabel and A. H. Halsey (eds) *Power and Ideology in Education*, Oxford: Oxford University Press, 487–511.

—— (1977b) *Outline of a Theory of Practice*, Cambridge: Cambridge University Press.

—— (1993) *Sociology in Question*, London: Sage.

—— and Passeron, J. C. (1990) *Reproduction in Education, Society and Culture*, second edn, London: Sage.

Bowles, S. and Gintis, H. (1976) *Schooling in Capitalist America*, London: Routledge and Kegan Paul.

Brown, J. S., Collins, A. and Duguid, P. (1989) 'Situated Cognition and the Culture of Learning', *Educational Researcher*, 18, 1: 32–42.

Brown, P. (1987) *Schooling and Ordinary Kids: Inequality, Unemployment and the New Vocationalism*, London: Tavistock Publications.

—— and Lauder, H. (1991) 'Education, Economy and Social Change', *International Studies in Sociology of Education*, 1: 3–23.

—— and Lauder, H. (eds) (1992) *Education for Economic Survival: From Fordism to Post-Fordism*, London: Routledge.

—— and Scase, R. (1994) *Higher Education and Corporate Realities: Class, Culture and the Decline of Graduate Careers*, London: UCL Press.

Bruner, J. S. (1962) *On Knowing*, Cambridge, Mass.: Harvard University Press.

Bull, H. (1985) 'The Use of Behavioural Objectives', *Journal of Further and Higher Education*, 9, 1: 74–80.

Business and Technician Education Council (1986a) *Assignments Help Students to Learn*, London: BTEC.

—— (1986b) *Teaching and Learning Strategies: General Guideline*, London: BTEC.

—— (1991) *Caring Services (Nursery Nursing): Unit Specification*, London: BTEC.

Business and Technology Education Council (1995) *Business Advanced GNVQ: Mandatory and Core Skills Units*, London: BTEC.

——, City and Guilds and RSA Examinations Board (1995a) *Mandatory Units for Advanced Health and Social Care*, London: NCVQ.

——, City and Guilds, National Council for Vocational Qualifications and RSA Examinations Board (1995b) *Unit Test Specifications for Advanced Health and Social Care*, London: NCVQ.

Bynner, J. and Evans, K. (1994) 'Building on Cultural Traditions: Problems and Solutions', in K. Evans and W. Heinz (eds) *Becoming Adults in England and Germany*, London: Anglo-German Foundation, 230–248.

Calhoun, C., LiPuma, E. and Postone, M. (eds) (1993) *Bourdieu: Critical Perspectives*, Cambridge: Polity Press.

Callendar, C. (1992) *Will NVQs Work? Evidence from the Construction Industry*, Brighton: Institute of Manpower Studies, University of Sussex.

Capey, J. G. (1995) *GNVQ Assessment Review: Final Report of the Review Group*, London: NCVQ.

Carey, A. (1994) 'What Makes for Modularity?', *Insight – The Magazine for Education and Business*, 30, Sheffield: Employment Department Information Branch (EDIB).

Carr, W. (1987) 'What is an Educational Practice?', *Journal of Philosophy of Education*, 21, 2: 163–175.

—— (1991) 'Education for Citizenship', *British Journal of Educational Studies*, 39, 4: 373–385.

—— and Kemmis, S. (1986) *Becoming Critical: Education, Knowledge and Action Research*, London: Falmer Press.

Child Poverty Action Group (1996) *Poverty: the Facts*, London: CPAG.

Chinn, C. A. and Brewer, W. F. (1993) 'The Role of Anomalous Data in Knowledge Acquisition: A Theoretical Framework and Implications for Science Instruction', *Review of Educational Research*, 63, 1: 1–49.

Clark, G. (1994) 'The Changing Context of post-16 Education and Training', Paper presented at Keele University (CSRE) Postgraduate Seminar Programme, December.

Clarke, J. and Willis, P. (1984) 'Introduction', in I. Bates, J. Clarke, P. Cohen, D. Finn, R. Moore and P. Willis (eds) *Schooling for the Dole*, London: Macmillan, 1–16.

Claxton, G. (1996a) 'Implicit Theories of Learning', in G. Claxton, T. Atkinson, M. Osborn and M. Wallace (eds) *Liberating the Learner*, London: Routledge, 45–56.

—— (1996b) 'Integrated Learning Theory and the Learning Teacher', in G. Claxton, T. Atkinson, M. Osborn and M. Wallace (eds) *Liberating the Learner*, London: Routledge, 3–15.

Collins, M. (1991) *Adult Education as Vocation*, London: Routledge.

Confederation of British Industry (1989) *Towards a Skills Revolution*, London: CBI.

—— (1993) *Routes for Success – Careership: A Strategy for all 16–19 Year Old Learning*, London: CBI.

D'Aeth, R. (1973) 'Youth and the Changing Secondary School', *International Studies in Education*, 34, Hamburg: Unesco Institute for Education.

Department for Education (1992) *Initial Teacher Training (Secondary Phase)*, Circular 9/92, London: DfE.

——, Welsh Office, Scottish Office Education Department, Department of Education for Northern Ireland and Universities Funding Council (1996) *Education Statistics for the United Kingdom*, 1995 edn, London: HMSO.

Department of Education and Science and the Welsh Office (1988a) *Advancing A-levels* ('The Higginson Report'), London: HMSO.

—— (1988b) *National Curriculum Task Group on Assessment and Testing*, London: HMSO.

Department of Education and Science, Department of Employment, and Welsh Office (1991) *Education and Training for the 21st Century*, London: HMSO, Cmnd 1536.

Duke, C. (1993) *The Learning University: Towards a New Paradigm?*, London: SRHE/Open University Press.

Economic and Social Research Council (1994) *ESRC Learning Society: Knowledge and Skills for Employment Programme* (research specification), Swindon: ESRC.

Eisner, E. (1993) 'Objectivity in Educational Research', in Hammersley, M. (ed.) *Educational Research: Current Issues*, London: Paul Chapman Publishing, 49–56.

Elster, J. (1983) *Sour Grapes: Studies in the Subversion of Rationality*, Cambridge: Cambridge University Press.

Erikson, E. H. (1968) *Identity, Youth and Crisis*, New York: Norton.

Esland, G. (1971) 'Teaching and Learning as the Organization of Knowledge', in M. F. D. Young (ed.) *Knowledge and Control: New Directions for the Sociology of Education*, London: Collier-Macmillan, 70–115.

Evans, K. and Heinz, W. (eds) (1994) *Becoming Adults in England and Germany*, London: Anglo-German Foundation.

Fenstermacher, G. D. (1986) 'Philosophy of Research on Teaching: Three Aspects', in M. C. Wittrock (ed.) *Handbook of Research on Teaching*, third edn, New York: Macmillan, 37–49.

Finegold, D. (1993) 'The Emerging Post-16 System: Analysis and Critique', in W. Richardson, J. Woolhouse and D. Finegold (eds) *The Reform of Post-16 Education and Training in England and Wales*, Harlow: Longman, 38–53.

——, Keep, E., Miliband, D., Raffe, D., Spours, K. and Young, M. (1990) *A British Baccalauréat: Ending the Division Between Education and Training*, Education and Training Paper No.1, London: Institute for Public Policy Research.

—— and Soskice, D. (1988) 'The Failure of Training in Britain', *Oxford Review of Economic Policy*, 4, 3: 23–53.

Fitz-Gibbon, C. T. (1990) 'An Up-and-Running Indicator System', in C. T. Fitz-Gibbon (ed.) *Performance Indicators: A BERA Dialogue*, Clevedon, Avon: Multi-lingual Matters, 88–95.

Furlong, A. (1992) *Growing Up in a Classless Society? School to Work Transitions*, Edinburgh: Edinburgh University Press.

Further Education Unit (1993) *Introducing General National Vocational Qualifications*, Bulletin FEU028, London: FEU.

—— (1994) *Initiating Change: Educational Guidance for Adults 1988–93* (Final Report of the National Educational Guidance Initiative), London: FEU.

——, the Institute of Education, University of London and The Nuffield Foundation (1994) *GNVQs 1993–94: A National Survey Report*, London: FEU, University of London Institute of Education, Nuffield Foundation.

Gardner, H. (1984) *Frames of Mind: The Theory of Multiple Intelligences*, London: Heinemann.

Garnham, N. and Williams, R. (1980) 'Pierre Bourdieu and the Sociology of Culture: An Introduction', *Media, Culture and Society*, 2: 209–223.

Gibbons, M., Limoges, C., Nowotny, H., Schwartzman, S., Scott, P. and Trow, M. (1994) *The New Production of Knowledge*, London: Sage.

Giddens, A. (1984) *The Constitution of Society*, Cambridge: Polity Press.

—— (1991) *Modernity and Self-Identity*, Cambridge: Polity Press.

Gipps, C. (1990) *Assessment: A Teachers' Guide to the Issues*, London: Hodder and Stoughton.

Giroux, H. (1982) 'Power and Resistance in the New Sociology of Education: Beyond Theories of Social and Cultural Reproduction', *Curriculum Perspectives*, 2, 3: 1–13.

Giroux, H. (1983) 'Theories of Reproduction and Resistance in the New Sociology of Education: A Critical Analysis', *Harvard Educational Review*, 53, 3: 257–293.

Glaser, B. G. and Strauss, A. L. (1968) *The Discovery of Grounded Theory: Strategies for Qualitative Research*, London: Weidenfeld and Nicolson.

Goffman, E. (1971) *The Presentation of Self in Everyday Life*, Harmondsworth: Penguin.

Green, A. (1993) 'Post-16 Qualification Reform', *Forum*, 35, 1: 13–15.

Grundy, S. (1987) *Curriculum: Product or Praxis?*, London: Falmer Press.

Habermas, J. (1972) *Knowledge and Human Interests*, London: Heinemann.

Hall, S. (1992) 'The Question of Cultural Identity', in S. Hall, D. Held and T. McGrew (eds) *Modernity and its Futures*, Cambridge: Polity Press: 273–316.

Harker, R. (1992) 'Cultural Capital, Education and Power in New Zealand: an Agenda for Research', *New Zealand Sociology*, 7, 1: 1–19.

—— and May, S. (1993) 'Code and Habitus: Comparing the Accounts of Bernstein and Bourdieu', *British Journal of Sociology of Education*, 14, 2: 169–178.

——, Mahar, C. and Wilkes, C. (1990) *An Introduction to the Work of Pierre Bourdieu*, London: Macmillan.

Haugaard, M. (1992) *Structures, Reconstruction and Social Power*, Aldershot: Avebury.

The Headmasters' Conference (1994) 'Education 14–19', an HMC Working Party Report, October.

Heinz, W. (1987) 'The Transition from School to Work in Crisis', *Journal of Adolescent Research*, 2: 127–141.

Hickox, M. (1995) 'Situating Vocationalism', *British Journal of Sociology of Education*, 16, 2: 153–163.

Hirst, P. H. (1965) 'Liberal Education and the Nature of Knowledge', in R. D. Archambault (ed.) *Philosophical Analysis and Education*, London: Routledge and Kegan Paul.

—— (1969) 'The Logic of the Curriculum', *Journal of Curriculum Studies*, 1, 2: 142–158.

Hodkinson, P. (1992) 'Alternative Models of Competence in Vocational Education and Training', *Journal of Further and Higher Education*, 16, 2: 30–39.

—— (1995) *Careership and Markets: Structure and Agency in the Transition to Work*, unpublished PhD thesis, University of Exeter.

—— (1996) 'Choosing GNVQ', Paper presented at the 1996 Conference of the British Educational Research Association, University of Lancaster, September.

—— and Sparkes, A. C. (1993) 'Young People's Choices and Careers Guidance Action Planning: a Case Study of Training Credits in Action', *British Journal of Guidance and Counselling*, 21, 3: 246–261.

—— and Sparkes, A. C. (1995) 'Markets and Vouchers: the Inadequacy of Individualist Policies for Vocational Education and Training in England and Wales', *Journal of Educational Policy*, 10, 2: 189–207.

——, Sparkes, A.C. and Hodkinson, H. (1996) *Triumphs and Tears: Young People, Markets and the Transition from School to Work*, London: David Fulton.

Holland, G. (1977) *Young People and Work: Report on the Feasibility of a New Programme of Opportunities for Unemployed Young People*, London: MSC, cited in Moore (1988a) 'Education, Employment and Recruitment', London: Hodder and Stoughton, 268–270.

Holt, M. (1978) *The Common Curriculum*, London: Routledge and Kegan Paul.

—— (ed.) (1987) *Skills and Vocationalism: The Easy Answer*, Milton Keynes: Open University Press.

—— (1996) 'The Making of *Casablanca* and the Making of Curriculum', *Journal of Curriculum Studies*, 28, 3: 241–251.

Honey, P. and Mumford, A. (1992) *The Manual of Learning Styles*, Maidenhead: Peter Honey.

House, E. R. (1986) 'How We Think about Evaluation', in E. R. House (ed.) *New Directions in Educational Evaluation*, London: Falmer, 30–48.

Hughes, E. C. (1937) 'Institutional Office in the Person', *American Journal of Sociology*, 43, 3: 404–413.

Husén, T. (1974) *The Learning Society*, London: Methuen.

—— (1986) *The Learning Society Revisited*, London: Pergamon.

Hutchins, R. M. (1968) *The Learning Society*, London: Pall Mall Press.

Hutton, W. (1996) *The State We're In*, new revised edn, London: Vintage.

Hyland, T. (1992) 'NVQs and the Reform of Vocational Education and Training', *Journal of the National Association for Staff Development*, 26: 29–36.

—— (1993a) 'Competence, Knowledge and Education', *Journal of Philosophy of Education*, 27, 1: 57–68.

—— (1993b) 'Professional Development and Competence-based Education', *Educational Studies*, 19, 1: 123–132.

—— (1994a) *Competence, Education and NVQs*, London: Cassell.

—— (1994b) 'Silk Purses and Sow's Ears: NVQs, GNVQs and Experiential Learning', *Cambridge Journal of Education*, 24, 2: 233–243.

Ilon, L. (1994) 'Structural Adjustment and Education: Adapting to a Growing Global Market', *International Journal of Educational Development*, 14, 2: 95–108.

James, D. (1995) 'Mature Studentship in Higher Education: Beyond a "Species" Approach', *British Journal of Sociology of Education*, 16, 4: 451–466.

Jenkins, R. (1992) *Pierre Bourdieu*, London: Routledge.

Jones, G. (1988) 'Integrating Process and Structure in the Concept of Youth', *Sociological Review*, 36, 4: 706–731.

—— and Wallace, C. (1992) *Youth, Family and Citizenship*, Buckingham: Open University Press.

Keep, E. (1991) 'The Grass Looked Greener – Some Thoughts on the Influence of Comparative Vocational Training Research on the UK Policy Debate', in P. Ryan (ed.) *International Comparisons of Vocational Education and Training for Intermediate Skills*, London: Falmer.

Kelly, G. A. (1955) *The Psychology of Personal Constructs*, vols 1 and 2, New York: Norton.

Kolb, D. A. (1984) *Experiential Learning: Experience as the Source of Learning and Development*, Englewood Cliffs: Prentice-Hall.

Labour Party (1993) *Opening Doors to a Learning Society* (Green Paper on Education), London: Labour Party.

—— (1996) *Lifelong Learning: A Consultation Document*, London: Labour Party.

Lacey, C. (1988) 'The Idea of a Socialist Education', in H. Lauder and P. Brown (eds) *Education: In Search of a Future*, London: Falmer, 91–98.

Lave, J. and Wenger, E. (1991) *Situated Learning: Legitimate Peripheral Participation*, Cambridge: Cambridge University Press.

Layder, D., Ashton, D. and Sung, J. (1991) 'The Empirical Correlates of Action and Structure: the Transition from School to Work', *Sociology*, 25: 447–464.

MacDonald, R. and Coffield, F. (1991) *Risky Business? Youth and the Enterprise Culture*, London: Falmer.

McGrew, A. (1992) 'A Global Society?', in S. Hall, D. Held and T. McGrew (eds) *Modernity and its Futures*, Cambridge: Polity Press, 61–102.

Maclure, S. (1991a) *Missing Links: The Challenge to Further Education*, London: Policy Studies Institute.

—— (1991b) 'Time to Bridge the Culture Gap', *Times Educational Supplement*, No. 3903, 19 April, 9.

Mathews, J. (1989) *Tools for Change: New Technology and the Democratisation of Work*, Sydney: Pluto Press.

Merton, R. K. (1968) 'Social Structure and Anomie', in R. K. Merton (ed.) *Social Theory and Social Structure*, New York: Free Press, 185–214.

Moore, R. (1988a) 'Education, Employment and Recruitment', in R. Dale, R. Ferguson and A. Robinson (eds) *Frameworks for Teaching*, London: Hodder and Stoughton, 264–280.

—— (1988b) 'Education, Production and Reform', in H. Lauder and P. Brown (eds) *Education: In Search of a Future*, London: Falmer, 99–130.

National Commission on Education (1993) *Learning to Succeed*, London: Heinemann.

—— (1994) 'After Learning to Succeed', NCE Briefing, 1, London: National Commission on Education.

National Council for Vocational Qualifications (1995) *GNVQ Briefing: Information on the Form, Development and Implementation of GNVQs*, June, London: NCVQ.

Nixon, J., Martin, J., McKeown, P. and Ranson, S. (1996) *Encouraging Learning*, Buckingham: Open University Press.

Oakeshott, M. (1962) *Rationalism in Politics and Other Essays*, London: Methuen.

Oates, T. (1996) 'The Development and Implementation of Key Skills in England', Paper presented at the 1996 Conference of the British Educational Research Association, University of Lancaster, September.

Okano, K. (1993) *School to Work Transition in Japan*, Clevedon: Multilingual Matters.

—— (1995) 'Rational Decision Making and School-based Job Referrals for High School Students in Japan', *Sociology of Education*, 68 (January): 31–47.

Parlett, M. and Hamilton, D. (1987) 'Evaluation as Illumination: A New Approach to the Study of Innovatory Programmes', in R. Murphy and H. Torrance (eds) *Evaluating Education: Issues and Methods*, London: Paul Chapman, 57–73.

Peters, R. S. (1973) 'Education as Initiation', in *Authority, Responsibility and Education* (third edn), London: George Allen & Unwin.

Phenix, P. H. (1964) *Realms of Meaning*, New York: McGraw-Hill.

Phillimore, A. J. (1990) 'Flexible Specialization, Work Organization and Skills: Approaching the "Second Industrial Divide"', in G. Esland (ed.) *Education, Training and Employment*, vol. 1, Wokingham: Addison-Wesley/Open University, 86–105.

Piore, D. and Sabel, C. (1984) *The Second Industrial Divide*, New York: Basic Books.

Postlethwaite, T. N. and Wiley, D. E. (1991) *Science Achievement in Twenty-Three Countries*, Oxford: Pergamon, cited in A. Smithers and P. Robinson (1991) *Beyond Compulsory Schooling: A Numerical Picture*, London: The Council for Industry and Higher Education, 8.

Postman, N. (1996) 'School's Out, Forever', *The Guardian*, 21 December.

Pring, R. A. (1976) *Knowledge and Schooling*, London: Open Books.

—— (1987) 'Confidentiality and the Right to Know', in R. Murphy and H. Torrance (eds) *Evaluating Education: Issues and Methods*, London: Paul Chapman, 278–290.

Quicke, J. (1996) 'Learning and Context: Constructing an Integrated Perspective', *British Journal of Sociology of Education*, 17, 1: 103–113.

Rainbow, R. (1993) 'New Models of 16–19 Provision: Case Histories and Emerging Frameworks', in W. Richardson, J. Woolhouse and D. Finegold (eds) *The Reform of Post-16 Education and Training in England and Wales*, Harlow: Longman, 87–100.

Ranson, S. (1992) 'Towards the Learning Society', *Educational Management and Administration*, 20, 2: 68–79.

—— (1994) *Towards the Learning Society*, London: Cassell.

——, Taylor, B. and Brighouse, T. (eds) (1986) *The Revolution in Education and Training*, Harlow: Longman.

Reich, R. (1983) *The Next American Frontier*, Harmondsworth: Penguin.

—— (1993) *The Work of Nations: Preparing Ourselves for 21st-Century Capitalism*, London: Simon & Schuster.

Republic of Korea Ministry of Education (1995) *Education in Korea*, Seoul: National Institute for Educational Research and Training.

215

BIBLIOGRAPHY

Richardson, W. (1993) 'The 16–19 Education and Training Debate: "Deciding Factors" in the British Public Policy Process', in W. Richardson, J. Woolhouse and D. Finegold (eds) *The Reform of Post-16 Education and Training in England and Wales*, Harlow: Longman, 1–37.

——, Spours, K., Woolhouse, J. and Young, M. (1995) *Learning for the Future: Initial Report*, Institute of Education, University of London and Centre for Education and Industry, University of Warwick.

Ritzer, G. (1993) *The McDonaldization of Society*, London: Pine Forge Press.

Robbins, D. (1991) *The Work of Pierre Bourdieu*, Milton Keynes: Open University Press.

Roberts, K. (1995) *Youth and Employment in Modern Britain*, Oxford: Oxford University Press.

——, Clark, S. C. and Wallace, C. (1994) 'Flexibility and Individualisation: a Comparison of Transitions into Employment in England and Germany', *Sociology*, 28, 1: 31–54.

Ryle, G. (1949) *The Concept of Mind*, London: Hutchinson.

Scheffler, I. (1965) *Conditions of Knowledge: An Introduction to Epistemology and Education*, Glenview, Ill.: Scott, Foresman.

School Curriculum and Assessment Authority (1993) *The National Curriculum and its Assessment* ('The Dearing Report'), London: SCAA.

—— (1996) *Review of Qualifications for 16–19 Year Olds: Summary Report* ('The Dearing Report'), London: SCAA.

Sims, D. (1987) *Work Experience in TVEI: Student Views and Reactions*, Slough: The National Foundation for Educational Research.

Smithers, A. (1993) *All Our Futures: Britain's Education Revolution*, London: Channel Four Television.

—— and Robinson, P. (1991) *Beyond Compulsory Schooling: A Numerical Picture*, London: The Council for Industry and Higher Education.

—— (1993) *Changing Colleges: Further Education in the Market Place*, London: The Council for Industry and Higher Education.

Spours, K. (1993) 'Analysis: the Reform of Qualifications within a Divided System', in W. Richardson, J. Woolhouse and D. Finegold (eds) *The Reform of Post-16 Education and Training in England and Wales*, Harlow: Longman, 146–170.

—— and Young, M. (1988) 'Beyond Vocationalism: A New Perspective on the Relationship Between Work and Education', *British Journal of Education and Work*, 2, 2: 5–14.

—— (1996) 'Aiming Higher than Dearing', *The Times Educational Supplement*, No. 4164, 19 April, 33.

Steedman, H. (1992) *Mathematics in Vocational Youth Training for the Building Trades in Britain, France and Germany*, National Institute of Economic and Social Research Discussion Paper No. 9, London: NIESR.

—— and Hawkins, J. (1994) 'Shifting Foundations: the Impact of NVQs on Youth Training for the Building Trades', *National Institute Economic Review*, 149, August, 93–100.

Stenhouse, L. (1975) *An Introduction to Curriculum Research and Development*, London: Heinemann.

Stobart, G. (1996) 'The Rough Guide to GNVQs', Paper presented at the 1996 Conference of the British Educational Research Association, University of Lancaster, September.

Stoney, S. M. (1987) *Consumer Reactions Two Years On: Fifth Years' Perceptions of TVEI*, Slough: The National Foundation for Educational Research.

Strauss, A. (1962) 'Transformations of Identity', in A. M. Rose (ed.) *Human Behavior and Social Processes: An Interactionist Approach*, London: Routledge and Kegan Paul.

Swartz, D. (1977) 'Pierre Bourdieu: The Cultural Transmission of Social Inequality', *Harvard Educational Review*, 47: 545–555.

Thomas, R. (1996) 'Little Comfort for Poor in Blair's Blanket Approach', *The Guardian*, 15 April, 14.

Thomas, W. I. and Thomas, D. S. (1928) *The Child in America*, New York: Knopf.

Thompson, L. (1996) *The Motivation, Expectation and Experience of 1st Year Students on a Full-Time GNVQ Advanced Business Studies Course in a College of Further Education*, unpublished MEd thesis, Westminster College, Oxford.

Thurow, L. (1992) *Head to Head: The Coming Economic Battle Among Japan, Europe and America*, New York: William Morrow and Company.

Toffler, A. (1970) *Future Shock*, London: Bodley Head.

—— (1980) *The Third Wave*, London: Collins.

Tymms, P. B. and Fitz-Gibbon, C. T. (1995) 'Students at the Front: Using Performance Indicators for Professional Development', *Educational Research*, 37, 2: 107–122.

Vygotsky, L. S. (1978) *Mind in Society*, Cambridge, Mass.: Harvard University Press.

Whitehead, A. N. (1950) *Aims of Education and Other Essays* (second edn), Tonbridge: Benn.

Whitty, G. (1989) 'The New Right and the National Curriculum: State Control or Market Forces?', *Journal of Education Policy*, 4, 4: 329–341.

Willis, P. (1977) *Learning to Labour*, Farnborough: Saxon House.

Wolf, A. (1995) *Competence-based Assessment*, Buckingham: Open University Press.

INDEX

A-level courses 39, 163, 189; assessment
24–5, 42–5, 60–1; chemistry 88–115;
combined with GNVQ 20;
descriptive curricula 88–136;
Higginson Committee proposals 18;
history 116–36; Leverhulme Study
7–8, 9; liberal education and 15;
prescribed curricula 42–7, 60–1;
variation in pedagogic practices5
A-level Information System 26
absorption of knowledge 97
'academic–vocational divide' 5, 15–16,
18–24, 195
accountability: assessment of vocational
education 55, 59–60; political 25–6,
35–7; quangos and management of
education 183–4
accreditation of prior learning 23
achievement, educational 36–7; *see also*
assessment
action 171; horizons for 143–6, 149–50,
178–80; ideological and cultural
change 186–7; learning careers
153–4; *see also* agency
adolescence 151–2
Advanced GNVQs *see* GNVQs
advice/guidance 26–30, 184–5, 203
agency 204–5; curriculum for the future
163–4, 191–2, 197, 204; curriculum
organisation 204; ideological and
cultural change 186–7; learning
careers 153–4, 156; new orientations
191–2, 197; reconceptualisation of
learning 167–8, 169–70, 172;
structure and 137–8, 172, 176–8,
181; *see also* studentship
aims: A-level chemistry 110; curriculum
for the future 187–204

alienation 132–3
analytical model of learning 167–8
answerism, culture of 185–6
application context 170–1
application of knowledge 46–7, 86–7
argument building 127–8
Aristotle 40
AS-levels 18
assessment 24–6; A-level 24–5, 42–5,
60–1; Advanced GNVQs 54, 55, 58,
59–60, 62, 184; BTEC 25, 59, 61;
education as a political act 36–7; new
orientations 193–4; NVQs 184; role-
play 64–6
Assessment Review Group 55–59
Audit Commission 25–6
Avis, J. 138–9, 158, 161, 202

Bacon, Francis 40
Bandura, A. 165
basic knowledge/skills: A-level courses
107–8, 114; curriculum for the
future 196
Beck, U. 152
behaviourism 88–90
Bernstein, B. 201
Bloomer, M. 5–6
Board of Education 193–4
books, using 125
Bourdieu, P. 139–42, 150
'brainstorming' 69–72
bridges 24, 29; *see also*
'academic–vocational divide'
British Baccalauréat 21, 195, 200
Brown, J.S. 165–6
BTEC (Business and Technology
Education Council) 48–9, 69
BTEC National courses 13, 39, 53, 163,